Social Theory and Human Reality

Social Theory and Human Reality

Pertti Alasuutari

SAGE Publications
London ● Thousand Oaks ● New Delhi

SAGE Publications Ltd
1 Oliver's Yard
55 City Road
London EC1Y 1SP

SAGE Publications Inc.
2455 Teller Road
Thousand Oaks, California 91320

SAGE Publications India Pvt Ltd
B-42, Panchsheel Enclave
Post Box 4109
New Delhi 110 017

British Library Cataloguing in Publication data

A catalogue record for this book is available
from the British Library

ISBN 0-7619-5164-4
ISBN 0-7619-5165-2 (pbk)

Library of Congress Control Number available

Typeset by C&M Digitals (P) Ltd., Chennai, India
Printed in Great Britain by Gopsons Papers Ltd., Noida

Contents

Preface

Writing the book at hand has been a long process. I wrote the first plan and signed the book proposal with Sage Publications in 1995, but because of my other book projects and publication activity, along with teaching and administrative obligations, progress was slow and I had to postpone the completion of the manuscript several times.

This was also a very challenging project for me because it has forced me to clarify my theoretical thinking into a (hopefully) coherent whole. The theoretical themes I discuss and the examples I take to illustrate them often reflect my areas of interest and previous studies. With one exception the texts have not been published previously. An earlier version of Chapter 6 has been published as 'The Discursive Construction of Personality', in Amia Lieblich and Ruthellen Josselson (eds) (1997) *The Narrative Study of Lives*, Vol. 5. Newbury Park, California: Sage, pp. 1–20.

The appointment as a Senior Scientist in the Academy of Finland for the academic year 2001–2002 was crucial for me. During that time I was able to put the pieces together into the first book manuscript draft.

Because of the long duration of the project, it is impossible for me to name all the people who have commented on my texts and ideas over the years. I want to thank you all collectively for your help and inspiration. I particularly want to thank Karen Armstrong, Jay Gubrium and Helmut Staubmann, who read the entire manuscript and gave me valuable feedback.

Pertti Alasuutari
Tampere, April 2004

1 Introduction

Recently a Finnish astronomer was awarded a prestigious prize for a book that uses the unity of natural scientific knowledge to build a story about who we are and what others out there could be. The book – written by Esko Valtaoja and entitled *At Home in the Universe* (2001) – addresses fundamental questions like 'where do we come from?', 'where are we going?' and 'what is the meaning of our existence?'. Moving across a broad area from astronomy to biology, it continues in the tradition of Stephen Hawking's huge world hit, *A Brief History of Time* (Hawking 1988).

It has always puzzled me why there are not similar books about social science: books that briefly and in a relatively uncomplicated manner sum up what we know about the object of our research, perhaps with some personal but empirically grounded speculation about the future and what lies around the corner. Or are there? There are introductory textbooks about the state of the art of separate disciplines such as sociology, anthropology or psychology, but often they inform the reader about different approaches and theoretical trends rather than showing any unity between them. It appears, as is often said, that the social sciences haven't as yet achieved the phase in their development that Thomas S. Kuhn (1970) calls normal science: scientists are not committed to the same paradigm, to shared rules and standards for scientific practice.

One proof of the social sciences' thus far poorly developed self-consciousness about a shared paradigm is that there are differing views even about what disciplines are counted within them. For instance, it is quite common to make a distinction between the social sciences and the humanities, which implies that disciplines such as history, linguistics, literature, and philosophy are separate from the social sciences, such as anthropology, political science, psychology and sociology. The disciplines listed in these two categories vary between countries and universities. The term 'human sciences' is quite commonly used to overcome this division, but 'social sciences' is also sometimes used as a generic term referring to disciplines that are not natural sciences. Because of my own training and background in sociology and media studies, in this book I concentrate on talking about social sciences or social science but – probably due to my ignorance about other human sciences – I assume that at the level of a general synthesis of what we now know about our object of study there cannot be any grave difference between social sciences and humanities.

Contrary to the common assumption, I think that underneath the surface of competing schools of social thought and research traditions there is a largely shared body of knowledge about the object of social sciences; that object I will call human reality. One of the reasons for writing this book was to see what an inventory of social science knowledge might look like. Naturally the outcome is only my personal view, my interpretation about the basic premises that are shared in social sciences. On that basis I suggest some ideas about what can be said about human reality.[1] Nevertheless, the motive of writing a general introduction to social science has largely set the tone of this book. Although the book deals with social and cultural theory, I have avoided the format of conventional theory books in which the author introduces and critiques competing theories and as a synthesis presents his or her own theory, which more or less differs from previous ones. Instead, I have deliberately adopted an eclectic voice that disregards differences between nearby camps that often use different concepts to formulate a similar point in slightly different ways and with different emphases. When there are closely related concepts that depict more or less the same thing I use them as synonyms. In addition, I introduce viewpoints that are commonly viewed as mutually contradictory and in that sense are competing theories. Such eclecticism is often denounced as an expression of intellectual laziness. It is expected that a proper theorist is able to present a theoretical structure that does not have such inconsistencies. My choice is, however, not the result of a failure to produce a consistent theory. My point is to argue that incompatible contradictions and anomalies belong to human reality. It is kaleidoscopic and elusive in such a way that one can describe it in terms of a contradiction-free theoretical system only by knowingly ignoring essential aspects of the way in which human reality works.

There is a particular reason why I talk about human reality. Since this is an introduction to social science knowledge, a more conventional choice would be to talk about the social reality or about human society. However, although social groups of more complex and large-scale organizations, such as nation states, often serve as objects and observation units of social research, the object of knowledge of social science cannot satisfactorily be defined that way. To talk about social reality implies that material objects are outside the scope of social science, which leads to an idealist conception of social groups and organizations. By talking about human reality I refer to the entire reality that we face and experience as human beings. It is not just words, ideas or interaction with other talking subjects; we are also living bodies coming to terms with natural and built environments. Although the natural sciences can and must exclude or abstract away from the influence of human subjects when analysing natural laws and processes, social scientists cannot perform a similar abstraction and ignore material reality. Even when we are dealing with objects that hardly interfere with human activities in any way – say, far-away galaxies or the tiniest particles of which atoms are made – natural science research can also be analysed from a social scientific perspective. That is because all knowledge is necessarily socially constructed. It is dependent on the human imagination – that is, on the intelligence and overall potential of the human race to reflect on the reality it encounters. Even if we think that it only takes a single exceptional genius to explain a particularly tricky phenomenon or aspect of reality, such inventions are worthless if they cannot be conveyed to others by using language, which is an essential part of human reality.

The way human reality was described above implies that in a sense all reality, including the reality that natural science studies, belongs to human reality. However, social science is interested in material reality only from certain perspectives. On the one hand, material reality – or, more precisely, the way it is conceived – sets conditions on human activities and social systems. On the other hand, knowledge about material reality and practices of gaining and utilizing that knowledge are essential elements in the formation and daily reproduction of human reality. Thus, as social scientists we are interested in material reality insofar as it plays a direct or indirect part in social action. In many ways material conditions necessarily affect social action, but on the other hand social systems and forms of knowledge possessed by humans affect or, rather, set conditions for an understanding of material reality. The title of this book, *Social Theory and Human Reality*, thus expresses my main objective: I discuss the main characteristics of the reality that we humans encounter in our daily life.

In this book I approach the world of social science from a particular perspective and emphasize one aspect which I think is of crucial importance and makes human reality an exciting object of knowledge. Routines, the culturally unconscious or non-discursive aspect of reality, are the main stronghold of social order, and they are also the reason why the human species has been so successful and able to adapt to varying conditions. The knowledge and experience of previous generations and of our fellow human beings is stored in language and institutionalized behavioural patterns, and yet we are far from being walking supercomputers because we are able to apply that experience unconsciously, by following routines. There is also a continuous interplay between routines and reflexivity. Each time we become reflexively conscious of something we also construct that something as a new object. In a paradoxical way, human reality as we live it is a dream world of our own collective making, in principle changed by every move or turn of talk that any of us makes. It is precisely because of this fictional character that human reality works as a great resource for human intelligence.

To give you a better idea of these main coordinates, I will now introduce them in more detail. I will start by explaining why I argue that routine, culturally unconscious behaviour, is the secret of the success of the human species.

Human Intellect and Adaptability

It would be only human to be self-satisfied and overestimate human intelligence, but there is no denying that humans have been the most successful species in adapting to all kinds of environments. The advances of physics, for instance, which have resulted in humans landing on the moon, are but one example of human adaptability. The human body itself does not survive extreme conditions but we have the ability to protect our body and make devices that enable us to adapt. Social and cultural adaptation is another component of human adaptability, one that has negative as well as positive consequences. The almost unlimited ability of humans to conceive of and organize their own or others' lives in most peculiar and sometimes inhuman ways has resulted in many horrors: degradation, massacre, mass suicide, all kinds of slavery, etc.

Often the question about human adaptability is approached by showing the superb intelligence of humans, which then explains our ability to use tools – clothes, shelter, hunting and farming technology, etc. – and in that way to survive even extremely harsh conditions. In this framework, language has been seen as still another proof of human intellect and as an additional tool enabling better coordination of the acts of, for instance, several hunters.

Anthropologist Bradd Shore (1996) combines the biological and cultural aspects of human adaptation by paying attention to the fact that at birth a human brain weighs only 25 per cent of its eventual adult weight. This implies that the development of an individual's nervous system is partially built according to guidelines provided by the local culture. Thus, although nature sets guidelines for human intelligence, even the way in which brains are developed, what kind of operations they are designed to perform, depends on nurture.

However, the human brain's capacity to store and process information in itself does not explain the specificity of the human species. Although an individual human being's brain is bigger than that of any other species, its capacity is still fairly modest. The incredible adaptability and flexibility of humans is mainly due to culture and society rather than a result of separate individual's intelligence. Or to put it more precisely, the human species' 'intelligence' cannot be properly located in the brain of any individual, although a single human being may sometimes, for good reason, be given credit for singular achievements in, say, science or technology. However, even in such a case the implementation and possibly vast consequences of an innovation are due to culture and society. More than probably any other species, humans adapt to their environment by learning and passing on information to others, rather than by following behavioural patterns encoded in their genes. Through communication and language we are able to learn about new ideas and put them into practice, for instance in the form of new institutions and organizations. Besides, as innovators we all stand on the shoulders of previous generations; we always rely on, criticize and make use of the concepts and ideas of our ancestors and a number of our contemporaries. The web of culture, including the social institutions and organizations humans always build, is the form in which our notions, knowledge and information about the world and about ourselves is encoded in a number of ways, ranging from social practices and built environments all the way to different sign systems and language, both in oral and written forms. Compared to that, the information stored in any individual brains, no matter how brilliant, is of minor importance when considering human adaptability.

Humans differ from other species precisely in their ability to exceed the physical and mental limits of individuals. We function, adapt to and build varying conditions such as societies and cultures, not as singular individuals provided with skills and capacities used in adapting to different environments but as social groups. Human adaptability is reliant on social institutions which store information (like written language) and which 'think for us' (Douglas 1986) by orchestrating routinized practices. Of course many other species, for instance bees, ants, lions and apes, build societies or hunt in groups, but without a highly developed language their experience and ideas are not as easily stored over generations, conceptually reflected on and further developed or rejected.

What do we know by now about human reality which accounts for humans' incredible adaptability? How is it that humans have been so successful in adapting to all kinds of environments and, as a consequence, conquering and controlling the whole globe? These are the questions to which social science gives answers and, despite disagreements between competing camps, social scientists emphasize that all answers cannot be found in biology. That is why in this book I discuss how sociability, culture and language explain human adaptability.

In natural sciences, for instance physics, science has made incredible achievements. In the early 1990s, when further observations in support of the so-called 'Big Bang' theory about the beginning of the universe made it a nearly unanimous view among cosmologists, even the scientists themselves expressed their wonder before the achievements of cosmology. They wondered how it was possible that they were able to describe the finest details of the beginning of the universe, the so-called 'Big Bang', which took place approximately 15 billion years ago. For instance, George Smoot, the team leader from the Lawrence–Berkeley Laboratory, said in 1992: 'It's like looking at God' (cited in Schaefer 1996).

When the social sciences are compared with the natural sciences, it is commonplace to wonder about how much less progress has taken place within them. Whereas the natural sciences have been able to describe and explain in a verifiable way the most complex phenomena taking place both in the microscopic reality of cells and atoms and in the macroscopic reality of the whole universe billions of years ago, social scientists do not really agree on a single theory. This pervasively messy status of the social sciences has often been explained by their recent birth, although in fact the modern natural sciences and social sciences were born at the same time in the seventeenth century.

Why is it that humans have been able to explore invisible and distant realities but have not been able to agree on practically anything certain about the human life-world, the way in which societies work or how they are constructed? Does this state of affairs prove that the social sciences are poorly developed?

If the paradigmatically uniform state of natural science is used as a yardstick in assessing social science, it indeed seems to be very poorly developed. However, this conclusion misses the point that the object itself – human reality – is extremely complex. The concepts and theories by which it can be sensibly understood are not as clear-cut and relatively simple as those explaining nature to us – otherwise we would never have been able to grasp the natural world as well as modern science has been able to do. Human reality is hard to understand precisely because of the human intellect's ability to gain knowledge and to provide accurate hypotheses even about the most far-out realities and the smallest particles of the atom. The huge capacity of human intellect is due to the complex nature of human culture and social life. Human intellect is not a property of individuals; it essentially resides in language, culture and social networks, which enable coordination and cooperation between individuals, groups and institutions, across distances, and even between past and present generations. It is incorporated in individual human minds, which may be able to come up with an explanation to difficult puzzles because they are invested with the collectively produced intellect of the human race. Because humans are able to theorize about, and make sense of, the most distant and incredible characteristics of nature, human reality as the basis of that creativity has to match in complexity its object of study.

Toward a Social Theory of Human Reality

What is human reality composed of, and how does it work so that it accounts for human adaptability? A social theory of human reality should be in accordance with, or account for, previous theories and findings of social research. I suggest that from a certain perspective, a great deal of social research and theorizing actually does share a common viewpoint or, to borrow a phrase from Talcott Parsons (1967: 722), even 'converges upon a single theory'. I suggest that the common ground is composed of two main elements. First, social scientists cannot entirely neglect habitual behaviour as a building block of society, although they may be more interested in individuals' reflexive moments. Second, in various ways we give credit to language for conveying information, coordinating action, and forming human reality.

The problem with my project is that the knowledge and theories of both the social sciences and the humanities form a messy field. Unlike the natural sciences, the scientific community of social sciences does not subscribe to a paradigm (Kuhn 1970), to a certain number of principles that are the bedrock of normal science. There is, for instance, no unanimity over what sorts of entities human reality contains (cf. Kuhn 1970: 7). It is not that there are competing paradigms that offer different explanations for the same findings. It is rather that different theoretical trends or schools of thought habitually find each other's findings and observations irrelevant concerning their viewpoints and areas of interest. For instance, structural theorists interested in macro-level phenomena are not interested in micro-level interaction or in the semiotics of language, and the latter may also find macro-level theories simply uninteresting. Sometimes a theoretical trend implies or explicitly claims that another trend is wrong about something, but if there is discussion between different camps, in most cases the argument is that the opponents have misunderstood the importance or ontological status of their findings. For instance, structural theorists seldom protect themselves from a constructionist critique by presenting a competing 'realist' theory of language, but rather argue that constructionists overemphasize the ideological impact of language. Similarly, ethnomethodologists refrain from assessing whether a macro theory is valid or not, and simply treat it as a form of 'members' understandings' of society.

Different social science traditions also deal with different levels of abstraction. Some of them perceive their object of study, for instance 'modern society', as a historically specific phenomenon, whereas others, such as 'behavioural science', are primarily interested in universally valid theories of human behaviour. However, writers are not always very clear about the level of abstraction at which they move, and hypotheses are seldom well formulated or expressed in a detailed manner. Rather, in the literature sociologists and anthropologists often make points about a particular, historically and culturally specific phenomenon, whereas their universal implications can only be seen by analysing the premises on which the arguments rest.

There are several reasons for the blurry condition of the field of social sciences. For instance, in order to distance themselves from competing and partly overlapping theories or traditions, different theorists often use different terms to refer to more or less the same concepts. That is partly because in the social sciences language has more roles than in natural science. It is always part of the object of study, and, on the other hand, language is the 'metalanguage', the means by which research results are communicated among scientists and conveyed to the general public. This also means that the research results have different effects on the object. If a scientific theory of human behaviour or the psyche is received favourably by the public, its metalanguage concepts become part of common property, folk theories and notions by which individuals inter-pret their own and others' actions. Thus, no matter how valid the meta-linguistic concepts were in actually describing and explaining human behaviour and social action in the first place, the concepts adopted by a community will become part of the object of social sciences. For instance, when it becomes common knowledge to conceive of heavy drinking as sign of a disease called alcoholism, the reactions of significant others to alcoholic drinking or the building of treatment systems and institutions derived from such a definition of the problem become part of social real-ity. In human societies language has a double hermeneutic character (Giddens 1984) or a double epistemological status (Alasuutari 1992a).

Another reason for social science's blurry state is that researchers are often more or less consciously partisans in the events they analyse in the first place. Often analyses about social phenomena have been inspired and mixed with different forms of critique about existing social arrange-ments. In that role, social scientists have in fact, for their minor part, affected the human reality they have discussed, since statements about social reality are always also interventions in routinized forms of action and thought, and in the forms within which it is reflected upon.

Much of sociological research and thought has been so interested in making sense of, and been so concerned about, the local and historical forms of social reality that it has been abstracted away from its cultural basis. Social facts have been perceived as if they were natural facts, inde-pendent from and unaffected by notions about them. Scientists have used their culturally induced interpretive resources to classify behaviours and institutions, and then to present theories about the mechanisms by which they relate to each other. By borrowing metaphors from different walks of life, societies have been likened, for instance, to organisms, màchines, plays or games.

In the quest for a scientific understanding of society, social scientists have been guided by historical cultural concerns. For instance, at its birth classical sociology was particularly concerned about social integration, felt to be threatened by the rise of industry and a capitalist exchange econ-omy in the eighteenth and nineteenth centuries. Continuing the traditions of moral philosophy and the French *philosophes* of the Enlightenment, Karl

Marx, Max Weber, Émile Durkheim and Georg Simmel wanted to understand what was going on in society: how and why social patterns and structures were changing in advanced European societies, and what kept the changing societies together. In addition to emphasizing different aspects of human reality in their theories, the classic theorists were part of the political imagination of their time. For Durkheim the salvation from disorder and anomie seemed to reside in a (new) morality and moral rules or norms, whereas Marx felt that the capitalist mode of production would inevitably result in an ever-strengthening class contradiction between the working class and the capitalists. For Marx this would eventually lead to a revolution and the birth of a socialist and communist society, where the contradiction between labour and capital would be resolved and where people would live in a more harmonious community, resembling Marx's picture of ancient pre-capitalist societies.

Since the golden era of sociology at the turn of the twentieth century, many later sociologists have had a nagging concern about the metaphysical nature of social theory. Although it is evident that social researchers and theorists may be more or less successful in explaining and predicting social phenomena and developments, it is equally evident that grand social theories can never rise above the ephemeral forms of social life. Concepts like social structure, social norms or personality do not have a referent in a reality outside language, although they may have a reality as social facts, as constructs by which people both within social science and in public discourse refer to different entities they have identified and defined in particular ways. By doing so, such constructs are, in different ways, real in their social consequences, for instance when social policies are organized and targeted by relying on them as maps of human reality.

 Several micro-sociological traditions of social thought have attempted in different ways to escape from the metaphysics of social science. For instance, phenomenological sociology conceives of social reality not as an objective reality but rather as an intersubjective reality of social meanings. However, the founder of ethnomethodology, Harold Garfinkel, denounces phenomenological attempts to interpret meanings, because, according to him, it means that one is trying to look inside the head of human beings. Instead, Garfinkel suggests that we must concentrate on studying the 'ethno-methods' by which people interpret each other and achieve a shared understanding of what is going on. Ethnomethodological conversation analysis (CA), in turn, denounces the Garfinkelian project of considering interaction as a 'screen' on which 'commonsense methods' are projected (Schegloff 1992a: xviii). Instead, CA treats the conversation as the prime object of study, and makes inferences about the devices (i.e., words or other utterances or gestures) by which the people involved in the conversation produce an intersubjective conception of what they are doing.

Yet there is no escape from the prison of language. No matter how detached sociologists want to stay from 'members' understandings', if their points about human interaction make any sense to the reading public, they will become part of the pool of concepts by which members interpret social reality. Besides, to be able to make observations about the things people do with different conversational devices, the researchers have to acknowledge that they understand the conversation. On the other hand, if sociologists indeed came up with such results about social reality that could not be reintegrated into the ever-changing pool of notions about it, it would mean that sociology would be totally incomprehensible or otherwise useless or absurd. It would indeed be a Pyrrhic victory.

The dilemma of the social sciences is not that its results always feed back into its object. Rather, the problem is that in grand theorizing researchers do exactly the same as humans do when adapting to a social environment: they tend to start treating as natural objects the constructs they make in order to manage their lives. In the case of cultural adaptation, it is the great human talent which enables us to feel at home and to cooperate smoothly. However, in theorizing it means that a theorist is trapped in the net of his or her own spinning.

On the other hand, postmodernists or social constructionists are in danger of being trapped in another kind of cage. Since it is true that any new theory or notion about human reality may be adopted by ordinary people who attempt to make sense of society and social life, from an extremely partisan viewpoint it appears that any theory is as valid as another one. It seems that the only value of a social theory is its contribution to the notions and metaphors within which people act and think in social reality. If social theory is nothing but an intervention in the frames within which we conceive of changing social reality, the question of the validity of a finding loses its meaning, and is replaced by the question of ethics: whether the intervention of a social scientist is for the good or to the detriment of human welfare.

All in all, it is obvious that the object of social science differs from that of natural science. Yet natural science is still commonly used as the model for truly scientific research. From this viewpoint, to acknowledge the complex role of language and the constructed nature of social and cultural phenomena appears to lead social science farther away from the goal of a real science of society. As a reaction to this dilemma, many trends of social science try over and over again to create a realistic and analytic meta-language and to reduce language to a merely instrumental role. They attempt to make language into a transparent channel through which knowledge about the object of research is described and theories about it are communicated. In that effort, scientific realism can be likened to the old belief in Judaism, according to which humankind initially had a single original language where there was a true name for each and every object in reality. Then, after the split of languages at the tower of Babel, the original language was lost. Similar to what Walter Benjamin (1989) hoped to do with his Marxist (or Frankfurt School) philosophy, scientific realism wants to recover the 'pure language', to call every object by its true name and to discover the laws governing this reality.

From the viewpoint of the quest for an original language, constructionist approaches to social reality are deemed to be too vague, complicated, relativistic and ambiguous. Although all grand, ambitious attempts to establish a positive scientific theory of society have failed, the proponents of scientific realism are convinced that a constructionist theory is the worst possible. In the face of all futile attempts to find even a single sociological law beyond all doubt in the scientific community, many researchers still anticipate gradually developing a positive social theory comprised of elegant, straightforward laws that explain the functioning of society.

In other words, some social scientists still seem to assume that one day social phenomena and individual behaviour will be able to be explained by relatively simple, universally valid sociological laws. Individual behavioural patterns will be explained partly by biological factors, and partly by social or cultural factors. Yet these cultural dopes or genetically programmed robots are supposed to have been able to crack the structure of the universe or the smallest particles of atoms! It really calls for a god to grant us the means and intellect to do that.

Instead of denying the complexity of human reality, let us accept it as the starting point for a social theory of human reality. The false ideal of natural science has led social scientists up the wrong track in their attempts to pile up positive knowledge about culture and society. We must not imitate the form of mechanics and assume that social reality can be grasped by mathematical formulae or causal laws explaining and predicting human behaviour. However, what we can learn from the natural sciences is that we have to accept the findings we cannot deny or explain in other ways. The complex role of language and the constructed nature of human reality are such findings. Without dismissing social research findings at other levels, a social theory of human reality has to incorporate language as part of it. Rather than just arguing that certain lines of reasoning and research results are uninteresting or inessential, a social theory has to be able to incorporate them in the theory. Instead of simply competing with other theories without any foundation for doing so, an integrative theory could be compared to Einstein's theory of relativity. It did not actually falsify Newton's theory of gravitation, but rather pointed out that it is only valid under certain specific conditions that humans happen to face on the globe.

Similarly, to formulate a social theory of human reality we have to realize the different ontological levels at which social sciences have gathered knowledge about social reality. In many fields of research, social sciences deal with historically and culturally specific local realities; this research can present more or less valid research results. However, we must not assume that out of these universal findings simply can be piled up to form a list of general characteristics of human culture and society. We always have at our disposal a more or less limited number of examples of cultural variability and relativity. The known past and present variability in social and cultural forms does not exhaust the human potential. That is why a social theory has to move at a level where local theories are treated as examples of the constructive nature of human reality, instead of theorizing about particular kinds of constructions.

Does a social theory of human reality have to be built from scratch? Does it still wait to be invented? It would be heroic to claim that it does, and then proceed to formulate it. However, I suggest that the common conception about a non-existent paradigm or paradigms in social sciences is a cherished myth. For social scientists it is so important to maintain radicalism and individualism in their self-image that it is nice to think that there is no 'normal science' in social sciences. However, different trends of social science are separated from each other mainly by the researchers' different conceptions about their roles in society: some identify themselves as theorists, others as researchers, as 'social engineers' or as politically active partisans. Despite the different perspectives that these different social roles open to human reality, I argue that even opposing camps agree on a number of ideas, or cannot deny them. There is, after all, a social science paradigm.

To formulate a positive theory of human reality we have to avoid treating the well-taken points about cultural relativity negatively, as obstacles. Nor should we get bleak because constructionists and rhetorical analysts have pointed out that all our knowledge basically consists of capturing constructs, metaphors we live by, and convincing stories by which we impose order on disorder. With our human faculties, we have been fairly successful in making sense of the universe; so why should we be totally hopeless in studying human reality? The only difference is that in this case the object of study is human reality itself: the home base that gives us the conceptual means to make sense of the material world.

To take the theses of cultural relativity and the constructed nature of human reality positively is to realize that that is something we already know about. We have to build on it. If human reality is a social and linguistic construction, how is it constructed and how does it work? Another obvious point is to notice that although human reality is a construction, in actual mundane practice we do not seem to notice its arbitrary character. Most of the constructs and social conventions go without saying. Let me formulate this important point by saying that daily life and social order are based on the cultural unconscious, on routinized, taken-for-granted lines of thought and action. However, such dormant routines are now and again reflected on. They are identified and conceptualized, rejected, changed or renewed, to be soon again taken for granted in their changed forms. In a sense, that is what human reality is all about, and this is the perspective from which I will discuss different aspects of human reality in this book.

The Constructed Nature of Human Reality

As has been said, human reality is at least as complicated as what we know about nature. And that is because of the role of language. Human reality consists of constructs piled upon constructs in a very complex fashion, and that is the secret behind our ability to imagine the structure of realities we cannot even see, let alone inspect directly from close range. Instead of dismissing the relativistic theories about the thoroughly constructed nature of social reality, I suspect that we haven't even realized all the social and linguistic constructs we take for granted as hard material reality.

That is not to say that the more wild the ideas, the more likely they are to grasp something essential about the nature of human reality. By being able to publish a total nonsense article in *Social Text*, the quantum physicist Alan Sokal (1996a, 1996b) showed that a great deal of postmodernist writing passing as science is really nonsense. To realize that human reality is constructs upon constructs, signs referring to other signs or metaphors upon metaphors, does not mean that anything goes. This character of human reality gives us a powerful imagination, but that does not mean that anything we imagine is true. On the contrary, because of the complexity of human reality, we have to be particularly careful when trying to say something sensible about that reality.

How do I know that human reality is so complex? In all science, there is no absolute certainty, which is a relief and a challenge at the same time. There is no other way than simply to trust the observations we cannot dispute, and to start forming a picture into which all the evidence can be fitted.

Strangely enough, language, the metalanguage in which all the theories of the world are eventually presented, is one of the easiest and most fruitful objects of study. And the things we know about language prove that human reality is indeed complex.

Take, for instance, what semiotics has revealed about language. Even though it seems natural in an everyday mode of thought to see language as a list of names for real objects, actually the reality is not as simple as that. In itself, language is a closed system, where the meaning of any single term is defined by, and dependent on, other terms. Although language obviously refers to observations humans make about material reality, on closer scrutiny it cannot be reduced to a mere list of names given to objects in external reality. There are all sorts of observations humans can make about reality, but a concept is always more than a name attached to an object, because concepts are abstract, generic terms referring to a class of observations. A class does not reside in nature itself, but can only be socially constructed (Barthes 1969; Eco 1979; Saussure 1966). This means that language consists of classes and classifications which organize our observations, but also help us in making them. Edward Sapir (1958) and Benjamin Whorf (1956) suggested that language organizes and guides our observations about nature, and that a culture's members are always socialized to a world organized by the concepts created by previous generations. They claimed that the limits of our imagination are the limits of language. In a sense that may be so, but we also have to remember that the potential of language as a tool of human imagination is practically unlimited and cannot be exhausted. By using their senses, imagination and conceptual tools, individuals make numerous observations all the time about reality and put their ideas into words, which sometimes means giving a new meaning to a word or introducing a totally new concept.

When language use is described that way, one may easily get the wrong impression that it is primarily an instrument by which individuals observe natural objects. It is that too of course, but language is also dialogical: a means of interaction. A great deal of concepts refer to human acts, actors and institutions. They interpret and describe the properties of ever-changing patterns of human interaction, often also materialized as human-made environments such as houses, roads and communication technology.

The role of tropes, metaphors and metonyms is another proof of the complexity of language. George Lakoff and Mark Johnson (1980) have convincingly shown how words such as 'role', 'journey' or 'structure' are used as models in expressing ideas and organizing experience. Language is full of tropes. Yet metaphors or metonyms easily go unnoticed; they become 'dead' or 'dormant' and are taken matter-of-factly, as if the words were just names for objects in the real world or as if the framework they imply was the only one possible. To lay bare the ways in which a speaker makes a convincing argument or describes an object as if language was transparent, one needs to apply rhetorical analysis (Perelman 1982; Perelman and Olbrechts-Tyteca 1971).

The Interplay of Routines and Reflexivity

Given all the complexity of human reality, one would assume that humans must be like supercomputers in order to function in it. Since not even the simplest possible thing can be communicated without directly or indirectly invoking a whole web or structure of concepts referring to other concepts, one would think that it takes a super-fast processor and a huge memory to sensibly cope in everyday life, not to mention intellectual conversations.

However, the most incredible thing about humans is that we manage the complex human reality with ease, often even without much need for reflection. After institutionalizing a social practice, fairly soon humans take it so much for granted that, if prompted about it, they will assume things have 'always' been that way. We manage our daily lives and also our more philosophical moments not because we are walking supercomputers but because we are rather like the bugs called water boatmen, which are able to walk on the surface of water. Similarly, we surf on the sea of culture, only invoking the frames and concepts needed on a particular occasion to find our way. Although adapting to changing conditions by means of concepts and practices requires a degree of reflexivity, we soon learn to take for granted a lot of what is going on, and to create routines of thought and action. Our natural and social environment, including the language we use, includes a vast potential of categorizations and points of interest, but a local culture soon enough makes it a home. According to Mary Douglas (1991), home is a place where a person wants to keep things in order, and in that sense a culture is a home, an order people try to maintain in the anarchy and disorder of human reality.

In that sense, human adaptability is first of all based on routines, now and again interrupted by reflexivity about the cultural unconscious. The cultural unconscious, the routinized and taken-for-granted aspects of our thought and behaviour, is not unconscious in the sense of being repressed from consciousness, as the concept is used in psychoanalytic theory. However, although we are not consciously aware of it, its existence is partly known to us in the sense that it includes tacit assumptions upon which our routines are based. Different kinds of tacit assumptions are invoked only when they are needed in a particular situation, for instance if smooth cooperation between interactants requires checking out the shared understanding of what is going on.

The general idea of the central role of the cultural unconscious expressed above, although not called by that name, has been formulated innumerable times in the history of social sciences. In that sense it truly forms one element of the paradigm that the social sciences share. However, for various reasons, it is often not placed centre stage in social theories. For instance, in classical sociology habit functioned as an important concept in the writings of both Émile Durkheim and Max Weber, not to mention American pragmatism, but was later purposefully excised from the conceptual structure of the field because sociology wanted to distance itself from behaviourist psychology (Camic 1986).

In fact, the idea about humans normally following habits is so self-evident and mundane that many social theorists have passed it with a hasty remark to concentrate on what appears to be its opposite, the more creative moments of human existence. Social scientists have wanted to explain the logic of social phenomena and institutions, perhaps by that means to change people's ways, which has directed attention to other, from their viewpoint, more fascinating aspects of human reality. Therefore, the concept of routine is not easily found in their conceptual structure. Consider Karl Marx and the way he discusses the relationship between material reality and human consciousness:

> In the social production of their life, men enter into definite relations that are indispensable and independent of their will, relations of production which correspond to a definite stage of development of their material productive forces. The sum total of these relations of production constitutes the economic structure of society, the real foundation, on which rises a legal and political superstructure and to which correspond definite forms of social consciousness. The mode of production of material life conditions the social, political and intellectual life process in general. It is not the consciousness of men that determines their being, but their social being that determines their consciousness. (Marx 1970: 20–21)

Apart from the conceptual difficulties of separating material life or social being from consciousness and inserting a causal relationship from the former to the latter, if social being devoid of consciousness or conscious thought could mean anything, it could be interpreted as Marx's reference to routines of everyday life.

Among classical social thought, American pragmatism has shed light on the role of habituality in human action (Kilpinen 2000). For instance, in summarizing the chapter on habit in his *Principles of Psychology*, William James put it this way:

> Habit is the enormous fly-wheel of society, its most precious conservative agent. It alone is what keeps us all within the bounds of ordinance, and saves the children of fortune from the envious uprisings of the poor. It alone prevents the hardest and most repulsive walks of life from being deserted by those brought up to tread therein. It keeps the fisherman and the deckhand at sea through the winter; it holds the miner in his darkness, and nails the countryman to his log-cabin and his lonely farm through all the months of snow; it protects us from invasion by the natives of the desert and the frozen zone. It dooms us all to fight out the battle of life upon the lines of our nurture or our early choice, and to make the best of a pursuit that disagrees, because there is no other to which we are fitted, and it is too late to begin again. It keeps different social strata from mixing. Already at the age of twenty-five you see the professional mannerism settling down on the young commercial traveller, on the young doctor, on the young minister, on the young counsellor-at-law. (James 1983: 121)

However, in addition to acknowledging the role of routines as a conservative element, the pragmatist tradition has shown particularly vividly how habits are an essential aspect of all human action, and also essential for creativity. This aspect of the pragmatists' concept of habit can be seen, for instance, in the way Charles Peirce conceives of abduction as the primary form of human perception and reasoning. This is how Peirce described abduction in 1901:

> Looking out of my window this lovely spring morning I see an azalea in full bloom. No, no! I do not see that; though that is the only way I can describe what I see. That is a proposition, a sentence, a fact; but what I perceive is not proposition, sentence, fact, but only an image, which I make intelligible in part by means of a statement of fact. This statement is abstract; but what I see is concrete. I perform an abduction when I do so much as express in a sentence anything I see. The truth is that the whole fabric of our knowledge is one matted felt of pure hypothesis that is confirmed and refined by induction. Not the smallest advance in knowledge can be made beyond the stage of vacant staring, without making an abduction at every step.

According to Peirce, drawing conclusions is never based on pure inductive or deductive logic. Instead, there is always an aspect of educated guesswork at play. Because of our abundant practical experience in perceiving the environment and in making sense of human reality, we are much more clever and creative than we can ever put into words. And this creativity in our reasoning is based on our habituality. All the time the human mind and body gather experience from circumstances and the conclusions drawn from them, and such accumulated knowledge is conditioned into habitual information processes that operate inside our conscious mind. Such culturally unconscious routines not only assist our self-conscious mind; they make perception and understanding possible. Consider language which we use as a primary means of communication. The fact that we can immediately understand a simple sentence and also get the emotions conveyed in it is based on the fact that we have stored up the uses of each term in our memory. Instead of having to consciously retrieve and process that information each time the word is used, we are able to routinely understand the word and the whole sentence without paying any attention to the whole procedure.

More recently, the role of habits has aroused interest in social and cultural theory under different terms. For Michel Foucault (1972, 1973b), the corresponding concept is the non-discursive or the unthought, while Pierre Bourdieu (1977, 1990a) has talked about *habitus* or *doxa*. Peter L. Berger and Thomas Luckmann (1966) explained the social construction of reality by the habitualization and institutionalization of routines, which for the next generation constitute *the* self-evident world. In a similar vein, the structuration theory of Anthony Giddens (1984) refers to the cultural unconscious in the concept of routines. In organization theory, Ikujiro Nonaka's (1994) theory of knowledge creation formulates similar ideas through a spiral model in which tacit knowledge embedded in practical consciousness is turned into discursive consciousness and put to a renewed routine practice. Stephen Turner's (1994) treatise on the social theory of practices also discusses the concept of tacit knowledge, but for him and for many others the umbrella concept is practice. It has even been argued that at present there is a practice turn in social and cultural theory (Schatzki et al. 2001).

Because habituality and the constant interplay between routines and reflexivity are at the centre of the paradigm of social sciences, it is evident that many more names and works could be mentioned in the list above. Likewise, it would be a task of its own to compare systematically differ-ent formulations of the theory with each other and point out how they dif-fer. Instead of that, let me just sketch the basic ideas of the spiral from routines to reflexivity and back again by quoting some of the relevant names.

As just noted, Pierre Bourdieu uses the concept *doxa* to refer to the uni-verse of undiscussed and undisputed knowledge, on the basis of which people's discourse, arguments and attitudes arise. 'Because the subjective necessity and self-evidence of the commonsense world are validated by the objective consensus on the sense of the world, what is essential *goes without saying because it comes without saying*' (Bourdieu 1977: 167). Here Bourdieu talks about knowledge, but, as said, it is questionable in what sense we can in fact talk about knowledge when we talk about routines and the non-discursive. It is certainly not knowledge in the sense of being consciously known to the participants, waiting to be put into words, because any formulation of it already transforms it, brings it into the realm of the discursive, and when doing that it changes its nature. We could per-haps speak about 'local knowledge' (Geertz 1983) – that is, the fact that people master and repeatedly perform certain practices without putting them into words or being able to give an account about them instantly. When stopped to account for such things, they may be puzzled or irritated by someone asking such a stupid question, or they may resort to a plethora of familiar repertoires within which such questions are usually dealt.

When talking about routines, or the non-discursive, we are dealing with observed or observable regularities or features of behaviour which are not articulated, put into words, in any way. Language is generally so flexible and rich in its possibilities that of course it can basically address anything, but without acknowledging that not everything is equally thor-oughly formulated and put into words we miss the point that any formu-lation and any discourse is a choice. While calling attention to something from a particular viewpoint, a discourse misses other potential aspects and viewpoints, perhaps to be taken up at a later instance.

In one sense the cultural unconscious could be seen as a consequence of the eternal incompatibility between things and words. Any description of an object or activity is incomplete in grasping every aspect and detail of it. Even if there is no lack but rather an abundance of formulations and articulations about and around a topic, there never can be a match between, say, an act and its account, or an object or a scene and its description. The words we use are not our own inventions; we have inherited them from the previous generations and the linguistic community. They carry with them their own history of contexts where they have been used. Besides, the elements from which they have been constructed leave their traces in the words by which we can communicate. For instance, the metaphors by which many words signify their meaning tell their own stories in the sentences where they are used. To paraphrase Michel Foucault (1973b: 323), we are formed as the subject of a language that for thousands of years has been formed without us, whose organization escapes us, and whose meaning 'sleeps an almost invincible sleep' in the words we momentarily activate by means of discourse.

On the other hand, we must not conceive of language merely as an incomplete system of description. The act of putting something to discourse, of becoming conscious of something previously unnoticed and reflecting on it within that framework, always changes or actually constitutes its (previously unnoticed) object, and affects the thinking subjects.

> What is essential is that thought, both for itself and in the density of its workings, should be both knowledge and a transformation of the mode of being of that on which it reflects. Whatever it touches it immediately causes to move; it cannot discover the unthought, or at least move towards it, without immediately bringing the unthought nearer to itself – or even, perhaps, without pushing it further away, and in any case without causing man's own being to undergo a change by that very fact, since it is deployed in the distance between them. (Foucault 1973b: 327)

When an aspect of the cultural unconscious suddenly becomes an object of reflexive attention, and subjected to articulation in discourse, it does not simply mean that an unknown subject is given a name; it always has a larger or smaller bearing on the whole discursive realm. Of course an aspect of the non-discursive may be noticed and pointed out by accident, for instance by a linguist interested in metaphors, in which case the finding is deemed uninteresting and simply forgotten, but often it begs the question as to why something that has gone this far without saying is now observed and put into words. It implies that old routines and practices are being questioned and changing.

For instance, among others, linguists and speakers of languages like Finnish, where the first-person singular pronoun does not have a gender, were conscious of the fact that the English *he* was often used to refer to a human being generally. However, it took the feminist movement to point out that this practice is sexist, and it must be changed by avoiding the first-person singular or by using 'he or she' instead. In that example, the previously unnoticed topic was formulated in terms of a moral issue and solved by introducing a social norm. Consequently, the avoidance of potentially sexist expressions adds a new aspect of reflexivity to language use, at least until the new rules have become routinized. Another consequence is that texts written before this renovation of English grammar call attention to the old practice, and connote sexism.

Here I have, mainly for pedagogical reasons, chosen to approach the non-discursive from the vantage point of something culturally unconscious becoming conscious and discursively constructed. That does not imply however that the non-discursive is outside culture, like a wilderness that has been untouched by any human being, or like a new realm of knowledge of which people now become conscious. We should think of the cultural unconscious not as a territory where no one has gone before, but rather as something once known but forgotten. I do not mean that everything is stored in the memory of a culture, if we only could manage to recall it. I just mean that our behaviour is always premised on conditions which are socially constructed: on assumptions about ourselves and our environment, and on policies and strategies planned to serve different functions and groups of people. Of course, plans never turn into practices exactly as they were drawn in the master plan for the simple reason that, even if there is a carefully made master plan, each participant has to strategize, apply and relate to the master plan. Actual practices developed on the basis of conscious plans and decisions then become institutionalized, which also means that some aspects of the practices become routinized: they are too self-evident to be borne in mind.

When an aspect of the non-discursive becomes an object of reflexive attention and is brought to discourse it is no longer the same object. The very discourse both enables us to identify the object and constructs the way it is perceived. Its place and position are defined by the discourse, but they also contribute to changing it.

We must not conceive of the cultural unconscious as a fixed entity with a certain content. We should not think of it as a pool of premises and tacit assumptions about reality that exists in a culture. Such a view implies that we could perform psychoanalysis of a culture and lay bare everything that is hidden from us, everything that is taken for granted. All the hazy veils of habit would be removed, society and culture would be totally transparent, and we would be speaking the original true language once again. As intriguing as this image is, it is impossible and misleading in many ways. For one thing, tacit assumptions should not be seen as a true, accessible, secret reality underneath a 'surface consciousness'. Most of what goes without saying in social practices are mundane shared premises, which can be easily laid bare if needed. Second, what is taken for granted and what is prompted and reflected on in social interaction changes from moment to moment. In fact, we could say that all communication takes place at the borderline between shared premises and reflexivity. The points individuals make in communication are always premised on certain unquestioned assumptions, while addressing others. Updating shared understandings in interaction means that different tacit assumptions are continuously evoked, questioned and rebuilt. Analysing *the* cultural unconscious of a culture is the wrong image because tacit premises change all the time. Third, when an unquestioned routine is called into question, it is not necessarily criticized or justified within the same discourse where it was once established. The original reason for a social practice may have been long forgotten, so that in the new situation the discourses of its legitimation are totally different. Even if they were more or less the same, we must bear in mind that to evoke a dormant routine is always an intervention and part of a new strategic situation.

Reflexivity about a routine of action or language use never means that all premises are deconstructed, laid bare or questioned at the same time. That would be simply impossible, because as subjects we are built of such dormant constructs, and because any meaningful act or communication requires some footing, some premises which are taken as 'firm ground'.

When a dormant routine is called into question and thus made visible, it means that the institution in question is changed, even if everything seems to remain the same from the outset. However the shattering of the natural attitude is reacted to, it means that a dormant routine becomes a topic, an object of attention. We could say that it moves from the cultural unconscious, from the non-discursive to the discursive sphere; it is articulated in one way or another.

The natural attitude may of course be shattered for varying reasons. The younger generation may assume new habits and manners that call some old routines into question. Another possibility is that a people comes into contact with other groups, which, for instance, happens as a consequence of migration. Different ethnic groups come into close proximity with each other, which makes them aware of some of their habits that they have thus far taken for granted, so they can now see that things can also be arranged differently.

A reaction to a change in default action may take varying forms. To do or witness something which goes against accustomed habits may even evoke physical emotions. For instance, Jewish people who break the Kosher rule not to eat pork may feel sick. Similarly, Norbert Elias (1978) shows that along with the 'civilizing process' people develop feelings of shame, embarrassment or repugnance for, say, not using 'proper' language or witnessing 'uncivilized' manners. As Harold Garfinkel (1967) pointed out in his ethnomethodological experiments, people may also get angry when someone deviates from accustomed habits. When a break from the ordinary takes place, thus calling attention to a dormant routine, one tries to interpret the deviants' behaviour in one way or another. One wonders whether the deviants are stupid, ignorant, sick, rude or up to something that isn't immediately obvious.

The change in accustomed habits also calls for a justification or legiti-mation of the new habits. One possibility is that old routines are simply defended by arguing that things have always been done that way. This 'tradition' argument comes very close to what Max Weber (1978a) dis-cusses in distinguishing 'traditional authority' as one form of domination. Another often related possibility is that a habit or a policy is justified or denounced by appealing to an unquestioned, sacred principle. It may be argued that certain habits represent the culture of a people or a nation, or they may be presented as civilized. Similarly, one film or novel may be preferred over another because it develops a new form or represents new thinking, implying that renewing and developing oneself is the divine meaning of life. Justification or rejection may also be based on moral grounds, arguing that it is right or wrong to behave in a particular way. In this instance, different moral principles such as fairness, equality or free-dom may be evoked. Related to that, a practice may be justified by legal arguments, although they can also be used to point out that it would be risky to break the law. The latter usage is an example of a whole range of utilitarian, practical and rational discourses within which a manner or practice may be considered. Often it is argued that it is more advanta-geous to an individual or to a whole community or society to act in a par-ticular way.

The discourses within which old or new manners are commonly dealt with in social life can lead to different policies or practices. We can distin-guish social norms, rituals, changes in ontology or cosmology, and coercion.

An explication of social norms is one possible way of reacting to the situation. It is also probably the most commonly discussed option in social theory. The grounds for the emergence of a social norm may be manifold: the norm may be justified by moral or practical reasons. In any case, we are talking about a social norm when members of a community express disapproval or approval for following a particular rule. The com-munity or a fraction of it may begin to defend the old way of doing things and organizing life by demanding that certain old habits are preserved – or already forgotten practices are revitalized in the name of tradition. This can be done, for instance, in the name of ethnic identity. The particular habits that are called into question are associated with the people, its par-ticular culture, values and tradition. To abide by certain habits, thus far hardly noticed dormant routines, now assumes the symbolic meaning of the particular ethnicity in question. Those who want to preserve their ethnic identity abide by the old habits, and possibly also raise their children to respect the habits in question. Thus, what used to be dormant routines, taken-for-granted ways of doing things – like addressing other people in speech, dressing up or preparing food – are now turned into social norms. Those who do not abide by them may be punished in some way, for instance condemned, but at least breaking the norms or abiding by them is given attention. Thus, to follow the norms may be interpreted as being polite, well-bred, religious or traditional, whereas breaking them may be seen as being naïve, impolite, ill-bred or rebellious. When a dormant routine is explicated as a social norm, it means that following or breaking it becomes a topic, and that it may then symbolize or signify something.

Following a certain rule may also take the form of a ritual. In the case of a ritual, such as taking off one's hat or shoes or washing one's hands or feet when entering a certain place, the action becomes relatively independent from the practical contents of the habit. Hands or feet are not washed because they are dirty, and the hat or shoes are not taken off because the room is warm or to keep the floor clean. Sometimes a ritual performed by an individual entails reciting texts, singing songs or making gestures which are unknown and incomprehensible to the audience. But whether or not the audience or the partakers understand the meaning of the particular gestures or words spoken, they know that the idea is not in the immediate contents but rather in what the ritual as a whole stands for. They may not even know the symbolic meaning of the particular ritual they attend, but they do know that it has some symbolic meaning. Through ritual people associate an idea, for instance belonging to a community, with an all-embracing cognitive and emotional experience.

In that respect, rituals come close to, but also differ from, habits which have become mere symbols. Manners of politeness, such as raising one's hat, shaking hands or asking 'How are you doing?' have diverged from their immediate content, and as dormant habits, they are seldom noticed or reflected on.

Breaking accustomed routines or questioning their basis may of course also lead to changes in common beliefs about ontology or cosmology. For instance, to show that a new method of treatment actually makes life easier, keeps oneself healthier or saves human lives may lead the community to believe that things like germs or viruses actually exist, and that they account for at least some illnesses. Old and new ontological or cosmological beliefs may then live side by side, but in any case the implementation of new technologies usually also leads to changes in world views.

Often, the spread of a new technique has only minor effects on shared world views or beliefs, but their introduction invokes notions about proper morals or decency. This takes place all the time at different levels of social life. For instance, new words are introduced into the language to depict new objects or to replace old terms. For some time, the new and the old are paid attention to, but soon enough the new things are taken for granted. When the microwave oven first became popular, it evoked questions about whether food cooked with it was safe, or as good as when prepared in the traditional way. Similarly, using a cellular phone has been associated with being modern, affluent or even pompous, but is now taken as a matter of course, as a necessity or simply as useful in some instances.

A community or a powerful group or individual, such as the state or the king, may also influence the way things are done by force. Coercion may take different forms. An old or new procedure may be instigated by mere force or threat of violence. Spatial or infrastructural arrangements are another way of forcing people to behave in particular ways. Fences, fortresses, roads, city plans, the architecture of houses and the technology of mass or two-way communication all provide conditions for possible forms of action and interaction.

Social organizations also set constraints, or we could say that infrastructure, architecture and social organization are always linked in many ways. For instance, we are not usually allowed to enter another nation state without showing a passport and going through certain procedures.

Coercion may often be conditional, drawing on individuals' more or less rational calculation of risks. For example, driving a car over the speed limit saves time; however, in addition to a bigger accident risk there is also the risk of getting a speeding ticket. Similarly, instead of buying the merchandise one needs one could just steal it, but then there is a risk of getting caught and being subjected to physical violence or facing a jail sentence.

These are all ways in which people may react to a habit or practice that does not go unnoticed, but is instead an object of reflexivity. It may evoke immediate emotions. It is also interpreted, objected to or justified in various ways. The situation may lead to different policies or practices. The different levels distinguished and the options listed for them are not meant to be exhaustive or even analytically crystal clear in the sense of being mutually exclusive. A new object of attention may be at once dealt with at all these levels, and the different options are only examples. There are no Platonic 'pure ideas' of things like the ritual or social norm. In actual practice, any social institution has aspects of norms, ritualism, forms of coercion, and so on. Besides, we must bear in mind that any typology about the forms of social institutions stems from the same source of culture and its classifications as does the object of this inquiry: how the objects that are part of human reality are cultural constructions. We must remember that there is no starting point, no fixed chronological order, for reflexivity about a previously unnoticed habit or practice. There is no untouched nature into which humans are thrown. There are no 'uncivilized' routines or practices that do not already have a social and cultural history behind them. Nor are there humans without social life and its institutions, policies and spatial arrangements, forming frames and constraints for reasoning and dormant routines. There is no starting point or an end result; instead, human reality and social and cultural change entail a conscious fluctuation between the objects of our attention and reflexivity and what is taken for granted. Anything may become a dormant routine: a habit, a policy or a classification. Similarly, a break in the expected practices or lines of thought may take place anywhere and trigger many kinds of processes. And after such a process, a new routine will be institutionalized and soon enough taken for granted at least from certain perspectives. One of the most amazing things about humans is that in about one generation we get so accustomed to a policy that we don't even notice it, and if asked, assume that things have been like that forever.

What is Reflexivity?

As was said in the previous sections, in this book I argue that a continuous interplay between routines and reflexivity is an essential part of human reality. Although in this context, as the opposite of habituality, the meaning of the concept of reflexivity is self-evident, on closer scrutiny it is quite as tricky as its opposite.

A popular concept, especially from the 1980s onwards, reflexivity is used 'with a diverse range of connotations, and sometimes with virtually no meaning at all', as Paul Atkinson and Amanda Coffey (2002: 807) put it. I suggest that it can depict different, more or less intertwined meanings, which fall into two classes. On one hand, the concept of reflexivity may refer to an attribute of the social science researcher. On the other hand, reflexivity may depict a characteristic of culture or an activity by ordinary people.

When reflexivity refers to the activity or attitude of researchers, the writers often point out that the methods we use to analyse human reality and the styles by which we report on our findings are – to some degree – constitutive of the realities they describe (Atkinson and Coffey 2002: 807; Gubrium and Holstein 1997). This realization, which owes a lot to Michel Foucault's treatment of discourses as practices that 'systematically form the objects of which they speak' (Foucault 1972: 49), led to a radical rethinking of ethnography after the publication of *Reflections on Fieldwork in Morocco* (Rabinow 1977), *Writing Culture* (Clifford and Marcus 1986) and *Anthropology as Cultural Critique* (Marcus and Fischer 1986). Consequently, people doing ethnographic research became engaged in reflecting on their activity with the understanding that 'the role of the researcher is subject to the same critical analysis and scrutiny as the research itself' (Carolan 2002: 8), or that they need to have an ongoing conversation about experience while simultaneously doing their fieldwork (Coffey 1999).

There are various solutions to that challenge. Standpoint researchers draw a radical conclusion by emphasizing that what you observe and how you conceive of reality depends on your perspective, and that different perspectives are mutually incommensurate. Consequently, as part of a research report the researcher must give an account of his or her characteristics and standpoint so that readers can assess its effect on the results. By contrast, in their reports postmodernist writers want to convey the idea that reality is many-faceted and that there is no ultimate truth. Thus, they ensure that different voices and perspectives are visible in the report so that readers have a chance to form their own picture of the phenomenon being studied. Reflexive sociology, as promoted for instance by Pierre Bourdieu (1990b), represents the third main solution. For Bourdieu, reflexivity depicts the means by which sociologists contextualize their own intellectual practice. In other words, in interpreting their data, researchers should take the positions from which the observations were made and the contexts in which the actions by participants took place as part of their data, part of the information that serves as clues in making the interpretations.

Reflexivity may also depict a characteristic or activity of ordinary people. This usage of the term in social theory was first introduced by the founder of ethnomethodology, Harold Garfinkel, who conceives of reflexivity as an essential condition of social life (Garfinkel 1967: 9–10). For ethnomethodology, reflexivity depicts routine practice that consists in the constant accounting for, and reporting of, the actions of members of society by themselves. It does not mean that members reflect on the premises or rules applied in giving accounts or assessing the adequacy of other accounts; such second-level reflexivity is reserved for the researcher engaged in ethnomethodological sociology.

In that sense, the concept of reflexivity used in more recent social theory is different because it refers to the reflexive monitoring of action, both at the individual and at the institutional level. Such a meaning given to the concept is in turn often associated with the assumption that, in particular, institutional reflexivity is increasing. Thus Ulrich Beck, Anthony Giddens and Scott Lash (1994) talk about reflexive modernization. According to Giddens, the reflexivity of modern life 'consists in the fact that social practices are constantly examined and reformed in the light of incoming information about those very practices, thus constitutively altering their character' (Giddens 1990: 38). This means, among other things, that the theories, concepts and findings which social research produces become part of lay knowledge and are thus 'fed back' to the social system. For instance, concepts like capital, investment or markets have become integral to what 'modern economic life' is: they actively constitute people's behaviour and inform the reasons for which it is undertaken. According to Giddens, despite the increasingly central position of knowledge about society, reflexive modernization does not advance certitude but instead destabilizes social life, changes the role of expert knowledge and creates a crisis of expertise.[2] At the individual level, it is assumed that these changes undermine people's 'ontological security' and increase self-reflexivity. It is assumed that we are constantly advancing (or retreating) to an era where everyone is increasingly aware of each institution, habit or concept as a social and cultural construction, and where common understanding has to be built from scratch every time. For instance, in the 1990s Ulrich Beck suggested that modernization had occurred in two phases: the first stage replaced estate society by class society, whereas in the 'reflexive moderni-zation' of the latter part of the twentieth century, the markers of class were fading at the expense of individual style and fashion (Beck 1994). Among other things, according to him, 'reflexive modernization' means enhanced individualization:

> Opportunities, threats, ambivalences of the biography, which it was pre-viously possible to overcome in a family group, in the village community or by recourse to a social class or group, must increasingly be perceived, interpreted and handled by individuals themselves. [...] And even the self is no longer just the unequivocal self but has become fragmented into contradictory discourses of the self. (Beck 1994: 8)

In a sense, the theory of reflexive modernization unites both meanings of reflexivity by suggesting that 'professional' reflexivity on the part of researchers in late modernity is to an ever greater degree united or in cor-respondence to the reflexivity of ordinary people, which is assumed to lead into a new, qualitatively different social system as compared with 'traditional society'. While there certainly is a point in emphasizing that in contemporary advanced societies research and theories on social pheno-mena have become an important institutional agent in social develop-ment and that public discourses on all aspects of human reality are informed by expert knowledge, it can also be argued that the assumed increased reflexivity in the social reality is a projection of a changed mind-set of the researchers and theorists about their object. It may be argued that whatever the society in question, whether it is 'primitive' or complex and technologically advanced, people have metacultural (Urban 2001) concepts or reflexive frames by which they describe, define and assess their action and the culture and society they live in, and such frames inevitably contribute to forming the reality they live in. Admittedly, less complex societies do not have social science as a specialized institution, but for this reason the feedback loop from innovations in reflexive perspectives to changed practices is even more direct. Therefore, reflexivity cannot be deemed a particular characteristic of modern societies, although forms of reflexivity vary between cultures.

When talking about reflexivity at the individual level, as the reflexive monitoring of action, to exaggerate and simplify a little we could say that the 'size' of the cultural unconscious in comparison to reflexivity, or the role played by it in everyday life, is a constant. Our brain capacity simply could not handle a situation where shared assumptions about each other's behaviour were close to zero and we would have to stop to question each concept and routine we have internalized. Instead, we remain functional and creative precisely because we automatically take certain things for granted in order to concentrate on what calls for reflexive attention at the moment.

It can be argued, first, that there is an accumulation of knowledge going on in human societies, but humans mould the accumulated knowledge into new routines, new given presumptions, which in a way collapse whole layers of knowledge and make them part of human institutions. Second, because social science by nature concentrates on pointing out what has been taken for granted thus far, and now comes into the open so to speak, it always misses the counterpart: the things that are becoming self-evident, culturally unconscious.

The grand narrative of the Enlightenment, wherein the modernization story is rooted, is based on a false ontology about the nature of human life and knowledge. There is no ultimate objective truth about social life, gradually revealing itself to modern humans, because through our cultural notions of life we also realize social reality and its institutions, and construct ourselves as actors in that reality. Our routines and notions of life are always based on certain premises that are seldom questioned in everyday life. But of course that does not mean that the contents of the cultural unconscious do not change, sometimes more radically than at other times.

The Structure of the Book

In the following chapters, I shall introduce the main characteristics of my discussion of human reality by outlining its key elements. Chapter 2 discusses the question of social norms and moral considerations in more detail. Chapter 3 deals with routines and reflexivity in the use of language. In Chapter 4, I argue that the ordinary conversations and institutional talk studied by conversation analysts show particularly well how the routines embedded in the cultural unconscious structure everyday interaction. Chapter 5 deals with the nature and role of rituals and ritual-like events as an interface between routines, reflexivity and the human body. In Chapter 6, personality is discussed as one of the key constructions of contemporary complex societies: how it is constructed and taken for granted as part of the cultural unconscious. Chapter 7 deals with a related issue, that is, how identity construction and identification with certain properties of a group of people play a role in the social order. In Chapter 8 I address why social and cultural theory tends to assume again and again that, along with what is known as modernization, routines will become a thing of the past. Finally in Chapter 9, I summarize the points of my argument and discuss their implications.

Notes

1   Naturally there are social scientists who disagree on what I suggest are the main aspects of human reality, or who argue that I have ignored important elements. Since it is also characteristic of different schools of thought in the social sciences that they concentrate on one aspect of human reality and explain social phenomena by it, it is likely that some scholars do not recognize themselves from the total picture drawn in this book. For instance, sociobiologists, economists and rational choice theorists typically concentrate on showing how a rational calculus of one kind or another predicts how individuals behave on the average, no matter if they express awareness of such egoism or not. In such trends of social research one is often not the least interested in how the motives for individuals' activity are dependent on or shaped by the concepts by which people conceive of human reality, or that language has a role in actively constructing and modifying social institutions. However, I suggest that in these trends of social thought one also builds a theoretical system on the assumption that patterned behaviour in human societies is based on routines, which is a central point emphasized in this book.

2   In this line of thought Giddens is clearly indebted to Jean-François Lyotard, who in his book *The Postmodern Condition* (1984 originally published in 1979) argued that the status of knowledge is altered when societies enter what is known as the postindustrial age and cultures enter what is known as the postmodern age. According to him, the postmodern age means that there is a general 'incredulity toward metanarratives': scientific knowledge loses its basis of authority.

2 Norms and Rules

As was said in the Introduction, I argue that routines are the mainstay of order for human reality. Within social theory such an argument immediately raises the counter-argument: what about social norms and values? Aren't they at least equally important, or should we not think that they are primary to routines? Aren't socially shared conceptions of what is right and what is wrong the original source of social conventions, practices and routines? Consider the fact that when people's habitual action is disturbed they often get irritated and express moral condemnation; doesn't that prove that they were following certain normative rules in their behaviour?

In recent decades, the norm theory has been criticized especially by scholars who suggest that the meaning of actions or objects is the key to understanding social order. According to such a cultural view, people's actions and social practices can be made intelligible by explaining how they conceive of reality and what things mean to them. Thus, for instance, the fact that people observe certain normative rules in their interaction can be made intelligible by showing what honouring those rules means to them. However, although the meaning theory is broader than the norm theory, it does hold the danger that we overemphasize members' consciousness of their action and forget about the cultural unconscious. In everyday life, the meaning of things is seldom readily available or fully thought through for the actors, and asking for or giving an account of what is going on does not simply capture the moment in an explanation; it is also an intervention in the routines.

Yet we cannot totally condemn the idea that social practices can be explained by explicating shared meanings. Similarly, the existence of norms is an interesting phenomenon in human reality. As will be argued in this chapter, it must not be ignored although norms do not constitute the founding principle of social order.

To address these problems of social theory, I shall discuss the role of norms and rules in human reality in the light of concrete examples. The questions are: how do we account for normative or constitutive rules in human reality? What is their place in the bigger picture?

The Meaning of Moral Rules: A Case Example

Let us take an example from the American Amish group, within which normative rules play an important role in keeping order and preserving their community. As one of the several Anabaptist groups that trace their origins to the Radical Reformation of sixteenth-century Europe, they are famous for their critical attitude toward modernization (Kraybill and Olshan 1994). To maintain the separation of the Amish church and society from the evils of the larger culture, the *Ordnung* – the understandings that prescribe the expectations of Amish life – embodies the dos and don'ts of the members. There are differences between the settlements, but in many of them it is, for instance, forbidden to drive a car, attend high school or join the Rotary Club. On the other hand, the members are prescribed to obey the teacher, to wear traditional dress, and to use horse and carriage. The long-standing taboo against using 110-volt electricity from public power lines effectively eliminates the use of electrical gadgets and appliances, although this restriction is partly circumvented in most settlements by batteries that provide 12 volt DC current. In addition, the Amish rejection of mass media, especially television, helps to preserve the cultural boundaries that separate them from the winds of pluralism.

The Amish are a vivid example of the role of social norms in controlling human behaviour, often thought to be of primary importance for the maintenance of social order. For instance, in Émile Durkheim's early writings social norms are more or less equated with 'the social' at large, and treated as the mortar that holds society together by being a counterforce to individual interests which, in his view, threatened to tear modern society apart. However, the dos and don'ts of human societies can be approached from a different perspective, as one possible form of reflexivity before something unexpected, something that stands out from the routine and therefore catches people's attention. When such routine-breaking things happen, as is frequently the case, one of the possible and actually most common ways to deal with it is to consider unexpected behaviour from the viewpoint of right or wrong, accepted or forbidden. We are used to referring to this members' reaction, in many walks of life already institutionalized into formulated rules or regulations, by talking about social norms.

The Amish are a good example because social and technical change often makes communities and societies face new conditions and situations, which often trigger moral and normative considerations. When new things and behavioural options become reality, members become more reflectively conscious than before of both old and new, and formulate that reflexivity in terms of behavioural rules one must observe. Although the Amish are an extreme case, in a certain sense their concerns are no different from those of the classics of sociology, for instance from

Durkheim's primary concern with the threatening decay of morality in modernity.

So the Amish are by no means exceptional in their struggle with modernity and technical development. Let us take another example. When television came to Finland and spread throughout the country in the early 1960s, one of the Finnish Protestant revivalist movements, the Old Laestadians, banned it. After informal discussions on the subject, the annual Old Laestadian board meeting in 1963 decided that 'the television set with its programmes does not belong in the Christian home'. In this extremist Protestant sect, the total ban on television was maintained until the 1980s (Melkas 1985). In the 1960s the Old Laestadians also banned all forms of birth control, and the prohibition prevailed up until the 1980s (Päivi Alasuutari 1992).

The Amish and the Laestadians have dealt with the experience of changing living conditions and everyday-life practices in the larger culture in terms of morality: what is right and what is wrong, and how should people – or at least good Christians – live? Part of this moral discourse has been to discuss and agree on the rules which the community has to honour. Since new technology, especially, opens up novel options and possibilities for action (such as driving a car, watching television, or using a telephone), they have to be negotiated: is it okay to do those things, and if so, under what conditions?

Although religious groups may be extremist in their reactions, they are not terribly different from larger cultures or from the concerns that lie behind the emergence of the social sciences. For instance, ever since the development of mass media, film and electric communication, there has been a much more general concern about the effects of mass culture. A great deal of research on mass communication is in one way or another motivated by such concerns. Researchers have addressed the impact of violence and other unacceptable models of behaviour in mass culture. The Frankfurt School (e.g. Adorno and Horkheimer 1979: 120–67; Marcuse 1968: 56–83) and the aristocratic tradition of mass culture critique (Swingewood 1977) have been concerned with mass culture as a medium of ideological indoctrination. In recent years, researchers have documented and reflected on the fact that mass culture is still very much a moral question in probably all contemporary societies (Abrahamsson 1988; Alasuutari 1992b, 1996a, 1999; Ang 1985, 1991; Hagen 1994).

Non-members of particular groups such as the Amish probably do not see how telephone use could morally harm, but it appears that, with the advent of cellular phones, using a telephone is again raising moral questions. For instance, in Finland, where cellular phone density is the highest in the world, especially when the technology was first introduced there was a lot of discussion about proper rules of conduct for using the phone in public places.

However, not all new goods or ideas are resisted or dealt with with special caution, even among the Amish or the Laestadians. Some may be welcomed with delight and enthusiasm, others may be adopted with little, if any, attention paid to the whole thing. Nor is the emergence of moral considerations and social norms regarding a new object of attention a necessary consequence. Of course how new things are reacted to depends on local culture; in Amish culture even buttons for clothes have faced a total ban, but one can always find changes which go practically unnoticed, without causing any need for new rules of conduct or moral norms. It is also not very insightful or requiring of elaborate thinking to only distinguish between two possibilities: either the emergence of social norms or the whole change going unnoticed. As was discussed in the previous chapter, reflexive attention on something may lead to different policies or practices. In addition to social norms, we can distinguish rituals, changes in ontology or cosmology, and coercion. An expressed awareness of some rules one is expected to follow regarding the object of attention is only one form of reflexivity.

So what is the specificity of social norms as a form of reflexivity? Under what conditions do social norms appear, and what are their different functions in human reality? In this chapter I will argue that norms must be seen as articulations of different sites of contradiction, and as factors in often unpredictable and unintended social change.

What is Wrong with Control Theory?

It is quite prevalent in the social sciences to discuss social reality in terms of rules or norms that people observe in their everyday life. Sound moral rules and the foundation of morality have been the central themes of philosophy for centuries before the emergence of the modern social sciences, and in many respects classical sociology carried on the tradition of moral philosophy. Sociologists shared with Enlightenment *philosophes* concerns for the discontents of modernization. After much enthusiasm for progress at the beginning of the eighteenth century, from the mid-1700s onwards Enlightenment philosophy had become increasingly pessimistic about the destiny of humankind (Pollard 1968). Classical sociology carried on that tradition in its concern for social integration when faced with industrialization, rationalization, individualization and the exchange economy. For instance, Émile Durkheim was concerned about the prospect of anomie, a normless state, and for him the cure was a morality that was in concert with modern, individuated society. For the classics of sociology, moral rules – or 'social norms', as Talcott Parsons later called all socially controlled rules – were not a question of their rightness, but simply an analytic concept with which to analyse cultures and societies. It was noted that different societies comply with different social norms, and studying them is important because that is how individuals influence each other and how a society holds together. This can be called the control theory of society.

Talcott Parsons especially ascribed social norms a central place in his social theory. He even compared the position of social norms in sociology to that of space in classical mechanics (Parsons 1967: 76). To put it briefly, Parsons thought that society is held together by social norms and normative control of each other's action. The norms, in turn, stem from the culture's shared belief system, including conceptions about right and wrong. According to Parsons' line of thinking, without social norms society would dissolve – or rather, there wouldn't be any society to talk about – because Parsons conceives of society in terms of social norms.

Social norms indeed seem like a self-evident concept for discussing social reality. Many common topics of social life are conceived in terms of it, both in the social sciences and in contemporary culture at large. For instance, power is ordinarily understood as a person's (or institution's) ability to carry out his or her will, regardless of resistance (cf. Weber 1978b: 926). In other words, power entails the capability to impose norms on others' conduct. Similarly, child-rearing and socialization are discussed in terms of norms that parents or other members of society teach the new generation, who then internalize them.

Despite its prevalent use and intuitive usefulness, there are severe shortcomings in the control theory of social order. The concept of normative rules opens a fairly limited perspective on social reality. For instance, Michel Foucault (1980) has pointed out that the prevalent (Weberian) notion of power, which is a prime example of a control-theoretical conception, captures poorly the nature of power relations.

According to Foucault, within the prevalent notion power is conceived as anti-energy, reduced simply to the procedure of the law of interdiction. Such a conception may be comforting, but only at the expense of hiding a considerable part of the mechanisms of power. Foucault suggests that part of the acceptance of power is due to that notion, within which power is seen as a pure limit set on freedom. Instead of this reduced conception of power as only limiting, blocking, censoring and prohibiting (which Foucault does identify as part of many power relations), he suggests that power should be conceived within a broader framework, as the name that one attributes to a complex strategical situation in a particular society (Foucault 1980: 93).

> The analysis, made in terms of power, must not assume that the sovereignty of the state, the form of the law, or the over-all unity of a domination are given at the outset; rather, these are only the terminal forms power takes. It seems to me that power must be understood in the first

instance as the multiplicity of force relations immanent in the sphere in which they operate and which constitute their own organization; as the process which, through ceaseless struggles and confrontations, transforms, strengthens, or reverses them; as the support which these force relations find in one another, thus forming a chain or a system, or on the contrary, the disjunctions and contradictions which isolate them from one another; and lastly, as the strategies in which they take effect, whose general design or institutional crystallization is embodied in the state apparatus, in the formulation of the law, in the various social hegemonies. (Foucault 1980: 92–3)

Foucault's 'dislocational' theory of power does not conceive of force relations within a single centre, but rather understands the networks of power as a multiplicity of sites of struggle. These relations of power are not in a position of exteriority with respect to other types of relationships, such as economic processes, knowledge relationships or sexual relations. Power relations also always entail forms of knowledge and of subjectivity or desire; 'they have a productive role, wherever they come into play' (Foucault 1980: 94).

Foucault's discussion of power is problematic in the sense that he sits on two stools at the same time. On the one hand he analyses the (prevalent) notion of power as a social and cultural construction; but on the other hand he suggests a broader and better definition, which we are supposed to treat as a truthful description of what power really is. Nevertheless, he shows clearly how simplistic and misleading it is to conceive of social order only within the trope of rules (which according to Foucault's interpretation is 'juridico-discursive', and stems from the institution of law). The same applies to Parsons' control theory of society. Normative rules, whether imposed and controlled by a 'higher authority' or by other community members, are not the only ways in which social systems operate and hold together. There are norms people follow or conform to in social life, but by stretching the concept of social norm too much one loses sight of a whole range of things, even the whole notion of rules themselves.

Let us take another example. Child-rearing is also commonly conceived of as certain rules that parents impose on their children's behaviour, and it is assumed that good parents control their children's television viewing. The fact that in social surveys only about a third of parents report controlling their children's television viewing has been interpreted as a sign of insufficient parental mediation. For instance, Svenning (1988: 190–1) accuses parents of being 'poor censors', whereas Baacke, Sander and Vollbrecht (1990: 334) say that they are 'appalled' at parents' indifference. However, the issue gets much more complicated if we ask what reporting about having or not having rules for children's television viewing means; that question quite simply was beyond the scope of survey studies, where the questionnaires only addressed it as dichotomous yes/no terms.

Juha Kytömäki's (1991, 1998) qualitative interview study of parental mediation of television viewing sheds light on this question. The picture that he formed on the basis of interviews with 90 families was quite consistent with earlier studies. Only 32 per cent of the families said they actually controlled their children's television viewing. However, the responses of all the parents he spoke to were in the form, 'no, but...'. Looking more closely at what came after these buts turned the results completely upside down. The parents said they did not control the contents of what their children watched because they were not allowed to watch the late-night shows that were for adults only, or because they agreed on what was suitable viewing for children and what was not. Therefore, active control had become unnecessary. On the other hand, in those families where the parents said they did control their children's television viewing, that control did not seem to be very effective, or parents and children did not have a very clear agreement on the rules of television viewing. In contrast to what earlier studies had led us to understand, the problems were worse in those families where the parents said they controlled their children's viewing. That finding is in accordance with ethnographic studies which emphasize that in most cases such family rules are implicit. They are 'embedded in the activities of daily lives, unintentional and unremarkable at the time' (Bryce and Leichter 1983: 310). Explicit rules are actually symptomatic of stress or a developing family crisis (Reiss 1981: 179–81).

The concept of social norms is in other words restricted in the sense that not all rules are explicit, consciously identified as rules by those following them. Besides, rules are not necessarily experienced as norms, as something one *must* observe despite an urge to do otherwise. They may also be taken for granted, followed as a matter of course.

Parsons' control theory is poorly capable of distinguishing between different kinds of rules. In that sense Parsons was actually less perceptive than Émile Durkheim, whose theorizing he drew on in this instance. In his interpretation of Durkheim, Parsons ignored the fact that Durkheim distinguished moral constraint from other forms of non-moral normative constraint. For Durkheim, the over-arching concept that referred both to normative and non-normative conditions and constraints was the social fact:

> A social fact is identifiable through the power of external coercion which it exerts or is capable of exerting upon individuals. The presence of this power is in turn recognisable because of the existence of some predetermined sanction, or through the resistance that the fact opposes to any individual action that may threaten it. (Durkheim 1982: 56–7)

For Durkheim, 'moral rules' were a special class of social facts (Durkheim 1974: 35–6). In addition to them, he at least identified social custom (*moeurs*), strategic action of the utilitarian type, and other than moral normative action. Yet for Durkheim, regulative rules, be they based on moral or practical grounds, were of particular importance, because he thought that social regulation of individual behaviour was the glue that held society together. In addressing the 'Hobbesian problem' of social order, Durkheim pointed out that the coercive capacity of social facts stems from several sources, for instance custom, notions about usefulness and a shared cosmology. In that sense he diverged from the tradition of moral philosophy, for which moral rules are universal categorical imperatives, and thus cannot be explained by social and cultural factors. Still we can say that, quite like his later interpreter Parsons, for Durkheim social order was essentially based on social control. According to him, the difference between customs and moral rules is only a matter of degree.

> If purely moral rules are at stake, the public conscience restricts any act which infringes them by the surveillance it exercises over the conduct of citizens and by the special punishments it has at its disposal. In other cases the constraint is less violent; nevertheless, it does not cease to exist. If I do not conform to ordinary conventions, if in my mode of dress I pay no heed to what is customary in my country and in my social class, the laughter I provoke, the social distance at which I am kept, produce, although in a more mitigated form, the same results as any real penalty. In other cases, although it may be indirect, constraint is no less effective. (Durkheim 1982: 51–2)

Although Durkheim's discussion of normative control is actually quite elaborate, the problem remains that a perspective of normative control of social behaviour does not enable one to see beyond it. It leads into circular reasoning. The consistent behaviour of individuals who are understood as separate from one another is explained by (negative or positive) norm pressure, and if there are no signs of norm pressure, then the consistency of behaviour will be explained by reference to internalized norms.

Regulative and Constitutive Rules

One way to get out of this impasse of circular reasoning is to make a distinction between two kinds of rules that people follow in their activity (Winch 1971). On the one hand there are *regulative rules* – that is, social norms which force or oblige the individual to behave in accordance with the rules. On the other hand people follow *constitutive rules* in their activity when they communicate with each other. The latter kind of rules constitutes the meaning of the activity in question. For instance, following the rules when playing chess is not normally felt as a normative obligation but rather as something that defines the whole activity as playing chess. A player's attention is normally centred on different possible strategies within chess (with its constitutive rules), not on the rules as something that restricts the players from acting the way they would like to. The same is true of speaking a language: we follow the grammatical rules in order to communicate, to convey the desired ideas, not because some normative rules order us to do so.

The concept of constitutive rules opens up a whole new perspective for explaining social order and reality. For instance, within it social action can be approached from the viewpoint of the actor: what are the actor's motives for behaving in a particular way? In this framework, to explain behaviour simply by 'social norms' is obviously too crude. In Max Weber's (1978a) classic typology of social action, norm following would perhaps be closest to what Weber called 'traditional' action, determined by 'ingrained habituation'. On the other hand, abiding by regulative rules could also be seen as 'instrumentally rational' action, because by so doing one avoids harmful consequences. Then again, one may follow regulative rules because one believes 'in the value for its own sake of some ethical, aesthetic, religious, or other forms of behaviour, independently of its prospects of success' (Weber 1978a: 25). There might also be a shade of 'affectual' action in honouring certain regulations.

This strategy of explaining social reality is often called the interpretive method: one explains phenomena by their social or cultural *meaning*. Weber spoke about *verstehende* or 'interpretive' sociology. Within this perspective, people's behaviour can only be understood if we know what the acts and objects concerned mean to them; how people conveive of their own and others' action. There are of course different ways of understanding the meaning of meaning. For Weber the meaning or 'sense' of social action was more or less the same as the motive or individual function of an act. On the other hand, in some semiotically and also psychoanalytically informed uses of the term, meaning refers to the symbolic aspects of words, objects or narratives. Meaning is understood as something individuals 'attach' to natural objects or to behaviour *per se*; as a cover in which objects are wrapped or a stamp used for labelling them. In more epistemological uses of the concept, meaning is conceived as the form in which reality exists for us humans (Alasuutari 1995: 26–30).

When the framework is opened up by the concept of constitutive rules, which constitute the meaning of the objects of social reality, it seems obvious that social norms or regulative rules are a much too restricted notion to be used as an analytic concept to explain social reality. Rather, it appears that social norms are an empirical phenomenon, an aspect of social reality, but to make sense of the significance of particular regulative rules one has to study the social meanings of social norms. Thus, in this framework, meaning or constitutive rules are used as the analytic concepts.

In this 'interpretive' perspective, there is, however, always the danger that one makes an equally metaphysical assumption about 'the meaning' of these or those objects, or the 'world view' or 'cosmology' of a people, which is then used to explain their actions. Part of this problem is that one easily pictures individuals as 'judgemental dopes' (Garfinkel 1967), although it is also obvious that a shared understanding of a situation is a constantly updated accomplishment of interaction rather than its precondition. This ethnomethodological point can of course be responded to by stressing that individuals do not enter a situation blank, without any prior shared understandings. Yet the fact remains that the 'meaning' of something is also a notion members of society use to interpret or to explain social phenomena. Media audiences and critics may for instance identify 'innuendo' or 'symbolic meanings', or wonder what someone 'means' or what is 'behind' something people say. If asked, people who are concentrated on an activity are able to tell that they are, for instance, 'playing solitaire', 'clearing a room to repaint it' or 'writing a report'. The meaning of something is an interpretive resource frequently used in everyday life, and in that sense not much different from norms used to explain social or individual action.

Rules as Reflexive Resources

When rules are approached from the vantage point of dormant routines, it makes sense to think of them as regularities people have in their conduct, as rules which enable us to explain that conduct, which constitute the structures of society, and which people may at times become reflexively aware of. Yet, in order to address the specificity of rules themselves as reflexive resources, we need to question this self-evident perspective. Let us do that by discussing Giddens' and Mouzelis' discussion on this issue.

Anthony Giddens (1984) discusses how following rules simultaneously constitutes social structures through a 'duality of structure'. Giddens uses this concept to refer to the idea that a social system has a double role: as people apply generative rules and resources, they have both intended and unintended outcomes; the system is both produced and reproduced in social interaction. Thus Giddens' idea of 'structuration' entails that structure is a set of rules and resources; it is both the medium for and the outcome of the conduct that it recursively organizes. It is a medium because social conduct is produced through its use, and an outcome because it is through the production of this conduct that rules and resources are reproduced in time and space. It is the same medium/outcome duality that can be seen in language use: language rules help us to utter sentences while at the same time these utterances contribute to the reproduction of language. In the same way, institutional orders are routinely reproduced through the duality of structure, through agents making use of and therefore reproducing sets of rules and resources.

As a critique of Giddens' rules/resources duality, Mouzelis (1991: 28–9) points out that, in addition to a practical, there can be either a theoretical or a strategic/monitoring orientation to rules and resources. Actors often distance themselves from rules and resources in order to question them, to build theories about them, or to devise strategies for their maintenance or their transformation. For instance, the linguists' orientation to the rules and resources of language is theoretical: they want to understand how language works, not how to use it for routine communication. Within the strategic/monitoring orientation, actors are concerned with measures that aim at maintaining, repairing or transforming rules and resources. In the case of language, attempts at reviving dying dialects, or at 'purifying' or purging a living language from foreign accretions, are good examples. In these cases Mouzelis maintains that, instead of a duality, we can talk about a dualism between the structure and a subject whose implication in the reproduction of the structure is more indirect.

Both Giddens and Mouzelis take it for granted that in routine conduct there are certain rules and resources that can be made explicit and viewed within a theoretical or strategic/monitoring orientation as objects of reflection. Although that kind of shorthand may be satisfactory for their purposes, as a simplification it does not take into account the fact that any consideration and formulation of routinely used rules and resources – even those made by a social scientist – not only enables us to identify them but also constructs them as objects of attention. When this is done, actors have already changed the ontological status of the routine in question.

But can we say that there are rules in our conduct that we are not aware of? It is certainly true that rational thought employed in (social) scientific research presupposes, and is very much geared to looking for, previously unthought regularities in human conduct. To what extent are those rules one then arrives at products of that scientific gaze and discourse? A rule is always identified by being formulated but can we still say that a rule *per se* existed prior to its discovery?

I suggest that it is indeed reasonable to make a distinction between practical and theoretical (or also strategic/monitoring) knowledge, as Giddens and Mouzelis suggest: we may follow a rule without being able to put it into words, or rather our discourses do not lay it out in as much detail as possible. Discursive knowledge circles around the routine in different ways, for instance by paying attention to deviations from it, to various ways in which members may fail to behave according to implicit default expectations. Yet the rationale behind those expectations is never laid out in full. However, it is important to notice that a routine is never described in full, as it is *per se*, and therefore the distinction between practical and theoretical knowledge is a continuum, not a binary division. In that sense it is merely a scholastic question to ask whether a rule exists prior to its discovery. I prefer to talk about a routine rather than a rule, because a formulation of a rule or a set of rules is always an interpretation and an intervention; it adds another viewpoint within which to reflect on the routine in question.

Yet routines – or the unthought – must be seen as a larger category than just unthought rules; they are things we recurrently or irregularly do, could do or could think of. Routines are endlessly rich raw material for all kinds of observations and formulations about rules which, as soon as they are formulated, then change existing routines.

Consider that a discourse directs our attention to not walk under a ladder by claiming that it brings bad luck to the one who does it. To avoid walking under a ladder is usually done more or less irregularly, and in that sense it is not a rule. It is only due to the discourse that recommends us not to do it that we avoid this action 'as a rule'. Nor is the formulation of a norm the only form in which we may direct our attention to a routine. Consider the belief that if a person sees a shooting star he or she can make a wish that comes true. Before the belief existed, who ever happened to see a shooting star was decided by chance, and they might not necessarily pay much attention to it even when they did. It was evoked as something worth noticing, not by a rule that commands us to do something, but as a sign of luck. It can be interpreted as a conditional proscription: if you see a shooting star, you may make a wish. But not all omens or signs are like that; they may tell us about ourselves or about our future without any norms attached to them.

As said previously, a routine may be called attention to within a variety of interpretive resources such as normativity. However, we must not mistake the discourse within which a routine is noticed for the routine *per se*. Consider Garfinkel's experiments. According to a common interpretation, the irritation aroused by breaking default expectations about daily interaction indicates that they have a normative aspect; that such rules of everyday conduct are moral and constraining by nature (cf. Giddens 1984: 23). Let me instead emphasize that the interpretive resource of norms is one of the typical frames which breaking the routine course of action evokes, but it's not the only one. In experiments investigating reactions to rule-breaking, Garfinkel (1967) also reports that the subjects urged the students to spell out what they 'meant', or to suspect that the experimenters were 'up to something'.

Thus, the concept of generative rule can also be seen as just another interpretive resource which members use to reflect on routine behaviour. Employing it does not merely disclose the essence of a routine in question but also calls attention to it from a particular perspective and thereby affects future behaviour. By bracketing the generative rule as one interpretive resource, we of course face the danger of finding ourselves in a corner where we can no longer say anything about social reality without having to resort to metaphysical assumptions of one kind or another. We run the risk of being deprived of all analytic concepts, unpolluted by everyday-life use, which could be used to describe social reality as it 'really is'. Let me insist, however, that this step is worth taking because without it we construct an oversimplified picture of human reality. Rejecting even generative rules as an analytic concept does not mean that we finally reach a neutral analytic language with which to analyse human reality; any concept may in turn be bracketed and its metaphysics or rhetoric laid out. Rather than treating our chosen analytic concepts as parts of the 'original language', let me suggest that they should be seen as stepping-stones used in crossing a stream (although we must conceive of it as endlessly wide, and crossing it as a life-long project). As soon as each has served its purpose, it can be left behind and analysed from the foothold of the next one.

For Foucault a main stepping-stone is the concept of discourse, which he uses to point out the interplay and interconnectedness of words and things. By using this concept, he holds on to the constant interaction between the discursive and the unthought, or to reflexivity and routines. Discourses are not only words or mere things. They construct objects, be they deeds or natural objects, by providing the frames and viewpoints within which the members conceive of them. Each time a discourse is evoked it is for the purpose of reflecting, monitoring and perhaps changing the prevalent state of affairs, but by the same token it is itself subject to change. We can say that things are again and again 'put to discourse', but that does not mean that reality is seen totally anew. Depending on the discourses evoked, certain aspects of the cultural unconscious become objects of attention, and the routinized conduct in question becomes subject to interpretive repertoires within which to conceive of it. It may be that the observed routine itself does not change at the outset, but yet its status is changed when it is also seen as a topic. Any conceptualization or account of a routine is not simply evidence that subjects are becoming aware of it; it is itself a move in the very discourse within which it becomes an object of attention and reflection. A reference or account is a local 'speech act' – or statement as Foucault calls it – that both reproduces and modifies the discourses in question; it accomplishes something, 'does things with words' (Austin 1962). It entails frames and subject positions. It not only constructs objects and subjects, but as a local statement it is uttered to 'make' or 'clarify' a point, to 'criticize', 'oppose', 'defend', 'suggest' or 'define' something.

By emphasizing that routines do not only consist of rules people tacitly follow I do not mean to deny that there are 'sets' of things and words, rules or definitions people habitually refer to as interpretations and accounts of objects or aspects of practice. Most of the time people behave routinely, without paying attention to the underlying rules, but if a routine is interrupted they will immediately resort to the interpretive resources linked to those behaviours, thus monitoring each other's practices. That is exactly what is meant by discourse, and in that particular sense we can talk about underlying rules and norms.

Norms as Part of Discourse

As has been discussed here, norms represent a form of reflexivity, and that requires that some aspects of unthought routines attract participants' attention. Consequently, the situation is articulated in terms of a contradiction between how things are or what one desires and how they must, should, must not or should not be. Although it is as simple as that, norms may appear in their larger discursive contexts in numerous ways, and thus serve many different functions. To take a look at the different ways in which norms emerge and exist in discourses, let me suggest a few initial orientating concepts, which will be useful in moving around the different terrains of normativity.

To start with, let us distinguish *official laws and regulations* as rules people commonly know to exist. Normally people are not reflexively conscious of following them, but they are easily invoked whenever the need arises. Second, let us distinguish *moral principles* as commonly known standards or virtues to which people resort when criticizing, justifying or assessing something from a normative perspective. For instance, laws and regulations are typically legitimized by invoking different moral principles. Finally, we need to distinguish *everyday normativity*, the different ways in which the normative mode is invoked in everyday discourses. To better understand how people resort to the normative mode, we also need to realize that our habits and expectations of others' behaviour are part of the ways in which we define and identify with the group of people to which we belong. Therefore, breaches of the expected may touch us deeply and become a matter of normative reflection.

The Emergence of Norms in Social Change

Social change continuously gives rise to contradictions articulated within a normative mode: owing to economic and technological development, people's living conditions change, and open up new options and environments of conduct in a variety of ways. For instance, new research may challenge old truths about reality and thus give rise to new techniques, legitimated by a more 'efficient' or 'healthier' way to do things as opposed to, perhaps, the 'traditional', 'familiar' and thus 'easier' or 'natural' old way. An innovation may also enable totally new things.

For instance, the invention of telephones made it possible to talk to a person from a distance, and cellular phones freed such communication from the confines of space. Cell phones made us conscious of the default assumption that phones are located in the privacy of homes or in separated and marked areas of public spaces: how to relate then to phone conversations that may take place anywhere in public spaces? The code of conduct in answering a call is open to change also, because on the screen of cellular and other new phones one can see the name of the person (or the person's number if he or she is not saved in the phone) who is calling. These changes made it necessary to pay attention to certain routines of conversation, and breaking old routines aroused anger. However, not all changes arouse strong emotions for or against. If technical changes do not affect key areas of a culture, they may be adopted quite smoothly, almost unnoticed.

If we look at social and cultural development over long time spans, we can see how references to explicitly expressed social norms change, thus indicating that the sites of contradiction between feasible practices change. In his two-volume monograph *Civilizing Process*, Norbert Elias (1978, 1982) shows that in early medieval etiquette and manners books people are instructed to do or not to do things that are later taken for granted. For instance, in the manners book by Erasmus, published in 1530, it is said that it is 'impolite to greet someone who is urinating or defecating' (Elias 1978: 130), but in later manners books this piece of advice is missing. As an explanation for that, Elias argues that over time there is a shift in the frontier of embarrassment. Even the writers of later manners books are ashamed to speak about certain private matters as openly as their colleagues could some decades earlier. Feelings of shame are also frequently mentioned in the discussion. For Elias, this development is proof of a process whereby 'the regulation of the whole instinctual and affective life by steady self-control becomes more and more stable, more even and more all-embracing' (Elias 1978: 230).

There certainly seems to be a gradual change in conceptions about civilized language and behaviour, but we must also ask why that particular instruction was given in the first place. What was the contradiction between two or more possible lines of action that the instruction implies? I suggest that the existence of the medieval instruction not to greet someone who is urinating or defecating can be explained by the contradiction between the expectation that one greets a person one knows, and the idea that one had better pretend that one does not notice that person in such a shameful situation. In other words, a necessary condition for the existence of a certain explicitly stated rule of politeness is that there have to be two or more feasible ways to deal with the situation in question. The given instruction clears up ignorance or uncertainty about the matter. Its later non-existence may be because a certain practice has become self-evident, or because talking about it indeed has become shameful.[1] There is an 'economy principle' in all communication according to which one does not state self-evident things (Geis 1982).

Norms and Ethnicity

Another common reason for the emergence of the normative mode of reflexivity is that a people or a community comes into close proximity to another culture with their own habits and beliefs. That event could in fact be argued to be the very moment that a people or a cultural group is born in the sense of becoming self-conscious of themselves as a people or culture amongst other cultures (Moerman 1974), and it gives rise to notions about certain rules or habits 'we' have, unlike the others.

The formulation of such rules, however, inevitably changes the discourse in question. It means that parts of old unthought routines are being observed and used as raw material for new objects of knowledge, that is, for notions about 'us' in relation to 'them'. In other words, in this knowledge formation we are not talking about introspection for its own sake (if ever it was possible), but rather about knowledge formation conditioned by the observed differences between the two human communities, and how each party interprets the other's signs of otherness. In this process, communities may end up paying attention to habits or phenomena that were at most peripheral features of people's previous self-image, but paradoxically may become central characteristics in defining a people or a community.

Communities often more or less consciously defend themselves against external influences by formulating and imposing certain norms on their members, but in so doing they may come to define themselves by regulative rules that were initially of fairly marginal importance for them. So, they are changed by their own means of protection against social change. The Amish and the Laestadians have applied a normative perspective to modernization in order to defend themselves from social change, but the defence itself has had many unintended outcomes. For instance, Kraybill (1994) points out that Amish parochial schools bridle interaction with outsiders and restrict consciousness, and in that sense they may have been successful.

> Amish children do not study science or critical thinking, nor are they exposed to the relativity and diversity so pervasive in higher education today. The Amish rejection of mass media, especially television, severely limits their exposure to the smorgasbord of modern values. The tight plausibility structure in the Amish community thus helps to hold the forces of plurality at bay. (Kraybill 1994: 27).

Similarly, Melkas (1985) explains the Laestadians' prohibition of television with the idea that it comes between the religious community and the family. Päivi Alasuutari (1992) argues that by refraining from contraception, the Laestadian movement guaranteed its own continuity and secured the traditional family structure. 'At the same time, women were tied down to their traditional place and role' (Päivi Alasuutari 1992: 179).

The adoption of strict normativity has profoundly affected these religious groups' whole life. Certain general principles in their life-orientation guided them to pay attention to all kinds of technical innovations and new manners in a particular way: are they acceptable or not? The social norms they have then come up with impose constraints on their everyday life, thus setting conditions for their practices and routines.

These examples illustrate how ethnic identity is constructed over time. The meaning of being Amish or Laestadian gradually comes to be expressed by signs that place members of the community apart from others. One identifies a (fellow) member of a sect or ethnic group by clothing or the lack of a TV set at home, not by some deeper values that the members are supposed to share. Members may well know that those are basically only external signs, but especially in a multi-ethnic and multicultural society they become important because they signify who belongs to and still identifies with 'us', and who have given up on the tradition, which may well be a late invention. That is how the Amish have ended up being tied to, and identified by, topics which all come from outside the creed and community they wanted to defend in the first place. The Amish struggle, which originated in a desire to stay 'inside the perfection of Christ', to fulfil God's assumed wish about how a true Christian lives, has resulted in a closed community with its ethnic identity attached to such topics as what kind of clothes to wear, what vehicle to use, whether to adopt electricity, and what appliances to accept.

Norms and Morality

Not all references to norms are related to an experience of social change. Normative assessments and norm references are a constant part of practically all social interaction. Consciousness of a situation in terms of official laws and regulations or newly formulated norms is needed, for instance, when children, newcomers, foreigners or apprentices are instructed about forbidden deeds and how to act in different situations.

Often such rules are practical, as in the case of traffic rules: it makes things easier when all know on which side of the street to pass others. However, consciousness about generally known principles, often referred to as *moral principles*, used in assessing, justifying or condemning human behaviour is a particularly interesting example of everyday-life norm references. That is because the control theory of society assumes that social order is primarily dependent on people's morals: how well people respect moral rules and how effectively social control works.

Moral principles can be described as the pool of typical standpoints people use in assessing something from a normative perspective. James Q. Wilson (1993) lists sympathy, fairness, self-control and duty as examples of what he calls moral sense, and he argues that they are universal sentiments:

> But when we behave in ways that seem to violate our fundamental moral sensibilities – when we abandon children, sacrifice victims, or kill rivals – we offer reasons, and the reasons are never simply that we enjoy such acts and think that we can get away with them. The justifications we supply invariably are based on other claims, higher goods, or deferred pleasures: we need to assure a good crop, reduce suffering, produce a son who can inherit our property, or avert a plague that would devastate the community. Our moral sense requires justification for any departure from it. [...] It is this feeling that we must offer justifications for violating a moral standard that explains the difference between a standard that is purely a matter of taste ('I like chocolate ice cream') and one that is a matter of moral sensibility ('I ought not to be cruel'). (Wilson 1993: 25–6)

However, if we analyse empirically the normative standards people use repeatedly in everyday normativity, we find that there are many other more or less sublime standpoints that people employ, for instance relaxation, usefulness, freedom or an individual's nature. I am not trying to argue that we are less respectful in real life than Wilson assumes. It is only that to construct his concept of a universal moral sense Wilson has chosen principles which most of us would assume to be universally valid.[2] However, in everyday morality people invoke several principles and standpoints which are often considered to be contradictory to each other. Invoking them is not nearly always done to correct someone, so that normative order will be restored. Instead, it serves a plethora of functions.

Norms in Everyday Interaction

My study of a Finnish self-help group for people with drinking problems, the so-called A-guild, (Alasuutari 1992a), provides a good example of a case where the function of invoking a normative perspective was not to change individuals' behaviour. Rather, it was often done to indirectly negotiate the contradictions between the cultural group and the society at large.

In the A-guild the members constantly told stories and anecdotes about their previous lives as drunkards or alcoholics. The tone of these often humorous stories was somewhat boastful. The men seemed to boast even about the amount of hardships they faced when drinking. If someone told a story about his (a great majority of members were men) less severe drinking history, his would typically receive a mitigating comment from someone. However, when that happened other members would typically express criticism for openly undermining the experiences of others. The group thus promoted tolerance toward individual differences. In other words, there was an openly expressed norm which forbade undermining the seriousness of others' previous drinking problems. Every time someone boasted about his previous drinking, it was disapproved of and he was reminded that it was inappropriate to do so.

The repeated references by guild members to the norm in question seemed to have no effect on the members' behaviour. They could of course be interpreted as failed attempts to change members' behaviour, but actually that wasn't their function. In the A-guild example the existence of continuous references to certain social norms was an expression of the awareness of the contradiction between the guild's philosophy and the default values of the surrounding society. For instance, these men who strove for sobriety tended to boast about their previous drinking because of their rejection of theoretical knowledge detached from concrete practice. By boasting of previous drinking the members cherished their 'field experience'. However, boasting about drinking in a group that propagates sobriety does not make any sense whatsoever on a conscious and rational level.

The guild example shows how ingeniously norms may be employed in interaction. As part of talk, norm references also employ humour and irony, but even solemnly expressed norms may serve other than apparent functions. To understand further the functions of norms in face-to-face interaction, we need to consider the role of language and discourse in relation to tacit routines.

When individuals for some reason need to stand back and reflect on their routines, they have to relate their experiences to the available discourses within which the topic in question is discussed. However, routines and discourses are two different things, and serve different functions. Personal or publicly shared routines are automated sets of acts whose very function is to think for us, and thus allow us to adjust the flow of acts to local conditions. Routines consist of the premises on which the coordination of individual acts is based, and each time we are only conscious of the premises that somehow need to be renegotiated. The function of language is not to simply mirror or describe human action; that would be all too impractical, and only satisfactory for professional theorists. Instead, discourses provide formulations about the different points and ways in which routines have been renegotiated in the past. They suggest interpretations about the problems and the actors involved, and ways of dealing with them. When individuals stop to think about their routines, they may notice that the prevalent discourses around the routine in question do not exactly speak to their own experience. The particular need to reflect on the routine may also open a new perspective to it for them.

Consequently, individuals realize that the way they used to think about their behaviour and how they now perceive it do not totally correspond to each other. Such discrepancies between discourses and individual experiences of routines often get expressed in individual accounts as normative talk, for instance as excuses or justifications.

For instance, in my study of people's radio listening, based on qualitative interviews (Alasuutari 1993, 1997), many interviewees first said that they listen to the radio quite infrequently, but in fact reported using the radio daily on many occasions. It seemed that when prompted about their radio listening habits many individuals discovered a discrepancy between their characterization of themselves as light or infrequent radio listeners and their accounts of their daily listening practices. This was because individuals tended not to count their overhearing listening occasions as proper, concentrated radio listening, although overhearing is the character of a great majority of contemporary radio use. For the same reason, the interviewees often apologized for not being proper radio listeners, the kind they assumed the interviewer was hoping to meet.

In the example, a discrepancy between one's own experiences and publicly available discourses invoked norms about what one should be like or how one should behave. However, people did not invoke the normative standard of a 'proper radio listener' in order to become like that, but rather to convey the image of their own behaviour as something that deviates from it.

To give a better picture of one's own habits often entails evoking normative standards as accounts or justifications. For instance, in a qualitative interview study of television viewing (Alasuutari 1992b), people accounted for watching less valued programmes in a number of ways. They would admit to watching a television series but would hasten to give an account about the reasons for doing so or the attitude in which they watched it.

This practice of employing normative ideals could be interpreted by saying that people always want to find the best possible justification for their habits. That may be true, but in everyday-life conversations the evoking of norms more likely serves a function that is related to politeness.

Imagine an individual saying in a conversation that she lives in a suburb because it's peaceful and safe out there, and because it's closer to nature. If the other conversationalist replies that she lives downtown, the first one would probably hasten to emphasize how nice it is to live close to all cultural events, and how she still misses this after having moved further from the centre. The two would probably negotiate an agreement by saying, for example, how it all depends on different stages in one's life or on individual differences.

In the example above, references to norms are part of what Goffman (1967: 5) calls 'face work'. Goffman means that participants normally try to preserve everyone's dignity in the role they have chosen to play in that encounter. Individuals may emphasize their justifications for behaving the way they do, but they also defend the others' faces by giving credit to their choices. Any subject position is constructed as contradictory, and potentially in need of justification. That does not, however, prove that firm, stable subjects are only an illusion, and that all we have is a multitude of subject positions where individuals are placed in everyday-life conversations. Instead, this shows that, at least for the sake of politeness toward others, individuals construct their subjectivity as a problematic rather than as a firm stance. Each miniature picture of a person is thus presented as a potential narrative about how persons manage the inherent contradictions in their lives. Simultaneously, any portrait of a person can be pictured in terms of norms about what one should or should not do.

Norms and Social Order

In this chapter it has become apparent that norms are an extremely pervasive aspect of human reality. But is that all we can say about them without already simplifying things and brushing something aside? What are norms anyway?

I suggest that a closer look at norms has proven that social order cannot be properly understood by solely conceiving of it in terms of social norms. It is certainly true that socially controlled regulations channel individual behaviour by ruling out and opening up the means by which people may pursue their ends. Deviations from such norms may be largely prevented by social pressure, such as strong emotions of disapproval: for instance, legal norms are often backed up by a threat of violence or other forms of punishment. Yet norms in that sense are far from the only, or even the primary, reason why societies function in a largely peaceful manner. Instead, I suggest that tacit routines are the backbone of social order, whereas situations where norms are evoked and enforced are already a sign of crisis.

Laws and regulations play a role in the structuration of societies, but only through intertwined processes of routinization and naturalization. As sites of conflict between contradictory principles or opposing interests, some norms may have a long life – that is, contradictions may be repeatedly located in the same sites and articulated in terms of the same norms. However, other norms may be forgotten, indicating that the practices that their application creates are massively institutionalized and naturalized, and that the old sites of contradiction disappear, maybe only to pop up in other places and become articulated in other ways. When laws and regulations channel human conduct, they do so as part of the discourses surrounding them. They modify routines and construct objects and subjectivities.

I have suggested that norms can be defined more generally as articulations of a contradiction between how things are or what one desires and how they must, should, must not or should not be. As such they are one of the prevalent forms in which routines become objects of reflexive attention. Aspects of routines are used, in other words, as raw material to formulate prescriptive or proscriptive rules.

That does not mean that norms are simply rules people have become conscious about, or that routines are culturally unconscious rules existing in people's action. Even if a norm is evidently a formulation of a previously common, dormant habit, it changes that habit's position in the discourse. Similarly, we must remember that any formulation of an unthought routine in terms of rules also changes action, because the rules by which something is described also construct that something as an object of attention, and make people reflexively conscious of it.

The normative mode of reflexivity is often aroused by social change, but that does not mean that a smoothly running society without major social changes is devoid of everyday normativity or official regulations. Instead, references to norms and moral principles are a regular part of all social interaction.

In dealing with recurrent or newly emerging normativity, people often use fairly constant normative principles by which to reflect on and assess the topic in question. These can be called moral principles, although not all of the ones people frequently resort to would necessarily rank as particularly sublime. Besides, it is in the nature of those principles that they are mutually incongruent. Indeed, in ordinary conversations normativity is often used as a resource to narratively construct personhood by presenting oneself as a subject that manages between conflicting moral principles.

Instead of treating the social norm as the analytic concept that explains social order, normativity should be seen as a phenomenon that has different uses and functions in world cultures. Since it is in that sense part of social reality, it cannot simply be dismissed and rejected. Instead, to understand human reality one must try to understand how central notions of a culture work: how they make sense, and how they guide people to perceive and act in particular ways. The social norm is certainly one such notion in Western culture. Among other things, it has positioned the individual in opposition to society in a particular way, thus contributing to the construction of both those notions. It has adopted laws and regulations as the metaphor within which to conceive of and explain all power relations, thus providing us with the central imagery by which to conceive of ourselves as subjects. The social norm is indeed an important notion to reflect on.

Notes

1   As Foucault points out, silence is part of discourse. It is an element alongside the things said, and therefore analysing a discourse entails that we try to determine the different ways of not saying certain things: 'how those who can and those who cannot speak of them are distributed, which type of discourse is authorized, or which form of discretion is required in either case' (Foucault 1980: 27).

2   Indeed, it is quite easy to understand why Wilson appears to list universal moral standards, because they are for the good of the community (and not necessarily respected by outsiders). As MacIntyre (1981) points out, initially morality referred to duties that members of a community had for each other.

3 Language

If we should name just one thing that is peculiar to humans as a species and to human reality as a whole, it would unquestionably be language. A highly developed language is probably the main reason why the human race has become so powerful in relation to other animals. But what does our use and mastery of language entail altogether? In what ways does it make us qualitatively different from all other animals; is it true that we alone have self-consciousness? These are very difficult questions because for us language is not only a tool but also the metalanguage. We answer questions like that in terms of the same language that enables – or leads – us to pose them. The same is true of our knowledge of nature: we can with good reason admire the breadth and depth of information that science has accumulated and give due recognition to human mastery of language for it, but that information can only be expressed by using the language; it cannot be separated from it. Beyond mechanical reactions to present conditions or automated computing of information, conscious human understanding takes place within (a) language. That is, to make sense of an event or a phenomenon that catches our attention or otherwise awakens our curiosity, we naturally resort to language to give an explanation.

For instance, in an article explaining what time means in present-day astronomical theory, Raimo Keskinen, a Finnish physical scientist, discusses the so-called 'Big Bang' theory of how matter, space and time were created. As to the question of what there was before the Big Bang, he says that the question is as equally absurd as to ask what there is in a place that is located one kilometre to the north of the North Pole: whichever direction you take, it will be southward. Similarly, there is no way to get further back in time from the Big Bang (Keskinen 1989: 178).

The ability of science to study all kinds of natural phenomena is very much based on our technology, on our ability to observe and measure very small and big, close and distant objects, and on the resources provided by advanced mathematics and computers in dealing with the data. However, the point is that we can only understand and explain such phenomena if we are able to relate them to familiar things: to objects or phenomena we already understand. Thus, according to Lakoff and Johnson (1980), our understanding relies on metaphors: we explain or make models of previously unfathomed phenomena by likening them to familiar objects. For instance, the theory of relativity could never have been devised without resorting to the accumulated human experience that is passed on to us via language, nor could it be understood and applied without it.

It is thus natural to assume that language is the resource that allows us to stop and think, to be reflexive about something that has gone unnoticed in our everyday-life routines. From the way in which routines are customarily defined, one could also easily get the impression that by routines we refer only to behaviour as opposed to the use of language. That is not, however, the case. Although it is hard to conceive of reflexivity without the use of language, without conceptualizing objects that have thus far escaped our attention, it does not mean that language would comprise a uniform sphere of reflexivity. In many cases it is precisely the self-evident, routinely used concepts themselves that prompt us to ask what is buried in them: how they programme our concerted social activities without us being aware of it. In that sense, reflecting on our everyday life quite often means that we reconstruct and deconstruct commonly used, routinized concepts.

Language is indeed a tricky thing for humans. It is beyond doubt that the great capacity of the human race is due to it in several ways. First, by using language we can spread information and pass on existing knowledge to new generations, who can build on that. Second, concepts help us use our mental capacities in a more effective way because when facing a new situation we still need not start from basics. A concept often captures the results of a whole thought process in one term and thus enables participants to take the next step in solving a puzzle. On the other hand, the gravest mistakes and false illusions also have been spun of language. Because of the human ability to construct almost entire illusionary worlds out of language, people have stubbornly refused to use their judgement or even believe their own senses. Thus language is an essential tool of reflexivity, but it may also prevent us from seeing the obvious.

In this, chapter I try to answer the question, 'how is it that language is such a rich and flexible tool?' The answer in a nutshell is because language is such a complex and many-sided phenomenon. I discuss different theories of language and attempt to show that they all adequately grasp one aspect of it, but all of them also have their limits; they all shed light on some aspects by leaving other aspects in shadow. My conclusion is that these partial views should not be incorporated into a holistic view. Rather, it is precisely the many-faceted nature of language that makes it such a powerful tool. And although this might seem strange, another important asset of language's ability to work so well is that in everyday use language very effectively hides its secrets, that is, the way we actually use it and how it is constructed. Although rational thought and systematic analysis reveal the culturally unconscious side of language, in actual use over and over again we fall back on what I call a mundane notion of language. This does not mean that more sophisticated theories of language are useless. Reflexivity around language use is a continuous part of social life, and scientific theories of language are used as resources, but even in such a reflexive mode the speakers rely on an analytical metalanguage which they use habitually within the mundane conception of language.

I will first discuss what I mean by the mundane notion of language. Second, I will introduce two main approaches to language: top down structural theories and bottom up practice theories. After suggesting how these two approaches can be incorporated into an integrative view of language, I will discuss, in light of Foucault's theory of discourse, what kind of change it makes when things are put into words. By way of conclusion I will return to the question of how language works at the interface and *as* an interface between routines and reflexivity.

Language and Reality: The Natural Attitude

In everyday life, the tacit notion of language treats it as a phenomenon that is apart from and placed against reality. It is used in describing or arguing about reality, and in that role it is conceived as a transparent lens which itself does not interfere with its role as an instrument that provides us with a view on reality.

This view of language is not only restricted to everyday life and lay people. It is also common within scientific communication, and in the social sciences. For instance, Joseph Gusfield (1981) shows that such a notion of language is prevalent in research papers dealing with the issue of drinking and driving. According to Gusfield, the articles he analyses follow a particular 'literary style of Science', a form of presentation that is supposed to convince the audience. Gusfield calls this underlying tacit notion of language the 'windowpane' theory: the style of the scientist 'insists on the intrinsic irrelevance of language to the enterprise of Science' (Gusfield 1981: 16–17). This means, among other things, that the active voice is rarely heard; it is as if reality itself, or pure reason alone, dictated the operations and revealed the results.

Within this notion of language, any problems with descriptions or arguments about reality are treated in terms of their truthfulness. Thus, statements about reality can be true or false, or more or less accurate. If, for instance, the statements of two witnesses contradict each other, it may be taken as proof that one of them is not telling the truth, or the jury may try to figure out a story within which both statements can be incorporated into the actual chain of events.

Within this view, testing the truthfulness of different accounts of reality is sometimes talked about as comparing them to reality. In this mode of talk, the different ontological status of the material world as opposed to language is forgotten or pushed aside as irrelevant hair-splitting, and the concepts of reality and truth are equated or blurred with one another.

This empiricist view assumes that we have an unproblematic, direct access to objective reality. It assumes that reality consists of objects that exist independently from our practical relationship to the world, of objects that the language we use simply names. In this sense Melvin Pollner (1987) talks about 'mundane reason', the way that we always presume the world is a 'thing' which is independent of the mode and manner in which it is explicated.

To paraphrase Pollner, we can call this attitude toward language the mundane notion of language. As simplistic as it appears when we come to think of it, it is very persistent and common in everyday language use. It works well for practical purposes in many instances, and not only among lay people. For instance, in the natural sciences the role of language is normally taken for granted as the means by which we describe the laws of nature. There is no question about the conditions of the account other than the true nature of the object being described. The fact that our theories actually work in practice, and that the theories not only account for past events but also predict things to come, are taken as proof of the truthfulness of the theory being formulated. The same is true of the everyday-life use of language. We rely on others to give us truthful accounts of how things are or what has happened. We are briefed about what took place in a meeting, told how to drive to a particular place, and we read instructions for use. Since, for instance, driving instructions lead us to the right place, it is only natural to assume that they correspond to an objective reality. This practical attitude toward language behind the mundane notion of language is actually wonderfully captured in Marx's words in the second thesis of Feuerbach:

> The question whether objective truth can be attributed to human thinking is not a question of theory but is a practical question. Man must prove the truth – i.e. the reality and power, the this-sidedness of his thinking in practice. The dispute over the reality or non-reality of thinking that is isolated from practice is a purely *scholastic* question. (Marx 1969: 13)

Although there is more to Marxian praxis theory than will be discussed here, the basic idea is the same as in our everyday tacit understanding of language: it doesn't matter how it works as long as it works in practice.

Language as a System of Its Own

Saussure's Theory

As compared with the mundane notion of language, the semiotic approach provides quite the opposite view of language. According to the theory first developed by the Swiss linguist Ferdinand de Saussure, language actually works as a system of its own, with no referents to external reality. As incredible as this may seem, Saussure is able to provide evidence that supports his view. In certain everyday-life instances, this is actually the view of language we tacitly apply.

Saussure starts from the conviction that general linguistics, as he called his programme, must concentrate exclusively on signs. His argument was that the tangible object, known as the referent, serves only to confuse things, and prevents us from realizing the essence of the sign. In his view language must be conceived of as a system which only consists of signs and their mutual relationships.

The sign, then, consists of two analytically distinct elements, *signifier* and *signified*. Signifier refers to the sound-image that makes up the word (such as 'tree'), while signified refers to the concept 'tree', the meaning of the said sound-image. These associations of individual signifiers with what they signify are, according to Saussure, the main idea of a whole field of research that he called semiology, according to which language is 'a system of distinct signs corresponding to distinct ideas' (Saussure 1966: 10). In practice this means that when we hear or see the row of letters forming the word 'democracy', we realize that it means democracy (provided that we are familiar with the language and the idea).

Saussure points out that the relationship between signifier and signified, between the meaning of the sound-image and the concept associated with that meaning, is wholly arbitrary and artificial; it is impossible to infer from the word's acoustic image what it means. Although some words that describe sounds are onomatopoeic, that is, they are formed by imitating that sound, Saussure points out that these words are different in different languages and do not provide a sufficiently solid and broad basis for theory-building. The meaning of a word must quite simply be learned.

What an individual term means depends on other terms. As Saussure emphasizes, language is a system of differences at different levels. Although there are some terms that sound identical (like roots and routes), as a whole the functioning of a language requires that the signifiers stand clearly enough apart from each other. The same holds at the level of signifieds: the meaning of a word is determined by how it relates to other words. A dictionary is a prime example of this. If you want to learn what a word means, you can look it up and find out that it is defined by other words. The words used in defining the original one are again defined by other words, and there is no ending to this. Thus, at least in theory all terms of a language take part in defining a single word. In other words, language is a *system of differences*, a series of differences of sound (or graphic figures in writing) combined with a series of differences of ideas (Saussure 1966: 120).

The Saussurean semiotic view of language succeeds in effectively shattering the mundane notion of language whereby we routinely tend to assume – as Saussure himself mentions – that language is a list of names for objects in the external reality. As confusing as it may seem to reject the commonsensical notion of language, on closer scrutiny we cannot but admit that this is how language works.

Language and Reality in the Structuralist View

These theses seem to conflict with the commonsensical notion that language names the objective reality we perceive, and that language provides a tool with which we can describe that reality. We are prepared to accept that the same object (say a tree) can mean different things to different people, as Blumer (1986: 11) observes in introducing the basic tenets of symbolic interactionism: 'a tree will be a different object to a botanist, a lumberman, a poet, and a home gardener'. Yet we will still insist that a tree is a tree. The problem with this way of thinking, Saussure points out, is that 'tree' is a *concept* which classifies reality, not the name of a specific object in nature. In Finnish, for instance, the word 'puu' refers to both growing trees and felled timber; the scope or 'value' (as Saussure has it) of the English-language concept of tree is thus smaller than that of the Finnish concept. The point must also be made that the distinction between a 'tree' and a 'bush', for example, depends on how a (linguistic) community defines a 'tree' in relation to other plants and living creatures.

This is not simply a matter of semantics, but a much more far-reaching issue. Structuralists who support the Saussurean semiotic theory suggest that reality presents itself as distinct objects and beings that are distinguished from one another on the basis of a collective system of distinctions. In a rainbow, for instance, there are no dividing lines at the places that we consider to mark the boundaries between different colours; the spectrum is simply a continuum in which the wavelength of the light increases across the arch of colours. The way in which we divide this continuum into colours with different names is based on a system of distinctions that is specific to our culture, not to nature. Indeed, different cultures divide the rainbow in different ways into different colours (Eco 1971). The same view is contained in the Sapir–Whorf hypothesis (named after American linguists Edward Sapir and Benjamin Whorf), which says that the structure of a language tends to condition the ways in which a speaker of that language organizes nature, slots it into different categories and interprets it (Whorf 1956: 213).

Structural linguistics would seem to support the hypothesis that systems of classification, as evident in different languages, are not determined by external reality. As to why classification systems are organized in a particular way in a particular culture, there are different answers. Within the structuralist trend, scholars have different views on the role of social structure, practice or world view in structuring or being structured by language and cultural classification.

According to the 'socio-morphic' idea, classification structures of a language are a continuation and reflection of the social structure. Probably the most influential person to promote this view was Émile Durkheim. His study, *The Elementary Forms of the Religious Life* (1965, originally published in 1912) has stimulated much subsequent research to test this theory. The indigenous tribes whom Durkheim studied were divided into clans, groups whose members said they were related to each other. This kinship is based on the belief that the clan is descended from its totem, often an animal or plant, sometimes a natural object. Each clan has its own sacred totem, a god-like creature. Furthermore, the tribe that is divided into clans is usually divided into two phratries, which consist of a group of clans united to each other by perceived bonds of relatedness.

Nature is divided into classes according to the same system that divided the tribe into phratries and clans. Each living or inanimate creature belongs to some clan. Not only animals, plants and humans, but also the stars in the sky and natural phenomena are classified according to the same principles. For the tribe, the universe is a major tribe with everything living and everything inanimate slotted into some department.

Totemism provides for the natives a complete world view, a cosmological order with its own systematics and internal logic. For example, the Mount Gambier tribe was divided into the phratries of Kumite and Kroki. While winter, rain, thunder, lightning, clouds, hail, the stars and the moon belonged to the Kumite phratry, the Kroki phratry had the summer, sun, wind and autumn. In other words, if the sun belongs to one phratry the moon belongs to the other one. The totemistic world view is thus based on comparisons, distinctions and oppositions.

Durkheim says that the key thing about his study of totemism is the discovery that the notion of class as well as any systems of classification used by world cultures have a social origin. Although the decision to slot two creatures into the same category may be inspired by visible similarities, the idea of the category comes from human society and not from nature. The same principles used to divide natural creatures and phenomena into clans and phratries are applied to the tribe's social organization.

On the other hand, the French anthropologist Claude Lévi-Strauss has suggested that totemism can be best explained by what all humans share: an intrinsic intellectual interest in constructing taxonomies. According to him, the natural taxonomies evident in totemic systems are used as a model for dividing human groups into cultural classes. In Lévi-Strauss' theory cultural relativism is combined with assumptions about universal constants. The classes tribes construct are according to him culture-specific, but he argues that humans think in terms of binary oppositions, and that all cultures include the distinctions between nature and culture and male and female. By emphasizing humans' intrinsic interest in creating taxonomies, Lévi-Strauss objects the assumption that people only focus their attention on those objects of reality that have a practical function for their livelihood. Instead, each culture has its own cosmology, a system of thought or world view which seeks to explain all aspects of that world. Special attention can be given to animals or plants that occupy a strategic place in the culture's cosmological system, although they are of no importance to the tribe's livelihood. Lévi-Strauss suggests this as an explanation for the incredibly detailed knowledge of many primitive tribes about their environment. It also explains why snakes, flies, mosquitoes, or the shooting star can serve as a clan's totem. For instance, the *Hanunóo* of the Philippines classify all forms of the local avifauna into 75 types of birds, identify more than 60 types of fish and classify insects into 108 named categories, 13 of which are ants and termites (Lévi-Strauss 1966: 4).

The structuralist view emphasizes the point that the 'savage mind' is quite as capable of what seems to be 'academic' thought, well beyond thinking that revolves around the necessities of everyday existence, because existential questions are important for all humans regardless of how 'civilized' – i.e., close to the 'Western' standard of living – they are.[1] Lévi-Strauss especially wanted to make that point against crude functionalist theories, which when studying other, materially less developed societies easily lead to a racist disparagement of the people, as was the case with the British anthropologist Bronislaw Malinowski. According to him, primitive peoples classified certain edibles as totems because they were good (or bad) to eat. He claimed that primitive peoples' interest in totemic plants and animals was inspired by nothing but the rumbling of their stomachs: 'The road from the wilderness to the savage's belly and consequently to his mind is very short, and for him the world is an indiscriminate background against which there stand out the useful, primarily the edible, species of animals and plants' (Malinowski 1948: 29). Against this formulation, Lévi-Strauss insisted that 'natural species are chosen not because they are "good to eat" but because they are "good to think"' (Lévi-Strauss 1963: 89), and it is indeed hard to disprove his argumentation. It would be very difficult to show a functional reason for the fact that people who live under very primitive circumstances are interested in classifying insects or identifying hundreds of barely visible stars in the sky.

Although cultural classifications cannot be reduced to nature or to the practical necessities of people's livelihood, empirical research has shown that total relativism does not work either. Human sensory organs are built to make certain distinctions in the environment, which appear to be reflected in the ways in which different languages classify reality. Semantic universals in the naming of colours are a case in point (see Palmer 1996: 79–88). The somewhat culture-specific colour classifications are conditioned by human neurophysiology, which according to research in that area, responds to certain basic colours (Kay and McDaniel 1978). Accordingly, comparative research on colour naming in different languages shows semantic universals. There appears to be 11 basic colour categories and universal rules that govern their appearance (Berlin 1970; Berlin and Kay 1969). Furthermore, the possible combinations of composite categories (such as red and yellow) obey a set of universal rules (Kay et al. 1991).

I suggest these findings show that the biological and cultural sides of human existence are intertwined in a complex way. There are universal features of cultural and linguistic differences between classification systems for the simple reason that the human condition is in many ways the same anywhere in the world. For instance, we have a limited number of senses, which are sensitive to particular ranges of physical stimuli. Our senses have obviously developed to register information that is relevant to us, and on the other hand, human cultures are adapted to handling only that kind of sensory data. To survive in their environment all cultures and languages organize these data into concepts in a relevant way, but that does not mean that classification systems are determined by, or can be reduced to, sensory data. Differences between languages show that there are several ways to organize experience into concepts in a way that enables interaction with other people and with the environment. Besides, only a part of cultural classifications deals with colours or other properties of the physical environment. Languages also include concepts that describe and deal with emotions, relations, dispositions, activities, lives, institutions and organizations. Concepts developed in such instances are often used as tropes, such as metaphors or metonyms, or cultural models to discuss other aspects of human reality (Holland and Quinn 1987; Palmer 1999). For instance, nature may be 'humanized' or social phenomena 'naturalized'. Yet cultural classifications cannot be reduced back to the social organization either. The two cannot be neatly separated from each other. Instead, social organizations and concepts that are used to deal with them mutually affect each other.

Language Use as Practice

While semiotic and structuralist theories approach language from the top down, there are a whole range of theorists that aim at revealing the secrets of language via the opposite route, from the bottom up. Instead of starting from a ready-made language system, these theories start from a more holistic view of human everyday-life practice and relate language use to it as just one aspect of the whole. This route to an understanding of language and meaning often moves towards a fully developed language system by starting from simpler forms of communication or activity. Examples can be drawn from animal communication, the way children learn language skills, or from action in which verbal communication forms only one small part. The representatives of this line of thought range from Marxian psychology of language all the way to American pragmatism and the later work of Ludwig Wittgenstein. As to more present-day research and theorizing, social constructionist thought and ethnomethodological conversation analysis also share many ideas with the above-mentioned. For the sake of convenience, let us call these views on language and meaning praxis theories.

As said, praxis theories tend to arrive at the construction of meaning from simple, routine and unconscious everyday practices. For instance, George Herbert Mead has emphasized the practical aspect of language development and use. According to Mead, meaning grows out of habitual interaction among animals or humans. He emphasizes that meaning is present already before any of the actors is conscious about it, and well before, or regardless of whether, any words are uttered. That is because, for Mead, 'response of the second organism to the gesture of the first is the interpretation – and brings out the meaning – of that gesture' (Mead 1934: 80). Meaning is thus the resultant of the social act which a gesture initiates, and in which both organisms are involved. It is 'a content of an object which is dependent upon the relation of an organism or group of organisms to it' (Mead 1934: 80), and therefore it is not primarily a psychical content, for it need not be conscious at all.

In ethnomethodological conversation analysis (CA), researchers share Mead's emphasis that when analysing interaction, we must not start from the assumption that terms or other objects in the environment have a fixed meaning. Instead, it is stressed that a shared understanding of what is going on is a continuously updated accomplishment of interaction (Heritage 1984; Nofsinger 1991). CA researchers also share the idea that meanings must be approached as public, not as internal psychic phenomena. That is because it is stressed that coordination of action between the parties involved in it is based on publicly available information, which in addition to speech or other utterances by the participants may entail all available sensory information about the environment. Within CA, studies that have taken other information than speech into account often go by the name of 'institutional interaction' research. In so-called 'workplace studies', in addition to or instead of face-to-face interaction, researchers have studied subjects who have audio-visual information at their disposal, for instance in the form of headphones and television or computer monitors (Heath and Knoblauch 2000).

From this perspective, it is possible to conceive any form of human activity as a process wherein the participants read signs from their environment and act accordingly. In that sense, a practice can be defined as a set of observable acts and conditions. The acts may be movements, utterances, sounds or other observable changes in the environment, and the conditions may be any characteristics of the observable milieu in which the practice takes place. The progression of the activity consists in the actors coordinating their joint action with the help of observable acts and conditions.

Consider a person hammering a nail into a board. He or she will adjust the direction and force of the hits and continuation of the activity on the basis of how straight and deep the nail is, but may also take into account utterances by a bystander. The hits may be adjusted to the other person's talk, but the hammerer may also take into account the bystander's utterances, such as, 'Are you sure this is the right place?' or 'Don't drive it fully in.' Likewise, the bystander may point to a detail on a paper sheet entitled 'Building instructions', saying 'Don't forget this.'

In any practice, the actors' ability to adjust their acts to changes in their environment in a relevant manner is based on learning and thus on prior experience. One has to be able to read the changes in one's environment as signs that one takes into account. For instance, a hammerer knows that if the nail bends too much and is not straightened, it will not be possible to drive it in fully by just continuing to hit it. If a person does not realize that or 'reads' the angle of the nail incorrectly, he or she will get feedback from the environment and will thus gradually learn how to read the signs successfully.

Linguistic signs uttered by fellow human beings work similarly. Little by little children will learn what different words signify by gaining experience from the different contexts in which they are used.[2] If they fail to interpret others' turns of talk in the way they were meant and react in an irrelevant manner, they will get feedback that helps them in better mastering the language in the future. And this not only goes for children. All communication is comprised of turns of talk and other changes in the environment that give feedback to the participants, so that a mutual understanding is continuously updated. As conversation analysts emphasize, a shared understanding must be conceived of as a continuously achieved accomplishment, not as a starting point.

When human practices are approached from this viewpoint, it becomes clear that the difference often drawn between language and practice or between mental and material practices is ill-conceived. Linguistic signs used in coordinating interaction in practices are not fundamentally different from the signs people read from their material environment. For instance, an experienced hammerer knows by the sound of the nail how deep it has gone into the wood. And of course even purely linguistic practices have their physical and physiological side. Spoken language utilizes sound waves and hearing, sign language and written language utilize eyesight, and so on. In other words, all activity is based on the actors' ability to perceive constant features and changes in their environment and to adjust their behaviour accordingly, so that the interaction serves its functions. In this sense human use of language is no exception, although it is much more complicated than many other signs people interpret.[3]

Toward an Integrative Theory of Meaning Construction

Often the different views of how meaning is constructed discussed in the previous sections are seen as opposing theories. However, depending on the dispute in question, the theories can in fact be grouped in different ways.

If theories approaching language either from top down or from bottom up are opposed, we arrive at the structure *vs* practice battle zone. Those defending praxis theories point out that the semiotic, structural view easily leads to a solipsistic conception of the language system. If language were a closed system where the meaning of a word only depends on other words, it would be difficult to explain how we can successfully cope in our daily life by using it. Furthermore, structuralist theories easily lead to an anti-humanistic view of actors, who are, for instance in certain trends of post-structuralism, portrayed as cultural dopes, as mere effects of the cultural codes that organize society. In this critical view of structural theories, symbolic interactionists, Marxian praxis theorists, CA researchers and social constructionists find themselves in the same camp.

On the other hand, when taken to an extreme the idea that a shared understanding and the meaning of a particular word or gesture depend on the context is equally untenable. As Palmer (1999: 39) puts it, 'in practice, words would have no dependable utility and dictionaries would be irrelevant and entirely useless'. In fact, language and culture would not exist; there would be only communication and flux. These critical points would find advocates among proponents of semiotics.

However, if we take the epistemological dispute between scientific realists and those defending relativism, we will find another constellation of camps. In this discourse Marxian praxis theorists can be counted among the realists. Although they arrive at the constitution of meaning from everyday-life practices, they want to emphasize that concepts are anchored in material practices and objects. It is emphasized that objects present themselves to us according to their *end-use* (e.g. Holzkamp 1976). A hammer, for instance, is seen specifically as a tool that is used for driving nails. In broader terms, in opposition to structuralists, who explain human classification systems entirely by social organization and religion, this position argues that the world view that a language provides has to be relevant in relation to the surrounding material reality and especially to the way in which people make their living; people tend to focus their attention on such beings (and from such a point of view) as have a direct relevance for their practical activity and livelihood.

As is obvious also from the observation that theories of meaning construction can be grouped in various ways, they do not fall neatly into mutually exclusive camps. Instead, there are shared views and attempts to bridge the gaps between them. Let us take the dispute about how meaning is anchored to material reality. Although it is hard not to accept the 'relativist' point that conceptual classifications are made by culture, not imposed by nature, it is still quite obvious that our practical relationship with the environment sets overall conditions for our sensory experience. Consider again the colours we distinguish: although there are minor differences between languages as to how they are classified, the main point is that the human eye is able to perceive a certain range of electromagnetic radiation, and our ability to make sense of our environment by using eyesight makes use of it. This means that as far as different objects in our environment can be characterized and identified by a particular area of visible light, it is likely that that area is distinguished from other areas by giving it a name of its own. Likewise, if a particular group of people, for instance a profession, for their practical purposes need to make finer-grade distinctions within an area that for lay people looks all the same, they will create a sharper eye for it, and probably also come up with specific words that name particular parts of that area. Thus, for instance, Bedouins are able to distinguish several shades of the colour of sand and the Inuit have several terms to name different kinds of snow.

This could be interpreted to mean that – contrary to the semiotic and structuralist view – language does have a correspondence with objective reality. That is not the point, though. Actually such a praxis theory of language comes close to Saussure's semiotic view. Consider the colour example. If one range of the spectrum is termed 'red', as a quality of certain surfaces it is in practice defined by reference to objects that have the colour red. Thus, the term is defined by relating it to other terms, just like Saussure suggested. However, unlike Saussure, praxis theory emphasizes that the linguistic system is conditioned by practice, by people's practical relationship to their environment. Thus, although a fully developed language creates a system of its own, through its link to everyday practice language has an in-built reality principle.

As Marx put it, to talk about the correspondence of our accounts to objective reality is a 'purely scholastic question', because accounts or descriptions cannot be measured against it. Practice is the only measure. Because practice is the test, a valid description of an object depends on the community's practical relationship to that object. When the community agrees that the concepts used in giving an account of an object are in accordance with the practices related to that object, the description is deemed truthful. In that sense, truth and reality are intersubjective categories.

To recapitulate what was said before, this does not imply that linguistic communities or cultures can define their world views at will, free from all practical constraints. Although the same phenomena can be interpreted in different ways, all interpretations need to be relevant for some practical purposes. The 'realism principle' of intersubjective world views means that the basic realities of human existence – for instance that we need to eat and drink – are in one way or another inscribed in the language we use.

All in all, the bottom up and top down theories of meaning are not mutually exclusive, and one cannot make sense of the way in which meanings are constructed by looking at the phenomenon only from one of the two perspectives. For instance, praxis theories do not save us from the perhaps threatening prospect of relativism and having to abandon the mundane notion of language. If we only stick to praxis theories, we can never go beyond discussing the constitution of meaning of very practical and concrete things such as gestures or hammers. The real challenge is to try to explain how language assumes its character as a system, wherein the meaning of a word depends on its relations to other words in such a complex manner that we cannot relate its meaning to any practical inter-action situation. We need to understand how language achieves its independence from simply being a tool in coordinating action between individuals.

One step in that direction is of course to note that practices that entail interaction between human beings are also language-learning situations. If a person is not familiar with a phrase or word, he or she will get immediate feedback and will become more familiar with it. Linguistic signs can also be learned by other means than by learning how to use them in a relevant way. Since as sound-images or as written words linguistic signs have a material existence quite like any other changes or properties in one's environment that are used to coordinate one's activity, they can be pointed at. For instance, fairly soon after learning their first words by practice, children will learn to point to an object and ask what it is. When they hear an answer like, 'It's a hammer', they will soon learn to reproduce the word unknown to them and ask, 'What is a hammer?' They will then be given a description of the word in other, more familiar words. That is possible because a great deal of the communication between people who speak the same language is based on words with which all are familiar, so that the shared understanding about the meaning of those words in the context in question need not be invoked.

This is how language begins to assume its systemic character. In a language, there is often an abundance of synonyms for a strange word, which can be used in explaining its meaning. Besides, the meaning of a word can be defined by using simpler words, for instance by explaining what a tool is used for.

It is of course quite difficult and hardly even worthwhile to explain how the grammars of languages have developed, because they have a history that goes well beyond recorded time. However, there is interesting research and theorizing about how new conventional features evolve in a language. Referring to Ronald W. Langacker (1990), Gary B. Palmer (1999) emphasizes that the basis for language acquisition and development resides in *usage events*, in which full, contextually grounded understandings are paired with phonological occurrences in all their phonetic detail. Langacker asserts that the theory of language as 'usage-based' also implies that all linguistic structure emerges from context – that is, from discourse itself. This means that all the common features between individual usage events assume conventional meaning. They are perceived as recurrent and thus to some extent decontextualized schemas, which can then be put into use in another context. Recurrent commonalities in our action that entail speaking then get entrenched into structural features of that language: grammatical rules and semantic contents of words.

The 'theory of cultural linguistics' that Palmer engagingly develops in his book opens a convincing perspective on the way in which language works and develops, and it is supported by several fields of research. For instance, it makes plausible why and how metonyms and metaphors are so central to our language use (Lakoff and Johnson 1980). This is obviously because in recurrent everyday use, ways of using a word or expression may get increasingly abstracted away from the previous usage events to which they refer and from which they acquire their meaning. In new contexts the link to the primary usage events may be only metaphorical, but if the new way of using a word or expression has a niche in the language community, it will also soon become conventionalized, even to the extent that the metaphorical nature of the word is forgotten. Thus, we have dormant metaphors like the *head* or *legs* of the table or, indeed, the *structure* of language or society.

This feature of language development from concrete usage events to the more abstract and general use of a word can also be seen in the way new words are introduced into a language. For instance, often in partly playful ways, the name of a person or the brand name of a product can be used to refer to something that he or she is famous for. Thus, in sociology the ethnomethodological test is often called 'Garfinkeling'. Similarly, vacuum cleaning can be called hoovering, which then again can be used more metaphorically as a reference to some kind of sucking. These are very simple examples, but they serve as a reminder of the fact that a language is like a huge archive of human imagination, dating back for thousands of years, inventing and recognizing schematic features of previous events and applying them in ever-new contexts.

Yet generally we do not need to work hard as archivists to make sense of what others mean by what they say. Even somewhat novel ways of using a word are normally easily understood in their context. Actually, the fact that new words or ways of using existing words are constantly introduced into a living language does not mean that the language in question becomes more complex, or that people need to be more reflexive about the meaning of words. Instead, new terms are normally introduced to reduce complexity. New words work as a kind of shortcut or shorthand to refer to an object we would otherwise need to explain by using several words. For instance, in science or technology, complex activities that take place in the object of scrutiny can be referred to by a noun, which appears to name a very concrete object. Thus, the complex thought process that led the speaking community to consider the object of attention at that level is collapsed into a single word. Often, conceiving of the new object is made easier by naming it metaphorically; an unfamiliar thing is made understandable by likening it to something more familiar. This enables speakers to easily rise to the new level, skip the basics and concentrate on various properties of the new 'quasi-object'. On the other hand, objectification and metaphorical familiarization of a complex phenomenon may be deceptive in various ways. The source object may guide one to conceive of the target in a misleading way. It may also be that we forget about the metaphorical nature of the shorthand for referring to the object in question, which may then mean that we take the new object for granted without questioning how it is constructed. Speaking about the 'structure' of society is a good example: we may speak about it unreflectively even in a context where it would be more relevant to bear in mind that the metaphor refers to recurrent features in social action (within a bounded region that forms a relatively independent political and economic unit).

The Discursive and the Non-Discursive

To recapitulate what was said above, the conceptualization and construction of an object of attention within language does not necessarily mean that we are reflexively conscious of it. Or rather, the event of framing and naming an object may indeed make us reflexively aware of it and enable us to concentrate on its aspects and properties, but it simultaneously means that we lose sight of, or forget about, its 'conditions of production' as an object. In that sense we can talk about the metaphysics of language: every word and every conceptualization not only enables us to see new things, or old things in a new light, but also hides other things. Words are like analytical instruments, whose ability to make us discern new things more clearly depends on the fact that they close out other possible angles or ways of seeing.

This brings us to an interesting and difficult question: what happens when something that has gone unnoticed is brought to our attention? In other words, what are the consequences when routine lines of thought and action are framed in a way that makes us reflexive about them? Or, how do such startling moments usually take place? In a broader sense this means that we try to go behind or beyond language and ask what is its role in human reality.

The Foucauldian Perspective

One of the most interesting thinkers who has worked in this area is Michel Foucault, who uses the concept of discourse to refer to the area between, and the interplay with, words and things. Foucault does not treat discourses merely as groups of signs, but as practices that systematically form the objects of which they speak: 'Of course, discourses are composed of signs; but what they do is more than use these signs to designate things. It is this *more* that renders them irreducible to the language (*langue*) and to speech' (Foucault 1972: 49). In this characterization of discourses, Foucault beautifully formulates his research programme, which looks at language use not only from the viewpoint of meaning – that is, how signs designate things – but also from the angle of action: the use of signs forms and affects the reality in which they are used. In his studies Foucault shows that the objects systematically formed by our discourses also include ourselves as subjects acting in human reality. In *Madness and Civilization* Foucault (1973a: 247) notes that in the late eighteenth century a new concept of madness, and a new method of healing the mad, was invented. The mad were freed from all chains, but only at the expense of being punished for any manifestations of madness. In this way the asylum organized for the mad a consciousness of themselves, a consciousness of the man of reason, of the Other – that is, their own madness. In *Discipline and Punish*, Foucault (1979) discusses the same phenomenon on a more general level by noting that throughout the seventeenth and eighteenth centuries, there was a gradual extension of the mechanisms of discipline. They spread throughout the social body and formed what might be called the disciplinary society. This meant that people were ever more effectively produced as disciplined individuals, as individuals who are conscious of constant but unverifiable surveillance, and of the possibility of punishment. Such an arrangement assures the automatic functioning of power; it becomes unnecessary to use force to constrain the convict to good behaviour, the mad to calm, or the schoolchild to application. 'He who is subjected to a field of visibility, and who knows it, assumes responsibility for the constraints of power; he makes them play spontaneously upon himself; he inscribes in himself the power relation in which he simultaneously plays both roles; he becomes the principle of his own subjection' (Foucault 1979: 202–3).

For Foucault, the 'disciplinary society', which created a new self-concept within those who became subjected to the new disciplinary techniques, not only refers to the forms and effects of punishment. It also refers to disciplines as the corresponding forms of knowledge and research, and he points out that the new principles of disciplining and surveillance affected the entire population. The point is that the ways in which people's living conditions and relations to each other are organized and institutionalized not only affect their perceptions of reality but in fact *create* new objects. As Foucault emphasizes, forms of power and knowledge cannot be treated as separate from each other because they are two sides of the same coin. Thus, according to Foucault, the seventeenth and eighteenth centuries created a whole new social organization and way of conceiving human subjects. Individualizing surveillance, first practised by the police, and later on continued by various disciplines, was generalized into a form of knowledge. By the end of the eighteenth century, the disciplinary techniques attained a level at which the formation of knowledge and the increase of power regularly reinforce one another in a circular process.

> First the hospital, then the school, then, later, the workshop were not simply 'reordered' by the disciplines; they became, thanks to them, apparatuses such that any mechanism of objectification could be used in them as an instrument of subjection, and any growth of power could give rise in them to possible branches of knowledge; it was this link, proper to the technological systems, that made possible within the disciplinary element the formation of clinical medicine, psychiatry, child psychology, educational psychology, the rationalization of labour. (Foucault 1979: 224)

What is Non-Discursive?

The Foucauldian perspective on the role of language and conceptualizing things in human reality – later applied and further developed by many others – is fascinating, but yet it is quite difficult to know exactly what Foucault meant by discourse. Reading his own descriptions of the theory of discourse and of the method he used in his studies (Foucault 1972) is not very helpful because he writes in a captivating but not terribly analytic manner. By analysing his empirical studies one gets a clearer picture. To put it briefly, in his studies he wanted to show in practice how discourses indeed 'systematically form the objects of which they speak'. To do it, he actually applies two perspectives to the historical source materials he analyses. On the one hand, he analyses the materials from a 'discourse-analytic' perspective, which means that he uses such concepts as statement, discursive practice or the enunciative function. On the other hand, he needs another mode of writing. He needs to use the 'factist' (Alasuutari 1995), 'empiricist' or 'mundane' mode, within which his own treatment of the events conveys the truth. Foucault not only needs that perspective on historical documents to show the effects of discourses; he also needs it to contextualize the statements he analyses within the overall situation in which they were uttered. To put it briefly, he cannot do this without referring to non-discursive social reality, which he reconstructs by looking at his material from another perspective. Therefore, I suggest that for Foucault the distinction drawn between the discursive and the non-discursive marks the difference between the two perspectives. Thus, to describe his method of reading human reality from these two perspectives, he maintains that the rules of formation of a discourse must be articulated with its non-discursive conditions, such as political events, economic phenomena, and institutional changes (Foucault 1972: 157; see also Torfing 1999: 90–1).

In other words, in his concept of the non-discursive, Foucault simply denotes such 'things that happen' that are not taken up or referred to in language use. For Foucault (1972: 157), certain events that take place simultaneously with the discursive are 'non-discursive practices' because he describes and uses them to understand the discursive field, consisting of utterances in language use. For instance, when analysing the psychiatric discourse in *Madness and Civilization* (1973) or the medical discourse in *The Birth of the Clinic* (1975), like any ethnographer he collected information about the society at large – institutional practices, economic processes, demographic fluctuations, manpower needs, levels of unemployment, and so on. That was done not only to give *background* to the texts but also to show how they are affected by each other. He constructed a 'realist' picture of the era in question to see in what ways aspects from that picture were 'brought to discourse'. Pieces of that picture are deemed non-discursive at least in the sense that they are gathered independently from the ways in which things were discussed in the particular era under scrutiny. They are the author's construction of possible 'raw material' that could find an articulation in the discursive field. Or they are the author's information resource when trying to understand what the texts are talking about or refer to.

Ernesto Laclau and Chantal Mouffe (1985) criticize Foucault for this problematic manner of using the concept of the non-discursive. In this instance Foucault talks about institutional practices as being non-discursive. Does he mean that they are not affected or constructed by language use, by the discourses at work when the institution in question developed? This is how Laclau and Mouffe understand it, and they criticize Foucault for that assumption. They reject the whole difference between discursive and non-discursive formations. In that distinction, discourse rests upon a definition that includes language, and Laclau and Mouffe refuse such a definition. On the contrary, for them discourse is the 'structured totality' that results from articulatory practice (Laclau and Mouffe 1985: 105). One aspect of discourse for Laclau and Mouffe is its refusal to be organized according to rules that are external to itself. According to them, behaviours, techniques, institutions, and other examples of what Foucault might label the non-discursive are in fact articulated discursively first.

Laclau and Mouffe are quite right in pointing out that it is imprecise to talk about whole practices, such as 'institutional practices', as non-discursive. For one thing, as they emphasize, there are never 'mute' non-discursive practices and then ways of bringing them to discourse. Second, although we can say that there are unthought, and in that sense non-discursive, aspects in all practices, it is equally true that any practice also entails discursive elements. We use language and resort to different discourses in coordinating our action in any institutional context, no matter how routinized the concerted action is between the parties involved.

Evoking the Unthought

Foucault's use of the concept of discourse is unclear, and it also varies in his writings. Laclau and Mouffe criticize him for using the distinction between discursive and non-discursive practices in such a way that it is equal to the old distinction between mental and material. They emphasize that it is impossible to make a distinction between mental and material practices, and that all articulation is both. Laclau and Mouffe use building as an example. They emphasize that while it is impossible to build a building using 'the idea of "building-stone"', it is nonetheless obvious that the idea was previously articulated in the material form of building-stones, and that every time a building-stone is employed, the idea is also being employed. No matter whether a given object resembles that which we normally associate with the idea of 'hammer', the idea itself guides our use of the object.

However, the way in which Laclau and Mouffe suggest that discourse should be used leads to the conclusion that everything in human reality is discursive. It means that the concept of discourse cannot be used to pay attention to anything special in human reality; it is just a characteristic of it. That is of course a possible way to use the concept, but to address the question of the role of language in human reality one would then need to introduce another concept.

I suggest that there is another way to understand what the non-discursive could mean for Foucault. The distinction between discursive and non-discursive can be used to address the role of language. We could say that there are non-discursive elements in our practices in the sense that they routinely go unnoticed. We cannot even say that certain discursively formed, known elements of a practice are simply overlooked because a new discourse 'systematically forms the objects of which it speaks'. Thus, previously non-discursive objects are not there before the moment of their formation within a new discourse. Even to name and refer to that which happens as a practice of a particular kind means that one frames it in a particular way. To name and to give an account of that which happens means that it is constructed as an object in discourse. It is brought into discourse, and into a particular discourse. From this viewpoint that particular object-in-discourse was previously non-existent, 'non-discursive'.

To give an example, let us take the question of homosexuality. The American gay and lesbian movement has quite convincingly attained a hegemonic position in public discourses with its story of coming out of the closet. According to it, before the 1970s, when the first homosexuals began to make their sexual preferences public, all homosexuals had to lead a secret life. They had to hide their real self. Coming out marked authenticity and the inaugural act of freedom. However, what is known as 'queer theory' challenges such a liberation narrative, following the Enlightenment tradition. This view points out that the change which has taken place in recent decades cannot be properly understood within the closet metaphor, as if the now visible gays and lesbians were always there, pondering whether to take the decisive step and show the world who and what they are. Instead, when the appeal of the gay and lesbian movement to individuals to be open about their sexual preference was increasingly successful, it shaped whole new ideas and practices. As Steven Seidman says:

> Clearly, visibility is a condition of community building and political mobilization. Yet, such an identity politic not only has marginalizing and exclusionary effects but reinforces a regime of sexuality. Affirming a lesbian and gay identity still sexualizes the self, reproduces the hetero/homosexual binary as a majority/minority relation, and subjects selves to normalizing sexual norms. (Seidman 1998: 185)

Seidman also argues that as homosexuality becomes a visible, even routine, part of public life, in a paradoxical way homosexual suspicion is generalized to all Americans (whom Seidman has studied and speaks about) as there will be a pervasive awareness of the closet and the practice of passing. 'If normalization and routinization generalize and heighten homosexual suspicion, there will likely be a more concerted effort by many Americans to project a heterosexual identity' (Seidman 1998: 183).

Thus, the emergence of the new discourse forms objects, such as gay and lesbian identities or ways to project sexual preference, that were not there before. Afterwards, we may of course argue that certain elements or seeds of the new discourse and practices can be found already in the past, but it is important to note that within the old discourses they were unknown, unnoticed or differently signifying objects. In that sense, they were non-discursive.

The Persistence of the Mundane
Notion of Language

In this chapter I have drawn an outline of our 'natural attitude' to language and then challenged it by contrasting it with different scientific theories of how language works. The discussion of different viewpoints about language use has, I hope, shown how naïvely the mundane notion conceives of language. The words we use do not just innocently name objects in the world but they actually form a system in their own right – a system that is not just a replica of the external reality, because the concepts themselves are part of human reality. Moreover, language use is many more things than reporting on reality. Above all, it is part of human interaction with others and with the environment. Thus the meaning of words is in their use; words are tools that work in a relevant or 'realistic' way when they enable us to coordinate practices with each other. Therefore, we cannot really compare our descriptions or accounts to 'objective reality'. The accuracy or truthfulness of our descriptions depends on our practices, on our practical relationship to our environment. Much of what we do is culturally unconscious in the sense that it goes unnoticed, but 'putting things to words', evoking and taking them up in language, does not simply mean that we remember them again; every formulation of what is going on is also a move in the game. It not only frames things in a particular way but it also potentially creates whole new objects in human reality.

Since we know all these 'secrets' of language, and since on closer examination of how we use language it is very difficult to deny that language is not what it seems at first sight, why hasn't our knowledge of language changed our attitude toward it? Why do we still persistently resort to the mundane notion of language in everyday life?

One could of course argue that this is not the case. The social sciences frequently draw on the different theoretical perspectives on language to destabilize the natural attitude and to question the cultural unconscious that guides our practices. Besides, reflecting on the way the words we use tend to hide or embellish things is common in ordinary life.

Yet at some level the mundane notion of language is almost inescapable. For instance, here we have discussed how the natural attitude is deceiving in several aspects, but it hasn't really affected the manner in which this discussion is organized. As the writer of this text I haven't questioned the analytical concepts I use or the very framework in which the true nature of language is revealed. At that level of this text – or any scientific text for that matter – I have resorted to the mundane notion that the reality (of language in this instance) is out there, and the concepts I use accurately portray that reality. There has been no discussion about the metaphors or other tropes I use or about the pitfalls of this whole perspective.

So why is it then that we normally rely on a mundane notion of language and human reality? What functions does it serve as opposed to a theory that would take into account our practice-mediated relationship to reality? What are its consequences?

For one thing, it would be too complicated to take into account all the complexities of human reality discussed above. What would everyday-life conversations be like if we remembered all the time that the concepts we use classify and organize the world for us, that our turns of talk are speech acts, and that – with our notions of ourselves and our sense of bio-graphical continuity – we are discursive constructs of identity? Instead, we routinely resort to a notion of authentic individuality and to a world view where there are words that refer to things in the world. Such mundane reason is easier to handle.

One of the reasons why the mundane notion of reality feels simple is that in thinking about our relationship to a complex human reality, we tend to use the immediate material world as the metaphorical model for all reality. We habitually conceive of our environment in terms of separate objects, such as houses, roads, trees, stones, living creatures and fellow human beings. When dealing with any aspect of human reality, we tend to assume that the same model of object reality applies to it, too. Quite like assuming that the object world has qualities which exist independently from our classification systems, our interaction with other people is built on the premise that they also possess qualities, such as a certain character, which can be observed by paying attention to the way individuals behave and what they talk about. In our practice of character assessment, we rou-tinely take into account the effects of the context in which we gather observational data, but all such uncertainties do not weaken our habitual belief in an authentic inner self, which lends itself to indirect inferences. Nor do we normally question the social nature of the qualities we attribute to individuals. People are simply assumed to possess such qualities as being cheerful, talkative or intelligent.

Yet this simple model, in which our observations are independent from our perspective and from the concepts we use in articulating them, works well in most cases. Although humans can use their language and imagi-nation to build totally imaginary conceptions of reality, the language we use has to pass the test of enabling us to successfully coordinate interac-tion with each other and with the environment. The outcome of an inter-subjectively valid account of an object or phenomenon works for all practical purposes. We just conceive of it in terms of a simple image where there is objective reality on the one hand, and language that is used to pic-ture it, on the other.

There are of course logical problems, anomalies and inconsistencies in the world view that we build for ourselves in this way. The attempts to solve and overcome such problems sometimes lead to further problems and peculiarities. For instance, as will be discussed in Chapter 7, the insistence that human individuals have, or should have, one and only one coherent individuality, coupled with the evidence that we may want different things, has led to ideas about a 'personality structure'.

However, the fact that our world view, the big picture we draw about our reality, contains inconsistencies and never totally adds up is a great driving force for human imagination, willingness and ability to be constantly on the move. The need of individuals and groups to continuously try to develop a sufficiently consistent and enjoyable relationship to their changing living conditions ensures that languages continue to be endless resources for imagining and critically researching new things. If we arrived at a situation where it would be commonly agreed that we have total knowledge of reality and that there are no anomalies or contradictions in our thinking, it would be the end of history.

Notes

1   In that sense Maslow's (1987) famous theory about the hierarchy of needs does not seem to hold.
2   This is also how Ludwig Wittgenstein defines meaning: according to him, in most cases 'the meaning of a word is its use in the language' (Wittgenstein 1999: §43).
3   By drawing a parallel between linguistic signs and other feedback from one's environment that humans read as signs, I do not mean to suggest that the entirety of reality is a text for us; a common metaphoric definition of culture often heard after the so-called linguistic turn. On the contrary, I want to relativize the special character often assigned to language, which is thus set apart from or placed against other human reality. Then, to restore the damage caused by a split between words and things, the entirety of human reality is 'swallowed' by language.

4 Conversations

In the introduction it was argued that social order is based on the 'cultural unconscious', on routinized, taken-for-granted trains of thought and action, rather than on regulative rules or on a uniform, shared meaning structure. Because of our routines, as individual members we voluntarily contribute to sustaining the peaceful and orderly character of human societies. In any society or community, there are of course times of greater or lesser disagreements and conflicts, in which the 'rules of the game' are negotiated and renewed. However, even radical and abrupt changes such as revolutions really only touch the surface of the deep waters of the cultural unconscious.

To better understand how this works, how we unconsciously reproduce the social hierarchies and power structures in our daily lives, an obvious object of scrutiny is everyday human interaction in its different forms, the simplest of which is ordinary conversation. In recent decades ethnomethodological conversation analysis (CA) has made great progress in advancing our understanding about conversations, and has argued that ordinary conversation is the key to, and foundation of, more complex forms of social interaction, often referred to as 'institutional interaction' by CA researchers.

Therefore, in this chapter I am going to discuss how conversations and more formal variants of social interaction are premised on taken-for-granted lines of thought and action. I am especially interested in addressing the question of how the tacit routines of interaction contribute to reproducing social order in such ways that, even in conditions where the underlying social structure is extremely hierarchical, open force and violence are much less often resorted to than one would expect.

This chapter is organized in the following manner. First, by way of introducing CA, I will show a culturally unconscious aspect of conversations – that is, the tacit rules of turn exchange, which we routinely follow and which constitute the overall structure of interaction. These 'syntagmatic' rules enable us to smoothly take turns in conversation and thus to achieve a shared understanding of the topic, but as essential as they are, perhaps precisely because of that, they are an easily missed aspect of conversation. That is because, when taking part in or listening to conversations, we tend to concentrate on their contents: what each participant has to say and what he or she is therefore like as a human being. That is why, as I will discuss next, in order to make readers pay attention to the 'structure' rather than the contents of conversation, CA researchers have to resort to a particular language that brackets the contents and suppresses agency. Next, I will discuss another culturally unconscious aspect of conversations – that is, the fact that participants in a conversation always rely on shared knowledge of the meaning of words or other signs used. There is the 'economy principle' in conversation that anything which is familiar to a speaker in what a previous speaker has said is left unevoked, but such shared understanding is still essential for the flow of conversation. Finally, I will discuss still another culturally unconscious aspect of conversation: as participants in varied forms of interaction, we also tend to take the institutional context for granted. This means that the restrictions imposed on our role as a participant in a particular context are taken for granted as the rules of the game in question.

Conversation as a Game

The ingenious idea of conversation analysis, developed particularly by Harvey Sacks, is to examine talk 'as an object in its own right, and not merely as a screen on which are projected other processes, whether Balesian system problems or Schützian interpretive strategies, or Garfinkelian commonsense methods', as Schegloff (1992a: xviii) puts it. Instead of making observations or interpretations about the topic of a conversation, as a member would normally do in day-to-day interaction, a conversation analyst instead approaches a discussion as a kind of game, for instance a tennis match. One makes observations about the ways in which participants with their turns, comparable to returns in tennis, contribute to the development of the game, of course constrained by the previous moves and by the rules of the game. For instance, in tennis a player has to take into account the speed, spin and positioning of the other player's strike when deciding how and where to hit the ball next, and to anticipate what options his or her strike opens and closes for the opponent. Additionally, the player has to make sure that the ball hits the court in order to continue the ball in play. Comparably, a question in a conversation puts certain constraints on the next turn of talk. The addressed recipient is reserved the right to talk next or expected to get the chance to respond in the near future. Additionally, he or she is expected to give an answer or give an account for not answering.

This analogy between tennis and conversation is not meant to imply that conversants necessarily compete against each other or try to win the game. We could quite as well imagine a practice or warm-up match, where the aim of the players is to keep the ball alive for as long as possible. Or consider a proper game where the other player fakes, trying to convey the impression that he or she is playing seriously but in fact wants to lose the match for one reason or another. In this analogy, the point is not in the possible similarities in the motives of the interactants, but rather in the way in which the turns of the participants impose constraints on the next ones, thus forming 'syntagmatic' structures of interaction. The analogy, when perceived from this viewpoint, highlights also how we can identify and name certain recurrent elements in a conversation, comparable to 'forehand', 'drop ball' or 'volley' in tennis.

Much of the research in conversation analysis has indeed been engaged in pointing out and naming basic, concurrent elements in conversation. One of the most fundamental of them is named the 'adjacency pair', for instance a question and an answer or an invitation and its acceptance or refusal. You are supposed to respond to a question posed to you or you are held accountable for not doing so, and similarly an invitation forms the 'first pair part' of an adjacency pair because the addressed recipient is expected to accept or refuse it.

Researchers have also paid attention to particular interactive strategies, such as 'angling' or 'circular questioning'. These point out different 'devices' by which conversants successfully achieve their goals in verbal interaction.

CA's ability to approach conversations from a distinctive perspective is based on the way it abstracts away from the 'natural attitude' towards human interaction. CA refrains from making inferences about what conversants mean by what they say in the conversation.

The CA perspective can be compared to other approaches to language and its use. For instance, it is comparable to narrative analysis in the sense that whereas narratology is interested in the logical and chronological structure of the narrative, the focal concern in CA is with the logical and chronological structures of the interaction between the individuals involved. Compared with the plot of the narrative, the difference is that the structures of the conversation are constituted through the interaction of several individuals. On the other hand, it is comparable to the semiotic approach, where one does not simply assume that the meaning of a term is known to the researcher, but instead he or she studies its meaning by inspecting how it is related to and contrasted with other terms. Similarly, in CA one also starts with empirical observations about the use of terms, utterances or other observable objects to see how they are used for different purposes in different contexts.

When compared to semiotics, there are of course differences in the CA approach. For one thing, semiotics concentrates solely on structures of meaning, whereas the CA approach particularly investigates conversations and talk as 'speech acts', whereby participants construct and reproduce social relations, for instance by imposing constraints on each other. Second, CA goes beyond studying terms which have a dictionary meaning. In addition to them, it can analyse anything that is publicly available to conversants, for instance laughter, pauses, hesitations, gestures, etc.

Let us take as an example the article by David Silverman and Anssi Peräkylä (1990), which discusses the treatment of delicate issues in AIDS counselling. According to their analysis, the counsellor's reference to a possibly sensitive topic, for instance sex, is marked in the conversation by hesitation or pauses between words. If the client also marks it as sensitive in his or her response, the counsellor will continue to do that. If not, the counsellor will discontinue to mark it as sensitive in his or her next turn.

Methodologically, the CA programme entails that the researcher refrains from all inferences concerning meaning beyond interpretations confirmed by observations about an analysed conversation. That is, in CA one mainly restricts one's attention to those details of a conversation that the participants themselves take up when responding to the others' turns of talk. For instance, the researcher is not supposed to speculate whether a turn presented in the form of a question was really meant as a question. It is treated as a 'question' if it produces an 'answer', which then means that we have a specimen of a question–answer adjacency pair. Thus, the researcher attempts to let the conversants confirm the meaning of an utterance or a word used.

In CA, therefore, the researcher has to avoid getting immersed in the contents of a discussion, but instead tries to keep a keen eye on the particular way in which things are accomplished. Conversation analysts do not completely stick to only those interpretations that the participants confirm. However, when CA researchers suggest an interpretation about a turn of talk that is not confirmed by another conversant, they typically put it in a more conditional form: 'Whereas the first part of C's turn (lines 1–5) could be heard as a part of an invitation to produce a description of external states of affairs related to Edward's life, the concluding line 7 unequivocally elicits a description of his mental state' (Peräkylä and Silverman 1991: 447). This rhetoric of suggesting interpretations to the reader reflects the principle, originating in Harvey Sacks' ideal about a 'primitive natural science' (Lynch and Bogen 1994), that a scientific community studying the empirical facts is the ultimate test of research results. Readers are provided with all facts; they are supposed to see with their own eyes and judge whether the writer's interpretations hold.

Another means by which CA researchers try to convince their readers about the validity of their interpretations of the function of an utterance or gesture in conversation is to point out how a particular object in conversation repeatedly produces the same outcome. By pointing out such a recurrent phenomenon and giving examples of it, the analyst is in a strong position to interpret, identify and name its elements: 'In the course of an examination of conversations in which people talk about their troubles, a recurrent phenomenon was found: A troubles-teller produces an utterance and then laughs, and the troubles-recipient does not laugh, but produces a recognizably serious response' (Jefferson 1984: 346).

Literal and Commonsensical Meaning

One objective of CA is to reflect on and point out how members construe intersubjectivity. This requires that the researchers identify and name largely unnoticed 'objects' in conversation. One is interested in the way the participants in the conversation *do* a 'question' or an 'answer' – that is, what sort of things conversants accomplish by different terms. As Harvey Sacks (1992a: 11) puts it: 'What we want then to find out is, can we first of all construct the objects that get used to make up ranges of activities, and then see how it is those objects do get used'.

To be able to do that, the author needs to bracket the commonsensical meaning of a conversation and point out the exact terms and other objects used in conveying it to the speakers. Oftentimes, the gist of a finding in CA is to point out the difference between the literal and the contextually shared interpretation of talk. Consider the following conversation from Jefferson and Schenkein (1978: 156):

```
11   S:   G'n aftuhnoon sir, W'dju be innerested in subsribing
12        to the the Progress Bulletin t'help m'win a trip tuh
13        Cape Kennedy to see the astronauts on the moon shot...
17   R:   Well I live in Los Angeles. I don't live around here
18        but these fellas live here, you might- ask the:m, I don't
19        know
```

In the excerpt, S's utterance in lines 11–13 is understood as a polite request to buy a newspaper subscription, although literally it is phrased as a question of whether the man would be interested in buying one. Similarly, the man's response in lines 17–19 is understood as a 'no' answer, although he did not actually say no. Thus, by a close reading of an excerpt of an actual conversation the analyst is able to make and pinpoint a difference between the 'actual' and 'literal' meaning of an utterance. This has then led conversation analysts to ask why things get done the way they do in conversations. For instance, the excerpt above serves as an example of the rules of politeness people usually follow in conversation (Brown and Levinson 1987).

By studying how speakers continuously display their interpretations about each others' turns, CA is also a way of conducting empirical analyses of the way in which participants produce and update intersubjective understandings (Heritage 1984: 259). Ordinary conversation and other talk display how participants understand one another's conduct, thereby building in a routine grounding for intersubjectivity (Schegloff 1992b: 1295).

Bracketing Contents and Suppressing Agency

Thus, by concentrating on conversation as a game that evolves turn by turn, conversation analysis manages to open up a whole new perspective on conversation; a perspective we easily miss although – or precisely because – we are very experienced as conversationalists. We can manage the rules of conversation in practice, but we could not identify them without the assistance of systematic research that shows the logic in the flow of human interaction. As mentioned, this is because in practising everyday conversations we have other, more relevant and pressing things in mind. Instead of paying attention to the structural rules that enable all verbal communication, we concentrate on what everyone has to say, and perhaps also what that tells us about the participants as personalities: what kind of people they are and what they really think.

The natural attitude toward conversations mentioned above is actually so predominant and persistent that CA has found it necessary, or useful, to create a particular vocabulary for pointing out and talking about the findings. This special CA language has two objectives. First, to make readers pay attention to conversation as a kind of game with its different moves, CA rhetoric has to 'bracket' the contents, i.e., to make the readers distance themselves from what people say in their turns of talk. The problem is that although the contents of a conversation are not the point, the 'higher-level' observations about the particular ways 'that persons go about producing what they do produce' (Sacks 1992, Vol. 1: 11) in conversation can only be made if readers understand the 'commonsensical' meaning of the words used. Thus, the contents must be bracketed, yet the author needs to refer to them. Second, to prevent readers from being immersed in unproblematically reading the mind of the conversants 'in between the lines' of what is actually said, the author needs to suppress their agency. In this there is also the problem that general knowledge about the participants' possible motives and intentions is an important resource in interpreting and making sense of a conversation. It is here that the particular CA rhetoric comes to play as a means of easing out and circumventing the dilemmas.

For instance, CA rhetoric typically talks about action by using forms that distance subjectivity in analytic descriptions. That is, a semblance of 'objectivity' is culturally accomplished by borrowing from descriptive forms that suppress agency. This rhetoric also helps the reader to bear in mind that in the CA approach one is not interpreting the intended meaning of particular utterances, but rather the focus is on how the participants publicly produce intersubjective understandings. Therefore it is preferable to write 'a troubles-teller produces an utterance' or 'P produces a narrative' to simply saying 'a person says something' or 'P tells a story', because the latter expressions read too much (subjectivity) into the analytic description. This is a rhetorical tool that succeeds because it incorporates the cultural signalling of objects as opposed to subjects. The rhetorical effect is mainly achieved by the choice of metaphors, such as 'device' or 'production', which are recurrently taken from the world of mechanics.

Building on and Updating Shared Assumptions

In addition to pointing out how we unknowingly follow certain rules of conversation, CA research also marvellously reveals how we routinely take into account all knowledge or 'default assumptions' that the conversants share. It is the constantly moving and changing 'foundation' on which is built all that is said. However, the way in which human interaction relies on the foundation of what the participants share is easily missed, because what is routinely assumed goes without saying. In that way the culturally unconscious rules of conversation also silently promote peace and harmony as opposed to disagreement and opposition. In that sense conversation is not just a neutral information exchange system, because to be 'on speaking terms' indeed means that one individual is, at a basic level, friendly and polite toward the other one.

The reason why we tend to miss a great deal of what goes on in a conversation is that only a small part of it is specifically taken up by the participants. That is because we routinely follow an economy principle in conversation so that all that is 'picked up' by the next speaker is marked relevant for the flow of conversation and thus directs it forward. Since everyone assumes that participants follow the 'cooperative principle' (Geis 1982) and thus say no less or no more than is necessary, a speaker's request for a confirmation about the interpretation of a detail in what another speaker said would be interpreted to mean that there was something unclear about it. Everything unproblematically understood is left unevoked; it is the 'task' of the other speakers to evoke it in a later turn if in their view there was something wrong with it.

In this way, shared knowledge, both shared views on reality and shared meanings of words used, gets continuously updated. For instance, Schegloff (1992b) has pointed out how speakers ordinarily address themselves to prior talk, thus displaying their understanding of it. In the next turn, the addressed speaker may then, if needed, display his or her understanding of the second turn, and possibly repair the other party's (mis)understanding. Let us take an example from Schegloff (1992b: 1307):

Dan:	...See Al tends, it seems, to pull in one or two individuals on his side (there). This is part of his power drive, see. He's gotta pull in, he can't quite do it on his own. Yet.
Al:	W'l-
Roger:	Well so do I.
→Dan:	Yeah. [I'm not criticizing, I mean we'll just uh =
Roger:	[Oh you wanna talk about him.
Dan:	= look, let's just talk.
Roger:	Alright.

At the arrowed turn, Dan first agrees with Roger's response to the perceived complaint and then specifically rejects that displayed understanding of his prior turn ('I'm not criticizing').

In this instance, CA researchers often emphasize the important point that we must not presume a collectively shared world view at the outset. For instance, Schegloff (1992b: 1295–7) contrasts ethnomethodological CA to social theories which assume a 'common culture' or 'shared' knowledge, and criticizes them for presuming more or less identical contents in separate minds. In their stead, he sees CA as an empirical and inductively developing research programme in which intersubjectivity is not taken as a precondition for human interaction, but rather is studied as a continuously updated outcome of ordinary conversation and talk-in-interaction. Because of this idea of empirically analysing how interactants in practice achieve a shared understanding, it is also emphasized within CA that the researcher must not resort to 'ethnographic information', i.e., to other information about a conversation being studied than what is publicly present in the conversation itself; participants' responses to a turn of talk, for instance, determine whether critique is critique or something else.[1]

However, the same research can also be read from the other perspective: updating shared understandings does not mean that everything is built from scratch. Much of what is said is left unevoked by others, because the participants have no problem in understanding it. For instance, in the excerpt above, the participants do not invoke objects such as 'power drive', 'to pull in one or two individuals on his side', etc. Since there is nothing problematic for the speakers in this context about the meaning of those terms, they are not addressed. Yet they are essential landmarks on the basis of which speakers invoke the parts they want to address.

Even the very act of invoking something in what the other one says normally makes use of a shared language: words whose meaning both parties know. This can also be seen in the way one does conversation analysis or reads a research report: we cannot do this without a basic understanding of the language used by the speakers. To pick up an object or format used by the conversants as the topic of analysis, we have to resort to our own understanding. In this instance, a distinction can be made between the value and meaning of terms, as used by Ferdinand de Saussure (1966). Saussure finds the meaning of a term in a particular sentence and context, whereas the value of a term depicts all its possible uses in the language: what sort of space or spaces it inhabits vis-à-vis other terms. Both the researcher and the readers need to know, and make use of, the value or 'dictionary meaning' of the words conversants use in order to reflect on their contextual meaning and their function in different 'speech acts' (Austin 1962).

Although in conducting an analysis of a conversation one does not and should not resort to any background information about the conversants and the situation, the language spoken is used as a resource. The dictionary meanings of the terms provide for potential interpretations about what is going on in the analysed excerpts. Although it is true that ordinary conversation is, in addition to, for instance, literature and correspondence, one of the means by which shared understandings are updated, such updating is also premised on taken-for-granted previous knowledge about the dictionary meanings of words and all kinds of default assumptions shared by the speakers. As Schegloff (1992b) emphasizes, in their turns speakers only address trouble in understanding, whereas comprehended parts of communication go without saying. One does not invoke everything in communication otherwise interaction would become impossible, and a shared understanding would have to be built from scratch each time. The objects which are not invoked in a conversation are equally publicly available to the participants and to the analysts, and in fact they are the foundation on which the descriptions and interpretations of CA are built.

In this sense, the method of CA puts us at the intersection between routines and reflexivity, between what is left unnoticed and what is invoked in interaction. By analysing what a speaker invokes from what a previous speaker has said, and in the ways that this is done and orchestrated, CA is not only able to reveal interesting things to us about how conversations evolve. It also enables an analysis of the underlying culturally unconscious assumptions on which the 'surface' – i.e., what is said – is made sense of by the participants. In addition to the obvious foundation that participants know the dictionary meaning of most of the words uttered, conversations give evidence of many other underlying assumptions in human interaction. For instance, conversation analysts have recurrently shown that speakers are commonly supposed to be polite toward each other. As Pomerantz (1984) points out, criticizing another speaker or disagreeing with him or her is, in general, the 'dispreferred action'. People do of course regularly criticize each other, but 'agreement turns/sequences are structured so as to maximize occurrences of stated agreements and disagreement turns/sequences so as to minimize occurrences of stated agreements' (Pomerantz 1984: 64). However, when a speaker produces a self-deprecating assessment, the recipient's agreement is the dispreferred action, so that agreeing with it is performed in 'dispreferred-action turn/sequence shapes' (Pomerantz 1984: 78).

The default assumption is that even when people criticize each other they are formally polite, or that they support each other's 'face'. According to Erving Goffman (1967: 5), 'face may be defined as the positive social value a person effectively claims for himself by the line others assume he has taken during a particular contact'. Goffman argues that a sacred principle prevails in conversation situations whereby the parties reciprocally maintain and defend each others' faces. This means, among other things, that the people involved in the conversation are considerate towards each other and try to sustain each others' self-image.

In everyday situations it is impossible to avoid face-threatening acts, but we do have various strategies for making them less threatening. Thus, according to the 'preferred action format', an acceptance to an invitation commonly occurs 'early'. Instead, the dispreferred refusals often occur 'late', thus also allowing for the first speaker to reformulate the invitation. And of course the preferred, 'affiliative' action format can be used as a polite way of refusing an invitation: 'I would like to but ...' (Heritage 1984: 273).

Institutional Interaction and Power Relations

The discussion above shows one way in which the human institution of conversation may contribute to preserving the existing status quo in society. It could be assumed that the culturally unconscious principle that we are basically polite toward others may decrease the likelihood that disagreements and dissatisfaction are expressed. That could be the case especially when an individual is having a discussion with a hierarchically superior person. However, that line of reasoning lays too much stress on our tendency to defer expressions of disagreement and thus present them in a polite manner. After all, people are perfectly able to disagree, protest and even rebel when they are willing to do so.

Another take on the link between conversation and power relations is to ask why social hierarchies are easily left in peace: does it have to do with the way in which interaction between people representing different ranks is organized? In other words, how are forms of interaction conditioned by power relations in society? In one way it could be said that speech situations reflect social hierarchies and power relations. According to this line of thought, power relations are formed and rearranged at a 'higher' level, and only displayed and played out in different institutional settings such as courtrooms or official ceremonies. On the other hand we could ask how relations of power are negotiated, produced and reproduced in actual interaction. Even if we reject the radical view, it seems plausible to infer that the tacit routines of interaction contribute to reproducing social order. What is more interesting, they seem to do it in such ways that, even in conditions where the social structure is extremely hierarchical, open force and violence are much less often resorted to than one would expect.

From this perspective, the CA research in institutional interaction (e.g., Boden 1994; Boden and Zimmerman 1991; Drew and Heritage 1992; Peräkylä 1995) provides us with interesting knowledge about how relations of power are locally and institutionally structured. In this instance, the term 'institutional interaction' refers to institutional or formal talk as distinguished from 'ordinary conversation'. In other words, 'institutional talk' refers to speech interaction where talk is 'at work'; it involves an orientation of at least one of the participants to some core goal, task or identity conventionally associated with the institution in question. As a consequence, talk assumes a relatively restricted conventional form (Drew and Heritage 1992: 22).

Studies in institutional interaction have shown that it is fruitful to identify and define different types of talk situations by comparing them with ordinary conversation: in what ways do they differ from it? For instance, before a lecture the speaker will address his or her audience, and in that sense a lecture contains elements from ordinary conversation. The main difference between different types of talk-in-interaction is that while in ordinary conversation listener and speaker roles can be freely changed, there are various kinds of restrictions in forms of institutional interaction. According to the studies, more formal or institutional types of interaction show systematic variations and restrictions on activities and their design relative to ordinary conversation (Drew and Heritage 1992: 19). Thus, forms of interaction can be seen as a continuum from the egalitarian ordinary conversation at one extreme to one-way communication at the other. Thus, it can be said that different kinds of institutions (with ordinary conversation as one of them) can be distinguished from each other by the degree to which they control and regulate the amount and forms of face-to-face, two-way interaction between individuals and social groups.

Such formal occasions are an interesting mixture of form, function and content. If we take courtroom conduct as an example, it is clear that the power relations between the accused, witnesses, trial lawyers and the judge can be seen in the options of conduct each has during the trial. The ones with less power are only allowed to talk when specifically asked to do so, and even then the ways of responding are restricted. In that sense one could say that the different speaker roles reflect power relations: for instance, the judge is not supposed to be interrupted. On the other hand, although there is variation in the liberties allotted to different speaker roles, no one can talk freely; the codes of courtroom conduct also tie the judge. We could even go so far as to say that the judge would not be the judge if he or she did not adhere to the rules of the role of judge. In that sense, the power position of the judge in relation to the others is jointly and locally produced by the people who play their part in the ceremony. Yet it would be naïve to assume that the power of the institution of justice would disappear if the people present refused to play their parts. Sooner or later order would be restored, that is, the existing relations of power would be reinstated – even if open force or threat of violence was required. However, in most cases the rules of the formal occasion in question are followed voluntarily, but not because the participants consciously reason that breaking them leads to trouble. Rather, the rules are taken for granted because they constitute the very institution in question. By restricting the means by which a 'player' can pursue his or her objectives, the rules of institutional interaction may put a participant in a disadvantaged position, but changing the basic rules is seldom suggested or considered as a possibility, because the rules are taken for granted. In that sense the routinized rules of institutional interaction indeed contribute to reproducing the status quo in a peaceful manner.

That does not mean that people just blindly follow the script of a play that has reserved a disempowered role for them. As an example, consider the problems journalists face in press conferences where they are not allowed to pose follow-up questions. As a consequence, they will try to make long, involved questions: 'Would you do so-and-so or not, and if not, then ... ?' This example, given by Harvey Sacks (1992, Vol. 1: 51–2), makes the point that people will always do their best to play their cards as well as possible and even to bend the rules. However, it also shows that even when strategizing under the given circumstances, participants have to take the rules of the game as given. And as we concentrate on making the best use of our possibilities in a particular institutional setting, we do not waste energy on the hypothetical question: what if we had better control of the situation?

Conclusion

Our mastery of the art of conversation is culturally unconscious in a variety of ways. To start with, we routinely follow rules of turn exchange, which form the basic structure of conversation as a game but remain at the back of our mind. That is because we normally concentrate on the contents of the conversation and on what it tells us about the conversationalists. Second, we routinely rely on the participants' practical mastery of most words or other signs used, and tacitly assume that they follow certain default codes of conduct such as basic politeness. Third, as participants in varied forms of interaction, we also tend to take the institutional context for granted. It means that the restrictions that a particular context imposes on our role as a speaker are taken for granted as the rules of the game in question.

It seems fair to say that the culturally unconscious routines we follow in institutional interaction contribute to reproducing existing relations of power in such a way that open force and violence are not needed. Because so much of what goes on in conversation is given for an individual, these given elements of interaction silently work for the status quo – not least because individuals become human beings by being socialized into the institution of conversation. The restrictions placed on the roles of the participants in an institutional setting are also very effective in preserving the existing order because questioning the rules of the game is seldom a reflexively considered option for an individual who is a participant. Such local conditions of interaction can be made favourable in an imperceptible manner for the one who designs them.

For example, consider how 'customer flows' are managed on the Internet. Registering and paying for products or services is made as easy and as automated as possible: the user just fills in a form, pushes a send button and receives an automatic message saying that the order was received. During the time from order to delivery of the product, the customer often receives email messages telling of the present stage of the process. All possible service or product information is made available on the company web page. In addition, usually there is a link called FAQs, or 'Frequently Asked Questions', where the company has collected answers to questions customers might want to ask. All this is designed to minimize direct contact between the customer and the company, which can be seen in the fact that contact information is often very difficult to find. There might be an impersonal email address, maybe also a telephone number to the company headquarters, but contact information for named persons is uncommon. In that way, the company saves in employment costs because answering questions from customers takes a lot of time. Customer satisfaction does not necessarily drop, however, because the 'architecture' described here channels customer flows in such a way that people feel they are getting immediate service. If a direct telephone customer service were provided, many people would use that just because it is so easy, and would be annoyed if they were put on hold.

Thus, restricting the need to deal with individuals at a personal level is key to managing a large number of people as customers in such a way that things happen in an orderly fashion. For the same reason companies often refer to their business as 'products' even if they sell services. The more standard the service 'packages' offered, the less need there is to individually negotiate each deal. If the purchase of a product needs to be tailored to meet the requirements of an individual customer, each element of the package is typically listed and priced so that the customer only needs to check the chosen options.

The same principle holds for the management of citizens as subjects of administration. The whole nation state and local-level administration can be described as a system that controls and channels forms of interaction between individuals in their different roles as citizens, clients or holders of administrative positions. For instance, taxation of citizens is set according to legal regulations and in practice handled as a direct deduction from the salary and as a percentage added on to prices. Thus direct contact between a citizen and tax officials is normally avoided; announcements about citizens' income tax percentage and their possible requests and complaints are handled by official correspondence. A great majority of the daily information that people need about changing conditions comes from the one-way channel of mass communication, and institutions such as money and traffic lights simplify the daily encounters where individuals would otherwise need to negotiate how to handle their mutual interaction. And if citizens want to change or influence the way in which public administration works, that is equally rationalized in the orderly form of an election: on a particular day they go and drop their ballot in the box. In that sense, democracy is one of the methods for putting restrictions on face-to-face interaction in such a way that participants take the local conditions for granted as the rules of the game.

When the organizational structure of society is approached in this way, it raises a larger question about what power relations actually mean. In his famous formulation, Max Weber defined power as the 'opportunity existing within a social relationship which permits one to carry out one's own will even against resistance and regardless of the basis on which this opportunity rests' (Weber 1969: 117), but on the other hand he made a distinction between power and sheer force: if a person realizes his or her objectives with force, the person does not have power but is simply stronger than his or her opponents. For that reason, Weber reasoned, legitimation of power is the critical question; without the consent of others, there is no power.

The discussion above, however, shows that the consent of others does not necessarily have to be based on a particular discourse that legitimates the arrangement in question. In most cases people are simply placed in a situation where they can do what they are doing in given conditions; questioning the rules is made impossible or difficult if, indeed, it comes to mind at all. Therefore, it could be said that people usually routinely follow the rules. The question is: can routine behaviour be considered as a form of legitimation? That is what Weber thought, and therefore he lists traditional authority as one of the forms of legitimation. According to him, it means that the power position of a person is not questioned because people do not question the legitimacy of an established tradition. However, here we are not necessarily talking about old habits that people are accustomed to. Even if people have followed a particular routine for a long time, it does not necessarily mean that it is followed because it is old. Routines do not need a justification at the time they are followed, and if their legitimation is addressed, the justifications given do not necessarily explain why they were followed in the first place.

Therefore, legitimation is not really the right word to discuss the concept of power, making the whole Weberian definition problematic. Michel Foucault's discussion of the concept appears to be closer to what is at stake here. According to him, power is not an institution or a structure, but 'the name that one attributes to a complex strategical situation in a particular society' (Foucault 1978: 93). For Foucault, basically all relations are also power relations. In this view,

> relations of power are not in a position of exteriority with respect to other types of relationships (economic processes, knowledge relationships, sexual relations), but are immanent in the latter [...]; relations of power are not in superstructural positions, with merely a role of prohibitions or accompaniment; they have a directly productive role, wherever they come into play. (Foucault 1980: 94)

Relations of power are also always coupled with a form of knowledge and with the production of identities, because different subject positions and strategies are immanent in relations of power and force.

As right as Foucault is in emphasizing that power relations are a complex set of intertwined issues and that there is seldom if ever a single centre from which power radiates downward, it is also problematic to say that power is everywhere. Then it simply becomes a synonym for social relations. Instead, I suggest that power relations are the possibilities and resources available to one person that can be affected and controlled by other people. This of course means that – as Foucault emphasizes – there is a power aspect in practically all relations and encounters between individuals, but of particular interest are the ways in which a clearly unequal allocation of resources is executed and reproduced in ways that minimize the risk of protest or revolt. The main technique is to control and regulate the amount and forms of direct, two-way interaction between individuals representing different power positions. This creates an architecture of institutions that places individuals in different subject positions. The instances of institutional interaction range from formal meetings or gatherings to written correspondence and sign language (such as traffic signs), and they form complex networks, so that changing one institutional arrangement requires measures taken in another. Within this network of institutions and organizations, one also usually finds the resources for the use of force in one way or another. However, the daily functioning of this network of power relations is based on people's habitual activity. The discourses used in reflecting on this network range from law, equality and justice, all the way to fear of punishment for deviant behaviour.

When power is defined this way, does it mean that the whole concept is reserved only to discuss the power of organizations? What about power relations between men and women or between ethnic groups? To talk about power relations between groups defined by gender or ethnicity implies that the groups in question have indeed organized and arranged forms of institutional interaction that work in favour of one group. However, the positions that the architecture of institutions gives to individuals may well 'radiate' into other fields: a high-ranking person may, for instance, receive special treatment also outside his or her 'office', not least because the person may have the possibility to affect others' lives. In addition, almost anything – love, sex, strength, wealth, knowledge – can be used as an asset in an interpersonal power play, which means that one person is able to manipulate another to act in a desired manner. On such occasions it might be difficult to observe the power relation from outside, but the more power one person has over another, the less symmetrical are the speaker roles that the individuals assume in their mutual interaction.

Notes

1   Other than conversation-analytic observations about the object of study have come to be understood as backgound information about the studied behaviour. Disagreements between 'purist' conversation analysts and others, and discussion about the different nature of CA-based and other observations about social behaviour have come to be known as the CA and 'ethnography' controversy (for this discussion, see Atkinson 1985; Bilmes 1992, 1996; Maynard 1989; Moerman 1988, 1992; Nelson 1994; Silverman and Gubrium 1994). In this discourse, the CA-perspective has emphasized that the analysis of human interaction should not rely on members' knowledge, as it does when knowledge about a situation is based on the participants' and ethnographer's account of it. The more interactionist or 'ethnographic' voices have, for their part, stressed that it is impossible to totally refrain from using ethnographic (or members') knowledge in order to recognize actions as, for instance, 'jokes' or 'boasts' (Moerman 1992: 33). Most participants in this discussion have agreed that the ethnomethodological distinction between 'topics' and 'resources' 'has been rendered in terms which are too rigid and absolute' (Atkinson 1985: 118).

5 Rituals

The previous chapter concluded with the idea that power relations in society amount to types of interaction between individuals. To simplify a little, the more powerful a position, the more interaction with the person in that position is restricted relative to ordinary conversation. It was also argued that with such an architecture of social hierarchies, power relations ingeniously hide themselves. When having to deal with powerful institutions we tend to take for granted the conditions of our role as a participant while concentrating on making the best use of our possibilities. Therefore, it was concluded that a power relation does not necessarily need any conscious legitimation.

On the other hand, as participants we know when we are dealing with a powerful position. When meeting a powerful person on official business or when attending an important ceremony, it normally means that we dress up formally and monitor our behaviour with special care. Or consider festive occasions, in which the stylized behaviour of the participants clearly overrides the practical function of the ritual in question. Yet the requirement imposed on the participants to play their part according to a predefined, detailed script may make the occasion full of excitement, even fear.

Obviously, when dealing with power relations we appear in different participant roles. First, there are sites of power whose interaction with those affected by them is so diffuse and indirect that the powerful players in the field easily escape our sight. Economic power is a prime example of this. The decisions – such as sales or purchases – of wealthy individuals or institutions may affect us in a number of subtle ways, although we may have no idea who has affected the changes. On the other hand, one's position in relation to other people, for example resources available to an individual, are often confirmed, decided or affected in the individual's encounters with certain institutions. As noted above, even in these encounters we may take our position for granted as just the rules of the game. That is especially the case if the arrangement is justifiable on a rational and functional basis. Thus, if we fill out and send an application or appear in court as a witness, we may not have any second thoughts about the way we are placed as a subject. At times, the architecture and dramaturgy of an interaction situation is in a conspicuous way designed only to serve as a display of power and hierarchy. For instance, those who are given an appointment to meet a powerful person, such as a king, are typically made to stand or be seated in a lower and smaller chair, and they are given specific instructions about proper behaviour.

From this viewpoint, ritual could be seen as an extreme case. It could be viewed as an occasion in which the physical arrangement – that is, restrictions imposed on individual participant's roles – hardly serves any other function than to demonstrate power relations between the participants.

Managing power relations in society is obviously one aspect of ritual, but it hardly solves the riddle as to why humans arrange rituals. They can indeed be used to place participants in strictly defined positions, but why do people participate if it means voluntary submission? And even if that can be explained by social pressures that create an obligation for individuals to attend, to make sense of rituals serving that purpose, one needs to assume that they extend their effects beyond the events themselves.

Indeed, at least the people who set up rituals obviously assume that they have long-lasting effects on the participants, and this brings us to another interesting aspect of ritual. That is, there are a lot of meta-cultural notions about rituals. They are an exciting interface between routines and reflexivity. For one thing, although everyday-life occasions may be more or less ritual-like, one cannot participate in a proper ritual unknowingly, which means that on such occasions we are reflexive about the rules followed. Second, although the concept of ritual stems from social science, especially from anthropology, it is also a lay concept that we use to categorize certain social occasions into a special class. Theories about ritual, for instance Émile Durkheim's assumption that ritual strengthens solidarity between members of society (Durkheim 1965), have become common knowledge and are used as resources in interpreting the rituals we come across in everyday life. In that sense, the notion of ritual also systematically forms the object that it appears to describe and analyse in the first place.

If we take a strong constructionist stance and deem ritual as one of the numerous concepts that simultaneously describe and form social phenomena, it would be difficult for me to justify why I have dedicated a whole chapter to it in a book that attempts to sum up what we know about human reality. However, I think that research and theorizing on ritual deals with an important aspect of human reality, an aspect that rightly deserves the attention it is given here. Although we cannot treat ritual as a clearly demarcated element of human reality, rituals and ritual-like activities highlight the importance of bodily experience. We may quite well be reflexive about a ritual-like event but it may still affect us, because it 'speaks' directly to our body. Rituals make us concretely do things, or they place us in different positions, and these bodily felt experiences effectively engrave on us a memory trace associated with the implicit or explicit meaning of the occasion. Such 'social engineering' is of course true of all behaviour. How we routinely behave or what we know or master is in a sense carved on our body, but the more holistic an experience is, the more both the mind and the body are involved in it, the more effectively it becomes a routine part of us as human subjects. Because the organizing and managing of power relations in such a way that open force is seldom needed is crucial to the smooth functioning of a society, it is no wonder that institutional interaction takes on ritual-like features.

To discuss this in more detail I will first define what I mean by ritual. By giving concrete examples of present-day rituals, I will show how rituals work as bodily felt, emotionally touching experiences.

What is a Ritual?

To talk about the uses and abilities of rituals for social engineering, one needs to define what they are. How does one recognize a ritual? Can we give a definition of it? Let me approach this task by giving a concrete example.

Some time ago I took part in the doctoral graduation ceremony of my university, a three-day event.[1] On Thursday afternoon there was first a rehearsal of the main ritual. How we would march to the hall, step to the podium, receive the top hat and sword, bow to the chancellor of the university – each detail was carefully practised. That evening there was a 'sword sharpening' ritual, followed by a dance party. On Friday there was the main ritual, after which we marched to church for a special service. After a short interval with just enough time to change clothes, there was a dinner party, followed by another, less formal party that lasted till early morning. Finally, on Saturday at noon there was a graduation boat trip to a nearby island, where there was a dance. For each occasion, there were detailed instructions about what to wear. These instructions were especially demanding for female participants: a formal dress, a certain colour of gloves, etc.

This series of ceremonies clearly fulfils the characteristics of rituals. All the features of ritual-like activities, as they are listed by Catherine Bell (1997: 138–69), can be identified. Action in the ceremony was *formalized*, *rule-governed* and *invariant*, and many of the ceremonies were obviously meant as *performances*, that is, dramatic and public events. In many ways the promotion ritual is *traditionalistic* in that it makes an appeal to an old tradition. Finally, the ceremonies made use of sacral symbolism, especially since a church service was part of the ritual. As Bell notes, since rituals aim to convey an air of sacredness, they often borrow elements that have been sanctified by older rituals.

Although it is easy to give a list of features that are characteristic of rituals, it is quite difficult to give a definition that is acceptable to all scholars interested in ritual-like activities. For instance, Erving Goffman (1971: 62) defines ritual by saying that it is 'a perfunctory, conventionalized act through which an individual portrays his respect and regard for some object of ultimate value to that object of ultimate value or its stand-in'. His definition is perfectly in line with those of many others, but still, in actual practice he stretches his treatment of rituals to the 'borderline cases' that he is interested in. His argument is that in contemporary society 'rituals performed to stand-ins for supernatural entities are everywhere in decay' (Goffman 1971: 63), and what remains are brief, interpersonal rituals. From his viewpoint, greeting a friend or shaking hands are prime examples of such modern rituals.

Let me argue, however, that in these instances we are not talking about rituals. Rather, Goffman adopts the common notion of ritual and uses it as an analogue or metaphor to reveal interesting things about our mundane, everyday-life reality. He shows that there are aspects in our routine social action that can be likened to rituals.

Instead of extending the meaning of ritual this way, I argue that proper public rituals are easy to recognize. I would say that, with only a few exceptions, you cannot participate in a ritual unknowingly. Even if one does not know the language or meaning of a ritual one happens to witness, the formalization of speech and action that sets rituals apart from ordinary life is quite easy to recognize. For natives, the fact that a ritual is taking place is of course clearer: people know that they partake in a ceremony organized for a particular reason. So one can say that rituals are formalized, rule-governed and invariant performances that people commonly refer to as rituals, or ceremonies, or by the particular names given to the ceremony in question.

Cognition and Emotion in Rituals

This way of defining ritual places rituals firmly within the realm of reflexivity in our lives. The gist of taking part in a ritual seems to be that we are particularly self-reflexive about every word we utter and each move we make. It is not even that in a ritual a participant needs to walk someplace or say something. Timing, style, bodily composure, facial expression, tone and pitch of one's voice, everything can be paid attention to and thus have meaning. The most mundane and routine things like walking ten metres and saying one's name can be 'lifted up' to another plane and have a special meaning (Bloch 1989: 78). Routine, culturally unconscious action seems to be miles away from rituals.

There is also a high degree of reflexivity about rituals in the sense that there are a host of public discourses available for people to discuss whether they are needed or whether individuals themselves want to take part. Let us take the case of the graduation ceremony I mentioned at the beginning.

Apart from its assumed solidarity-strengthening function, within the university management it was also thought that the graduation provides a good opportunity for the University of Tampere to improve its visibility in the national public sphere: to show off by displaying how many doctors graduate. The publicity acquired also provides a forum to justify the need to increase public funding for the university.

The design of the actual contents of rituals is also publicly discussed, which means that their nature as invented tradition is no secret. For instance, in the 1990s the Finnish Lutheran church revised its services and other rituals so that they were closer to the more colourful rituals of the Roman and Greek Catholic churches, whose rituals are assumed to be more emotionally touching.

However, to what degree people are reflexive about rituals depends on how you look at it. Rituals may accentuate our awareness of a situation or a particular act, but, as such, they are a taken-for-granted aspect of every-day life. At some level people know that rituals are made by human beings, that they are specially arranged events, but even the individuals who organize them do not necessarily question whether they want to do so. That may be the case even if people do not share the faith or ideology that the ritual in question symbolizes. As Bell (1997: 167) puts it, 'they are more apt to perceive themselves as simply responding to circumstances – whether the circumstances are a birthday party, a death in the midst, or the gathering of Friends at a Quaker meeting house'.

Why is it then that certain rituals are a self-evident part of our everyday life, even if we have lost our faith in the values that the ritual acts typically sanctify? Why don't we discard such contents from our rituals altogether?

It is partly because of this line of reasoning that many sociologists have predicted an end to public rituals. Since proper rituals are often linked to the sacred aspects of tradition and organized religion, it can be easily assumed that ritual is at odds with secularized modernity, which sub-scribes to a rational, scientific world view. It is also argued that increasing privatization and individualization will gradually make collective rituals obsolete. For instance, Etzioni (2000: 44–59) has recently suggested that the privatization of holidays – that is, a decline in participation in shared com-munal events – correlates with the rise of diversity in society. Correspondingly, following in the footsteps of Freud, who likened obses-sive-compulsive disorders to rituals, Giddens (1992: 71) notes that com-pulsions usually take the form of stereotyped personal rituals. According to him, this is because large areas of a person's life are no longer set by pre-existing patterns and habits in our post-traditional society. Instead, the individual is continually obliged to negotiate life-style options in all walks of life. In their attempt to create a sense of ontological security, individuals are prone to create their own personal rituals, which, if they are focused in socially unacceptable ways, are known as compulsions or addictions.

The trend outlined seems clear. According to this scenario, public rituals will be transformed into more diversified family rituals or even – at least in the case of pathologies – into personal rituals, so that each participant will only pay tribute to the values he or she believes in. Such a development could already be seen in Western countries in the 1960s and 1970s. The spirit of the times, a kind of modernist radicalism, strongly subscribed to reason and science and opposed all stiff formalities and conservative ritualism. Consequently, many individuals refused to take part in graduations, for instance; people even got married without arranging any wedding parties (or they rejected the whole institution and simply lived together). However, there now seems to be a sea change in the opposite direction. Recently, brief therapists have begun to utilize rituals as part of family therapy or marital counselling. Clients may be instructed to organize ritual-like sessions in their homes. In many areas of life, for instance the academic world, the younger generations are willing to respect or revitalize old traditions.

If we believe in the modernization theory of rituals presented above, we should assume that the revitalization of rituals shows that people again share the values behind those rituals. However, that does not seem to be true. Those who like to arrange or take part in old rituals do not necessarily consider themselves conservative. One could argue rather that postmodernism – a doubting of the grand narrative of modernization and rationalization – has enabled a more playful but still respectful attitude toward public rituals.

My interpretation about a changing climate of opinion concerning rituals may be wrong, or only applicable to some countries like Finland. But that does not change the point that I want to make. Rituals are not so much about belief or cognition as about emotions and bodily felt experiences. This means that rituals do not die out even if people lose faith in the values they sanctify or if they realize that a ritual they partake in is a recently invented tradition. The high talk or other kinds of references to official values or ideologies characteristic of rituals are not the main point. Rather, they serve a dramatic function. To exaggerate a little, even the worst cynics or humorists, who love to make fun of any official values, need to have sacred words or symbols in their rituals, because otherwise the requisite feeling denoting a ritual would be absent. A ritual would not be a ritual without the solemnity and formality typical of at least one part of it, and there is no better way to reach that than by making a reference to authoritative ideologies and by emphasizing social hierarchies.

So, one could say that rituals are surrounded by a curious mixture of doubt and belief, playfulness and seriousness. Cognitively – at least at some level of cognition – people know that rituals are invented traditions, whose contents can be developed and modified, and even that totally new rituals can be constructed. People do not even need to really believe in the values or ideologies that the rituals sanctify. Still, there is an air of solemnity around well-organized rituals, and that seriousness which creates the feeling of the ritual being a special occasion amongst the participants can best be achieved by making use of references to official authoritative ideologies or to sacred symbolism.

Because people seem to need sacredness for their rituals, all kinds of ideologies and organizations, such as religions, political movements, private companies or nation states, have eagerly developed rituals or sacred symbols, or have borrowed elements from older rituals. For instance, Christel Lane (1981) describes how the state adopted and actively used ritual as a tool of cultural management in the former Soviet Union. Soviet citizens came across these rituals during various stages of their life-cycle. Lane lists such familial life-cycle rituals as the birth rite, wedding rite, funeral rite and Remembrance Day. In addition, there were a host of rituals of initiation into social or political collectives, such as initiations into the communist youth organizations, educational rites of passage, introduction into the armed forces, etc. Moreover, there were all kinds of labour rituals and rites related to holidays of the calendric cycle. All these rituals had been carefully scripted, produced, tested and finally promoted to the general public, and in this planning process it was made sure that they were firmly rooted in the 'holy' Soviet traditions. On the other hand, very often the new rituals were not really that new: they were revivals or adaptations of old pre-Soviet rituals or merely joined together into an agreeable whole various elements which, up to then, had existed in isolation from each other (Lane 1981: 50).

There certainly always are, and will be, people who are devoted believers in the ideologies directly or symbolically expressed by the rituals they attend, and many other people are probably affected by them to a lesser extent. If rituals did not have any effect, they would probably die out. However, we have to reject the idea that (at least) ordinary people are defenceless victims of the rites of rulers, who by skilfully using ritual as a tool are able to manipulate people and modify their thinking and behaviour at will. It is rather that the needs of the high and mighty to promote their ideologies and to strengthen existing relations of power, and people's longing for something sacred, find each other in ritual. Political or religious leaders probably think that rituals are very effective, and it is in the interest of their advisers – that is, all kinds of experts – not to shatter their faith in ritual.[2] Yet there isn't really any science of ritual, no hard evidence that proves how effective ritual is, or how a ritual must be designed to make it work ideally. Rituals have assumed their form over time through trial and error, and the dramatists of new or revised rituals have copied ideas or elements from older ones.

Hierarchies and Solidarity

In the previous section I argued that people want their rituals to convey an experience of sacredness, to have something that lifts these occasions up to another level and sets them apart from ordinary events. That is why rituals refer to authoritative ideologies and emphasize social hierarchies.

Maurice Bloch (1989) has made the point that rituals play out social hierarchies. As noted, rituals are largely based on highly rule-governed and formalized modes of behaviour, and in a ritual certain objects or persons are considered sacred and worshipped. Usually rituals have a leader, a priest who directs the festivities. The forms in which sacred objects are worshipped (such as bowing to a person, picture or statue, taking off one's shoes when entering a sacred building or place, etc.) resemble the ways in which hierarchically superior persons are shown respect. Anxiety, fear and respect are an essential element of rituals.

The point that hierarchical relations are characteristic of rituals seems to be in stark contrast with the functional approach to ritual espoused by Émile Durkheim (1965). Durkheim thinks that a ritual's main function is to strengthen solidarity between members of society. According to him, when the members of a society or social group worship shared objects and share their experiences, it helps to form and sustain deep emotional bonds among themselves. According to the functionalist view, ritual is thus a counter-force to the centrifugal effects of profane, routine daily life.

Why did Durkheim lose sight of the fact that rituals emphasize hierarchical relations between participants, including imagined participants such as gods or spirits? It was partly because of his grand idea that in worshipping sacred objects as representatives of God, or gods, the members of a society are in fact worshipping society. That was coupled with the stress that he laid on the ritual's function in strengthening solidarity.

Durkheim was not totally wrong to say that rituals strengthen solidarity between participants. Rituals typically contain two parts: a formal event and a subsequent informal party. The formal parts tend to emphasize hierarchies between the participants, whereas the informal parts promote a feeling of communion across status lines.

Consider the graduation ceremony again. The first and second event, i.e., the graduation itself and the service in church, were formal and emphasized the social hierarchy. For instance, in the graduation, after receiving the top hat and the sword, we had to bow to the chancellor and vice-chancellor of the university, who were sitting in the front row. Similarly, when entering the church we had to take off our hat to honour the sanctity of the church and what it represents. Moreover, the seating order in the graduation and in the church reflected the social hierarchy. The chancellor, vice-chancellor, deans, leaders of the ceremonies and honorary doctors sat in the front row, and the rest of us were seated according to faculties, which were organized in order of their age, and within each faculty, in alphabetical order. In the more informal events, such as the dances and graduation dinner, we had more possibilities for free socializing, although there was a strict dress code for each event, and the way in which participants were seated at the dinner table reflected social hierarchies.

Even if many arrangements in rituals emphasize hierarchy, this does not exclude feelings of solidarity. A hierarchy itself means that people are organized into ranks – that is, classes of people – which may mean that those slotted into the same class are drawn closer to each other because they share the same position. For instance, the prospective members of a community, who are put through tests before they are accepted as full members, share the same experiences of anxiety and excitement, and this contributes to establishing closeness among them. The same is true of course for those who are higher up in the hierarchy, for instance those who are in charge of the festivities. As said previously, rituals are often comprised of two parts, a formal and more informal one. The latter part especially often serves to create an emotional bond among all those who have successfully played their role in the ritual drama.

Through another route I seem to have come to the same conclusion as Durkheim: rituals may indeed draw people closer to each other and thus enhance solidarity. But this is not so much because they strengthen a community by reinforcing the sacredness of the principles on which it is based. We may not have very high ideas about the values promoted, or we may be critical of the hierarchical organization reflected and represented in the ritual, but we get the thrill, the feeling of a special occasion, from the formality and sacredness of the event. Perhaps a minimum requirement for the sacred symbolism used in a ritual is that we recognize it, and know that at least some people regard it as holy.

Ritual as a Train

Ritual may not be as effective in promoting an ideology as one might assume. After all, many people who take part in rituals have a playful attitude toward them. Being formal and serious during the event is part of a play, so to speak, and one does not have to disclose to others what one really thinks about it all.

That does not mean, however, that I deny the effectiveness of rituals as a tool in reinforcing social order. Rituals and ritual-like activities are crucial in establishing – or changing – power relations, but not by being able to somehow convince people about an ideology. Rituals are 'non-discursive' and in that sense they do not encourage reflexivity. Even if an individual would like to express his or her opinion about a ceremony and about the things said in ritual language, it is made particularly difficult, and in that sense rituals are effective in controlling people's behaviour. Ritual is like a train: once you decide to get on board, it is very difficult to step off midway. Rituals make people – even untrained outsiders who decide to participate – act according to the script.

Rituals have that capacity because they are prime examples of what conversation analysts call 'institutional interaction' (Drew and Heritage 1992). Compared to ordinary conversation, this means that the options of interaction are restricted. For instance, the graduation ritual included an 'examiner's question' posed to one pre-selected doctor, the symbolic function of which was to test that the doctors possess the knowledge required to be entitled to graduate. This 'primus doctor' represented us all; the rest of us were quiet throughout the ceremony. In addition to that, there were some talks given by prominent people and words uttered in Latin by the leaders of the ritual at its different stages. That is, the speaker roles, and in most cases also the form and content of words uttered, were restricted and carefully planned beforehand.

That is typical of all rituals. Although what people say in a ritual may have significance, even legal consequences (like an oath), it may be that everything that is said, by whom, and at what moment, is written in the script beforehand. Despite all the jokes about what a bride or groom answers to the priest's question in a marriage, one rarely hears any other answer than 'I do'. If a breach of the script occurs, it is normally considered a scandal. Such formality also binds the leaders of the ritual. For instance, although a person who delivers a speech during a ritual may speak more freely, it is assumed that the theme and style of the talk fits in with the ceremony in question. Again, breaking such more or less explicitly stated rules would be considered a scandal that no person in his or her right mind would cause.

Such formalization is said to be effective in promoting a general acceptance of what is going on. Bloch (1989: 33–7) formulates this by saying that in ritual, propositional force of communication is excluded and illocutionary force is increased. As Bell (1997: 140) puts it, 'while people might challenge the expression of specific or concrete ideas, they tend not to challenge the routine expression of formulas or clichés'. In a ritual context, to publicly question or challenge the content alone is difficult, because it is so closely tied up with the form and style – that is, the whole event. That is why rituals that are an integral part of the human life-cycle – such as naming ceremonies, weddings or funerals – can easily be put to the service of a religion or an ideology, even if people are not devoted followers. Such rituals give the religious or political leaders an excellent opportunity to preach about their ideology and to associate it with important moments in people's lives.

The formality of rituals not only plays out social hierarchies in a symbolic form and makes participants silently accept the content of ritual talk;

rituals also effectively force participants into particular roles within a hierarchy. As Bloch puts it, the script followed has 'illocutionary force'. It can be said that rituals produce hierarchies, albeit that they may only be in force during the ritual.

In various ways rituals contribute to legitimating and routinizing social hierarchies and power relations. It must also be remembered that practically no power relations are 'put to use' without the support of rituals. For instance, a legal trial can be regarded as a ritual because speaker roles and forms of talk are carefully defined (Atkinson and Drew 1979). To put it another way, one can hardly speak about a hierarchy or power relation if it is not symbolically expressed, and those forms through which hierarchy and respect are expressed make it more difficult for individuals to challenge the existing order.

Why Do We Have Rituals?

As I have tried to show in this chapter, rituals are an ingenious and deceptive social institution. On the one hand they are harmless in many ways. We do not need to believe in the values promoted in the sermons or expressed in the symbolism. Purely as cognitive experiences, they do not seem to be very effective. They do not even try to present an argument, speak to us or try to convince us as individuals.

On the other hand, it is precisely because propositional force is diminished or totally lacking in rituals and ritual-like activities that they are able to affect us. When taking part in a ritual we step on a train that takes us where it is going, and we do not have much chance to argue against it. That is okay when we are dealing with a harmless ritual we ourselves have chosen to attend, but we must bear in mind that there are many institutions in society that follow the same principles as proper public rituals. In various forms of institutional interaction, our abilities to freely communicate with a person who is hierarchically above us are restricted. In these ritual-like activities we are also 'trained' so to speak, taken on a ride, and there isn't much we can do about the situation; we just have to play by the rules imposed on us. That is how power works.

Although there is a lot of reflexivity involved in and around rituals, in the above-mentioned sense we tend to routinely accept the existing conditions arranged around ritual-like activities. We may reflect on and question the existing social order in many ways, but institutional arrangements and interaction easily escape our attention, because they powerfully present social reality for us. For instance, a court of law would not be a court of law if the actors did not follow certain formal rules in their behaviour; thus it is difficult to ask whether things could be different. Similarly, the rituals people typically arrange at certain stages of their lives make such thresholds concrete and memorable and in that sense contribute to naturalizing – or rather routinizing – our notions of the phases of the human life-cycle.

So why do we arrange rituals? One way of answering this is to say that without them our lives would be very dull and monotonous. Ritual is one of the few ways in which humans are able to take a break every now and then from their mundane routines and arrange a special occasion. Another means would be psycho-active substances, but even their intake often assumes ritual forms. The thrill we get out of a ritual – as modest as it can be sometimes – is primarily based on its totality as an event. Ritual is also a bodily felt experience. When taking part in a ritual we do not just listen to a sermon or watch others perform; we are also made to do things like singing, walking, dancing, and we are put into particular postures. It is these bodily, physically and emotionally felt experiences that make rituals, if not unforgettable, at least hard to forget. The bodily experience is linked with what the ritual stands for: it is strongly associated with it in our minds because it is carved on our bodies. In that sense, rituals and ritual-like activities are important for our understanding of our human reality because they remind us of the fact that we are physical creatures, not just bodiless minds spinning human reality out of concepts and thin air.

Emphasizing the importance of the body does not belittle the role of language. Quite the contrary, for throughout this book I have stressed that the most fascinating thing about human reality is our ability to form and adapt to social constructs and to make them real in their consequences. However, for us this reality, although composed of constructs upon constructs, is very real, self-evident and resistant to sudden radical changes, and that is partly due to the mechanisms that rituals highlight. When certain ideas and principles, upon which social order is built, are played out in more or less stylized and formalized occasions, these ideas and principles leave a memory trace on our mind and body. Therefore they are harder to resist because we indeed know them by heart, as the saying goes: they are routinely observed and emotionally felt.

Notes

1   In Finland these graduation ceremonies are rare occasions. For instance, at the University of Tampere the previous ceremony was arranged in the 1980s. That is why many participants, like me, were now being ceremonially graduated as doctors although we had received our doctorate degree a long time ago.

2   The same is true for the effect of advertising. It is not in the interests of professionals, who directly or indirectly make their money from the business, to question the possibility of effective manipulation, although many social scientists agree that (fortunately) no social science can provide a ready formula. Advertising is a craft of using words and images, not a science.

6 Personality

The Case of Modernity

To illustrate how the main building blocks and working principles of human reality function in specific cultural and historical contexts, in the following two chapters I will discuss how some of the cultural features of modern societies are constructed and how they routinely work. In this chapter, I deal with the formation and routine reproduction of the modern notion of personality especially with the means of narrative work, whereas the next chapter discusses how social identity construction plays a part in the routine functioning and change of modern society.

One could of course argue that all humans have a personality structure and that differences between world cultures can be seen in the range of personality types found in a given culture. This viewpoint can also be justified by the cross-cultural variation of personality types as evidenced by personality tests. However, as has also been pointed out, such personality tests always have a cultural bias. More importantly, they only provide circumstantial evidence about an object called 'personality', which as a social construct is an element of a historically and culturally specific way of conceiving the relationship between individuals and the society at large. Therefore, analysing the historical formation and day-to-day reproduction of personality must be approached as a case analysis, not an analysis of a universal constant.

The notion and routine lived experience of personality is certainly an interesting case example of the functioning of human reality, because one of the fascinating things about it is how humans manage the relationship between individual actors and the social whole. As was discussed in the introductory chapter of this book, the reason why the human species has been so successful as compared with other animals is because of our institutionalized intelligence. In addition to the fact that the human brain is the most developed of all species, the knowledge and experience of previous generations and of our fellow human beings are stored in language and in institutionalized behavioural patterns by which we handle things and coordinate individual acts into a sufficiently orderly or functioning whole. This means that, on the one hand, everything rests on individuals and their behaviour, but, on the other hand, mutual coordination is achieved by what the actors share, and how they are socialized members of the society in question.

Among animal species with smaller brain capacity, social coordination between individual animals is primarily programmed in the genes, and at some level that is also true for humans. For instance, even a small dysfunction in the brain may severely disrupt an individual's social skills, and physical damage to the brain may change an individual's personality in aspects that we would easily be inclined to ascribe to the individual's social background. Nature and nurture are intertwined in complex ways. But although biology has its role to play in at least setting certain conditions for human sociality, for the most part the coordination of action among humans is programmed by culture, not genes.

That is why the answer to the question 'how do humans manage the relationship between individual actors and the social whole?' is that it depends on the society. The general model of human reality that we have been using does not say anything about how much autonomy individual members have in a community at large, nor does it say how people conceive of their selves. In this respect, cultures and societies are different. For instance, in some non-Western societies individual members are less 'individual'.[1] Within the sociological modernization narrative it is commonly assumed that in contemporary 'Western' or 'modern' societies, people are particularly individualized, whereas in non-Western societies people conceive of themselves less as separate from others and more as part of the community. Although it is certainly true that in many respects contemporary Western societies require quite considerable autonomy from individuals, the modernization narrative is problematic in that it flattens the diversity of human cultures into a linear picture of cultural evolution, with the notion of the Western individual as the inevitable end point of history. Instead, we must bear in mind that the degree of autonomy given to individuals depends on the local conditions.

On the whole, I suggest that we can say that the relative freedom given to individuals within human societies depends on the way in which social life is organized and how people gain their livelihood. If getting along requires independence and making individual decisions, it is also likely to be reflected in the local cultural notion of the self. Of course, the measure of individual independence also depends on the cultural history of the group in question. If people previously cherished a communal view of life, even changing material conditions do not alter that overnight. Moreover, material conditions do not determine the cultural notion of the individual; cultures in which the community overrules the individual tend to organize their life accordingly, including the way in which they gain their livelihood. But even though there are big cultural differences in the relative autonomy given to individuals, in human reality, in which coordination of action is programmed by culture rather than by genes, there is always a measure of autonomy given to individuals. Gene-programmed behaviour among animals may be very mechanical, so some animals may be poorly able to adjust their patterns of behaviour according to unexpectedly changed conditions, but – even if people stubbornly following their culturally conditioned routines may sometimes look pretty stupid – the competitive edge of culture over biology is that people are able to flexibly adjust to new situations, and that requires a measure of individual assessment.

Thus, when this chapter discusses the way in which personality is socially constructed and put to routine practice in advanced contemporary societies, we are dealing with a specific example.

The Formation of the Individual and the Inner Self

One reason for the still prevalent assumption about a linear universal development toward increasing individuality within the human race is that, internationally, dominant academic history writing is very Eurocentric. This often means that the development of individualization from the European Middle Ages until the present is mistaken for a universal evolutionary path from time zero to the foreseeable future. Within that time span, in that geographical area, a process of individualization indeed took place, but it does not mean that European modernity gave birth to the individual. It only serves as a case example of the dynamics by which social conditions and character formation mutually affect each other, thus giving shape to different forms of human agency.

Historians of European culture are more or less agreed that people's ways of thinking changed quite dramatically in the late sixteenth and early seventeenth century. In his studies of the civilizing process, Norbert Elias (1978, 1982) observes that manners began to change rapidly from the sixteenth century onwards, both in courts and among ordinary people, so that table manners, for instance, corresponded (among the upper classes) to present-day manners by the end of the eighteenth century. From there on it was mainly a matter of customs spreading and establishing themselves. The same applies to the history of sexuality; the period of modesty, silence and increasing prohibitions is usually said to have dawned in the early seventeenth century (e.g., Foucault 1980). According to Frances Yates (1969), the early part of the seventeenth century was an important period for the birth of modern European and American personhood.

The changing notions of personhood, and in particular an increasing demand for privacy, are commonly linked with urbanization and the rise of capitalist exchange economy, which required new kinds of individualizing administrative practices. A profound change in the style, or mode, of government took place. In antiquity and during the Middle Ages order was maintained by public demonstrations of the repressive apparatus and its power to rule and to punish criminals, allowing law-abiding citizens to remain in the background and live their lives in peace. But from the eighteenth century onwards, power and the centres of power became increasingly invisible, while citizens became targets of continuous and visible surveillance and control. The threat of chaos and disorder that lay dormant in the faceless crowds of modern society was countered by means of systematic surveillance, control and data collection on individuals.

Initially this method was applied in the late seventeenth century to combat the chaos that was created in urban areas by the plague. Houses were boarded up and closed from the outside, all public meetings and gatherings were prohibited, and guards were placed everywhere, at all gates and in every quarter. The same means were employed in eighteenth-century Paris to combat social unrest and crime. An invisible network of intense surveillance consisting of police inspectors, observers, police informers and prostitutes was set up, its job being to lay bare, to make everything visible (Foucault 1979). Modern society also saw a movement away from the brutal, public means of punishment that were favoured in the Middle Ages towards more humane forms of imprisonment and towards closed institutions that were committed to the ideals of moral education. However, as Walter Benjamin and Michel Foucault have shown, this has not necessarily translated into progress. The new system is one of relentless, all-embracing surveillance and control which leaves no one untouched, not even the most law-abiding of citizens. The key thing about the change, however, was not that people were subjected to non-stop surveillance. Rather, it is our awareness of the ever-present existence of the administrative apparatus, our knowledge that the system can intervene at any time and at any place, our anticipation of the embarrassing consequences of such an intervention, that keeps us on the straight and narrow path. External discipline and overt coercion have largely been replaced by self-discipline. In this process of civilization, the general mentality of the modern individual has changed quite considerably. The growth of self-discipline at the expense of external discipline over the past few centuries has made the latter more and more redundant and contributed to a growing sense of freedom among individuals. In this sense, as far as people's own experiences are concerned, modernization has implied a growth of *freedom*. It is not that people today feel they are *subjecting* themselves, against their own will, to imposed order and discipline, but they *take into account* the social coercions which set the conditions for their voluntary actions. For the most part the advanced form of social order becomes a natural environment, the activity it expects of people becomes *consistent with one's own will*. These variable conditions, which seem to appear all by themselves, and which no longer represent the personal power of the ruler or the coercive apparatus, are now perceived as representing a mystical society that is opposed to the individual.

The process of individuation related to the new kind of administrative and disciplinary apparatuses and to the formation of the capitalist exchange economy gave rise to a new conception of the self. As people were increasingly often treated as individual decision-makers, responsible for and made to 'pay' for their own choices with the help of a 'self-seeking' language borrowed from the Protestant Christian religion, a whole new vocabulary was created with which to deal with one's self. With the gradual emergence of the notion of the individual as a personality, who more or less effectively keeps his/her desires in check, there is an interesting shift in the location of the ego. Whilst people in the Middle Ages seemed to be familiar with their wants, and unaccustomed to forcing themselves to do anything, from the sixteenth century onwards the position begins to reverse.

Take, for example, Emanuel Le Roy Ladurie's (1978) study of Montaillou, a French village at the turn of the thirteenth and fourteenth centuries. Among the peasants, the notion of self-discipline was hardly known. Even though they appreciated living by their own work, they worked only as much as was needed to survive. If something more interesting happened, the work could be interrupted for weeks. The peasants' conception of sin was in concert with their relation to work. If, say, prostitution or an extra-marital relation attracted both parties, it was conceived of as innocent. As soon as it became unpleasant, it was understood to become a sin. The later Protestant notion of sin was quite the opposite. Especially in Calvinism, everything sensual and emotional was prohibited as sinful; not only sexuality – which was accepted only if its function was to multiply – but all diversions, and even an interest in high culture, were suspect. Work was conceived as a profane form of sacred devotions (Weber 1971).

The tension between the individual's self-discipline and desires was first conceived of as a religious question, and a question of moral conduct. Heavy drinking, for instance, was not perceived as a sign of disease or a loss of control; it was condemned as immoral behaviour, as a sin. But from early on, Christian asceticism has also included the idea that certain behaviours, especially pleasures, represent *nature* in the individual, and that is why they have to be overcome, controlled by *reason*. According to Weber, Western monasticism, in the rules of St Benedict, among the monks of Cluny, with the Cistercians, and most strongly the Jesuits, had become emancipated from otherworldliness and self-torture:

It had developed a systematic method of rational conduct with the purpose of overcoming the *status naturae*, to free man from the power of irrational impulses and his dependence on the world and on nature. It attempted to subject man to the supremacy of a purposeful will, to bring his actions under constant self-control with a careful consideration of their ethical consequences. (Weber 1971: 118–19)

Another source for the new language of personality can be found in the 'sciences of man', as Foucault called them, which emerged as a complement to new disciplinary institutions. Individualizing surveillance gave the surveyors new information about individual reactions to different 'stimuli', which led to the formation of new forms of knowledge, or disciplines, as 'regimes of truth'. They, in turn, gave feedback to the professionals in charge of further developing the disciplinary institutions (Foucault 1979).

The developing vocabularies of the self and personality can also be seen in the birth of a new genre of literature in which the language of the self is put to use, so to speak. I'm of course referring to the rise of autobiographies, which several scholars have treated as reflection or an indicator of the rise of individualism. For instance, Paul Delany notes that the emergence of autobiographies in Italy was preceded by family histories. And the same goes for Britain: 'In early British autobiographies we often find similar transitions from genealogy to autobiography; by placing his own story in the context of family tradition the writer could avoid giving the appearance of an unseemly egotism' (Delany 1969: 12). The historical studies of autobiography also suggest that individuality is a specifically modern form of self-conception, which began in the Renaissance and blossomed at the time of Goethe (Misch 1969; Weintraub 1975, 1978). Weintraub (1975: 834) points out that autobiography is inseparably linked to the problem of self-conception: 'The manner in which men conceive of the nature of the self largely determines the form and process of autobiographic writing'. Autobiographies reveal the gradual emergence of that form of self-conception called individuality. From Hellenic and Roman times onward, there has been, according to Weintraub, an ever sharper turn toward an inner-directed personality. Since the time of the Renaissance, 'Western man has by a series of complex and gradual developments formed a particular attachment to the ideal of personality we call individuality. This ideal is characterized by its very rejection of a valid model for the individual' (Weintraub 1975: 838).

Life-Stories and Biographical Reasoning

The fact that life-stories appeared as a new literary genre in the Renaissance is certainly an indicator of a new self-conception, but people did not start to write them just to please future cultural historians by providing them with material through which to study the modern self. Autobiography writers – and their readers for that matter – had to have a motive for going to the trouble, and that motive reveals an intimate link between life-stories and personality construction. Autobiographies do not just reflect or document modern individuality; rather, they are an outcome of the fact that people are engaged in biographical work (Gubrium and Holstein 1995a, 1995b; Gubrium et al. 1994) or biographical reasoning (Alasuutari 1986, 1992a).

This means that as agents in modern society we conceive of ourselves or our fellow members of society in terms of a 'personality frame'. That is, we think that what we do in a particular situation is – or should be – internally linked to how we behaved in previous similar or dissimilar situations. This does not mean that our behaviour is totally predictable, let alone determined by our past experience or past actions, but we do think that each person has his or her own style or personal way of acting and behaving in different situations. If people's actions are too predictable, they are easily considered simple-minded and close to robots or less intelligent animals, but if their action seems to depend only on other people's acts and opinions, they are deemed as opportunists lacking character.

Therefore, since having one's own character or personality obviously is a moral obligation, individuals are held accountable both to each other and to themselves as to how their past acts are related to their present acts and opinions, or to their future plans. This is especially the case when things change or when people could be seen to behave in a totally uncharacteristic, perhaps opportunist manner. In such a situation, an individual needs to partly, or entirely, re-narrate his or her past life, thus in one way or another maintaining continuity, or a socially acceptable reason for a total change of perspective and fundamental principles in life, which is the case in accounts about a conversion experience. In such situations, people are privately or publicly engaged in autobiographical work, which on some occasions leads to published life-stories.

In other words, autobiographies are the outcome of everyday-life autobiographical work, by which people construct their individuality and personality. Life-stories are narratives that tie together a chain of events from an individual's life by pointing out how they characterize the personality in question, thus constructing that personality. As Lejeune (1989: 4) puts it, an autobiography is a 'retrospective prose narrative written by a real person concerning his own existence, where the focus is his individual life, in particular the story of his personality'. Linde (1987: 344) broadens the definition by saying that a life-story is all the stories told by an individual during his or her lifetime which (1) make a point about the speaker, not about the way the world is, and which (2) 'have extended reportability' – that is, they can be told over the course of a long period of time.

Written autobiographies are a special case, but on the whole life-story narrating is an everyday-life phenomenon, which serves certain functions. Individuals do not have their readily narrated life-stories in their back pockets or at the back of their minds, waiting for a researcher to collect them. Any account of one's personal past (also when told to a researcher in a life-story interview) makes a point and serves a function.

A particular case of life-story narration must be related to its local setting in order to see what it is needed or used for.

The claim of a personality often justifies one's present behaviour, but the claim itself is justified by biographical work. For instance Gergen and Gergen (1984: 173) considered the way people's daily accounts of themselves require a biographical interpretation and, if needed, a longstanding story of self: 'Suddenly and momentarily to see oneself as "aggressive", "poetic", or "male", for example, might seem mere whimsy unless such concepts could be secured to a series of earlier events'. Thus, life-stories consist of retrospective accounts of the past; accounts which are given for particular reasons and in particular situations, such as the onset of chronic illness (Williams 1984).

Although life-story narrating may also take place as an individual's 'inner speech', needed for creating a sense of continuity of self in changing conditions and situations, the concepts, discourses, explanatory systems (Linde 1987) or interpretive repertoires (Potter and Wetherell 1987: 146–57) used in such accounts are not private language. People always use the interpretive resources available to them, even when it comes to creating a sense of self.

These considerations lead to a discursive view of self (see Harré and Gillett 1994). This view maintains that to accomplish their plans, projects and intentions, people have certain linguistic resources or repertoires at their disposal: 'The resources people have available in some roughly delineated, cultural system have been called an "...-ology". So an emotionology is a representation of the linguistic and other discursive resources people have available for describing emotional phenomena' (Harré and Gillett 1994: 98). From this viewpoint, we co-construct the individual as a personality by using particular repertoires within which to interpret people's acts in everyday life. Thus, emotions are not out (or in) there to be described with words; rather, they are a product of the ways in which they are talked about.

The Cultural Premises of Self

It is obvious that individuals use life-story narration and autobiographical accounting to construct their individuality, i.e., continuity over time. That is how a sense of self is discursively accomplished. This, however, leads to the question as to what are the cultural premises on which the understanding of a life-story as a story about an individual life, a story of a 'personality', is based. If self and personality are discursively constructed, how is this done? What implicit frames or cultural premises are required of a reader of a life-story? I suggest that we can identify two intertwined premises for the understanding of a life-story: the narrative implicature and the concept of face.

Narrative implicature refers to Herbert Paul Grice's (1975, 1978) idea of conversational implicature, which means that in ordinary conversations everyone assumes that participants follow the cooperative principle, which is realized in certain maxims of conversations. Micheal Geis (1982) lists six such maxims. It is not necessary to go through all six here; let me just say that the maxims we automatically follow require us to avoid unfamiliar language, to be truthful, relevant, and to say no less and no more than is necessary. These maxims are not regulative rules; it is rather that people use them regularly in interpreting each other's utterances in conversation (Nofsinger 1991: 40).

Similarly, when a person is telling a long story, we assume that there is a logical and thematic link that connects different sentences of the story together. Teun van Dijk (1980) actually makes the same point by showing that, in addition to semantic macro-structures, we assume that texts have a thematic coherence. He gives an example: 'John was ill, so he called the doctor. But the doctor could not come, because his wife wanted to go to the theater with him. They were playing Othello, which she thought they could not miss because Shakespeare is one of the few dramatic authors who ... ' (van Dijk 1980: 40). Each fact is a condition for the next one; participants are also kept identical for a while but the fragment has no coherence because a uniting theme is missing. We expect to find a theme or topic in a story, and if we fail to find it, we will soon ask what is the point. In story-telling and listening to stories we accept irrelevant details up to a point, but since we follow the cooperative principle we also try to make sense of the details of, for instance, a life-story. Consider the following sentences: 'I was never a good liar. When Paula asked me if I knew how to swim, I said yes.' Formally there is no link between the two sentences, but by following the cooperative principle we automatically read them as a way of saying, or emphasizing the point, that the speaker is telling the truth. However, in addition to narrative implicature, the example illustrates another, related self-evident frame. We automatically assume that upon hearing that the person was 'never a good liar' he continues to be that way.

This leads us to the concept of face, the expectation that a person should be self-consistent. Although the concept has initially been applied to human interaction, we can assume that it also holds in the telling of longer stories. In the act of story-telling, participants in human interaction are supposed to give a consistent picture of themselves as characters. We are supposed to maintain our face: to successfully and consistently play the role we chose to take when entering the situation.

Erving Goffman (1967) argues that a sacred principle prevails in conversation situations whereby the parties to the conversation have a reciprocal system of maintaining and defending each others' face. This means, among other things, that the people involved in the conversation are considerate towards each other and try to sustain each others' self-image. Brown and Levinson (1987) have shown that there is a universal principle of politeness based on avoiding face-threatening acts, which can be of two types: they may threaten our negative or positive face. *Negative face* refers to the wish of every competent adult that his or her actions be unimpeded by others. *Positive face*, in turn, refers to the wish of every adult that her or his needs/wishes be desirable at least to some others (Brown and Levinson 1987: 62). When we say 'You couldn't by any chance tell me the time, could you?' rather than 'Tell me the time', we are conforming to conventional expectations of politeness by showing that we are aware of, and honour, the negative-face wants of the addressee. In face-to-face interaction maintaining face also means that if I introduce myself as a specialist in a field, it is considered humiliating if my next turn of speech shows that I know very little or nothing about it.

In choosing to tell my life-story I enter an interaction situation by giving a presentation of myself. It may of course be that the audience of a written autobiography is unknown to the story-teller, but the story is nonetheless a presentation of self, a character, and as such the consistency that implicature applies. In a life-story presentation, the consistency principle means that the characteristics by which the story-tellers describe themselves are consistent with the life events told in the story. In a sense this is obvious because any events included in a life-story are there precisely because they make a point about the person. Life-story narrating is usually employed when accounting for possibly face-threatening acts, public acts that might be seen to contradict the public self-image the person has previously claimed for him- or herself.

Consider a job interview or an autobiographical statement required in the application for a vacancy. The events of past life mentioned must be truthful enough not to contradict one's personal records and documents. On the other hand, the story constructed on the basis of them should convey a longstanding interest in precisely the kind of job for which one is applying. This means that, for instance, previous work in a totally different field should be presented as a mistake finally realized. Another possibility is that one is able to plot an account that identifies the common element, the personal calling, between the tasks preferably in such a light that in the new job the desired element can be better realized than in the old one.

Are such life-story narratives totally false, and thus useless in trying to get a grasp of an individual's true self? Not really. As job interviewers know, if a person is able to depict a life-story where the new job can be presented believably as the realization of career development, he or she will probably adjust well to the new task. First, the same account can be given to friends and relatives. Second, biographical reasoning also works as a personal device by which we get a sense of continuity for our selves. If we need to remodel our self-concept in order to better fit into the changed role requirements, we can depict our life-story anew. Memory and forgetfulness are also excellent tools in shaping and reshaping the personal self.

Rescuing the Split Character: The 'Freudian' Narrative

We can say that the telling and reading of life-stories is based on the implicit assumption that there is a coherence in the past actions of the protagonist, that is, that he or she maintains face. To approach it from the perspective of everyday-life interaction, the function of life-story narrating is to construct a face, or self. I will now discuss how the particular conditions of face protection in complex societies result in the modern notion of personality, as it is formulated for instance by Sigmund Freud.

As historical studies have shown, autobiographies are a story genre which developed along with modernization (Delany 1969; Misch 1969; Weintraub 1975, 1978). However, if we accept the idea that life-story narrating is a means of face protection, it is not that obvious why this should be the case. According to cross-cultural research reported by Brown and Levinson (1987), there seem to be universal rules of politeness based on the notion of face, and thus the requirement of maintaining one's face seems to be a universal phenomenon. So why do autobiographies as a genre emerge along with modernization?

In complex societies individuals have multiple roles: one's face changes from one contact to another. However, as Mauss (1979) and Geertz (1973: 360–411, 1983: 62–8) have emphasized, in pre-modern society people are identified as collective stereotypes, as personages rather than persons, or as dramatis personae rather than actors: 'on the one hand the clan is conceived of as constituted by a certain number of persons, actually roles; and, on the other, the purpose of all these roles is really to symbolize, each in its own portion, the pre-figured totality of the clan' (Mauss 1979: 65). In such a social system the maintenance of one's face throughout one's life would sound like a natural point to make in a life-story, but that is precisely why biographical work became important along with modernization. The simplicity of the role system does not cause face-threatening tensions to the same extent that modern society does. Life-story narrating makes a point in a situation where role expectations radically vary from one social encounter to another, but one nevertheless holds on to the moral obligation to maintain face. The impossibility of actually maintaining face in the traditional sense of the word leads to narrative innovations, a changed conception of characters and personhood.

The formation of new notions of personhood can be seen in the development of European folklore and literature. Consider the characters of folktales (Propp 1975): each character – hero or villain – pursues an obvious, simply stated goal with the means of rational action. With modernization, such fictional characters came to be considered and scorned as too 'black-and-white'; modern novels introduced more complex characters with ambivalent views, and motives hidden from others and even from themselves.[2]

The new notions of personhood, canonized as Freudian personality theory, reflect the same development. In effect, Freud constructed and gave names to parts of a split self; a self – or personality – which was a solution to the difficulty in accounting for the behaviour of the modern individual. The modern individual appears in several, often contradictory roles, but the prevalent cultural notion of self still holds on to a single face that one is supposed to maintain and defend. Freudian personality theory and its popular version are commonly used as a resource in accounting for face-threatening situations or personal histories.

Narratologically, this personality structure is constructed by dividing a self into two or more characters with their separate goals or, to put it another way, by uniting several lines of action into one self. As a consequence, the otherwise incoherent account of face is rescued by inscribing an inner structure for the character in question; a personality which accounts for contradictory lines of action in a single self.

A Case Example in Personality Construction

How is the reading of life-story narrating as the reflection of a personality structure actually accomplished? What frames are required of a reader who hears the life-story as a reflection of the Freudian paradigm of the personality?[3] How is a picture of the supposed object-like construction called personality made and empirically defended? I will address these questions by using a case example from a study of mine (Alasuutari 1992a: 57–84).

In the study, a group of men (all manual workers and half of them alcoholics) were asked to tell their life-story. Each man was first asked to draw a continuous line depicting the ups and downs of his life, and then to explain them in an unstructured interview. In many of the interviews, the men expressed an ambivalence toward the schooling phase of their lives. The ambivalence about schooling could often be seen in the fact that school was drawn as a downturn, but when asked about it, it was described as a jolly good time.

Q: I understand you were held back a year. What was it like?
A: Actually there was a lot happening that year. I was sixteen and it was the last year of my schooling. I, for example, had an affair with my teacher. It was a wild experience.

Q: Was it an upturn in life?

A: I suppose I was held back as a consequence of all this. So it really can't be perceived as a highpoint.

The ambivalence about a phase in life comes from the fact that it can be evaluated from two points of view. If the men pay attention to what they liked and wanted at the time, schooling was boring and ending it was a relief, a liberation from a strait-jacket. From this perspective, having fun during school hours was the positive part of that phase. If, on the other hand, they consider how they got on at school and the usefulness of con-scientious schooling for a future life, the values turn upside down. In reflecting on and assessing a phase in life, the past moods and inclinations contradict long-term interests as presently perceived. This often leads to remorse, to second thoughts about what one or others should have done.

I wish I had gone on with my schooling. Not then but now, afterwards. I sure would have handled it, even though I wouldn't have liked it then. Father should have forced me, but it was a question of money and the fact that I didn't like school.

The frame within which the narrator reflects upon his past behaviour is very close to the Freudian notion of personality, as consisting of the 'libido' and an 'ego' (Freud 1978), although the narrator does not use those concepts. However, he does refer to a popular Freudian notion of the tension between desire and self-control in one's self.

What are the steps we take to arrive at such a split image of an objecti-fied personality as does the character of the narrative? The first step is to abstract away from different views of personal conduct, to make a typol-ogy of them. The lines of action in concert with things usually considered pleasures, sins or socially unacceptable behaviour are – as options for future action or as views of past action – named 'libido' or 'desire'. The views of action usually thought to be in accordance with socially esteemed values, moral codes or with an individual's long-term interests are named 'super-ego' or 'self-control'. After constructing this typology of separate lines of action into two classes, the next step is to conceive of them as object-like elements in an object-like structure called personality.

In the extract we read the Freudian personality structure off of the man's narrative, regardless of his own interpretations. However, often this personal-ity theory is written into the life-stories themselves as the narrators' frame within which to interpret their own behaviour. Charlotte Linde's (1987) analysis of explanatory systems in oral life-stories is similar. She mentions 'popular Freudian psychology' as one of the explanatory systems people use in accounting for their past life, but in a broader perspective another that she identifies as 'behaviourist psychology' falls within the personality structure frame as it is used here. Both of these common-sense theories include a split of the self into parts that are in contradiction.

In its perhaps clearest form, this view of the self as split into contradictory elements can be seen in everyday usage in accounts of some socially unacceptable behaviours, such as heavy drinking. Among the alcoholics, the drinking often becomes interpreted as an uncontrolled craving, alien from the man himself.

> It was a highpoint when I got a job and became a sailor, although I drank a lot. Before I went to the army it got out of control really, I couldn't hold back.[4]

From a narratological point of view, the 'personality structure solution' to a difficulty in preserving face, to maintaining an image of a separate, autonomous self pursuing his expressed line of action, is indeed an interesting one. The diverse and often conflicting logic for the actions identified in one's 'self' are objectified into evidence of parts of an inner structure. In his structural theory of narratives Greimas (1987) deconstructed such a notion of character by making a distinction between the actors and actants of a story; actors may consist of several actants.

Freud was one of the first to work out a sophisticated theory of the modern notion of personhood. It is often said that with the invention of the libido and the unconscious he shattered the self. Partly this is true; he did shatter the rational homogeneity of the self by inventing its inner, contradictory structure. However, by doing so he actually rescued the Western object-like notion of the self as distinct from other selves. It was only much later, with the emergence of family-systems theoretical therapeutic models and conceptions of their object of therapy, that the conception of the individual self as a centre was challenged and surpassed (Gubrium 1992). It turned out that many families or social networks were best helped, not by treating the identified patient, but by making an intervention in the system (e.g., Haley 1985; Watzlawick et al. 1974).

Biographical Narration and Self

To sum up the argument of this chapter, personality can be considered as an accounting strategy. It is used in accounting for the behaviour of a person who has appeared in more than one role, and in doing so has followed contradictory logics, if one assumes that each person only wears one face.

Does this imply that we should forget about the self or personality, that it does not really exist? Such sentiments have indeed been raised in some postmodernist discussions. However, it seems premature to announce the death of the subject. Instead of approaching the discursive view of personality as proof of a recent mentality change in late modernity, it must be seen as a logical outcome from the project of the social sciences. When we take a close look at the routinely given notion of self, we see how it is constructed in Western societies. What we are dealing with is a view of the ontological status of individual selves that differs from how we tend to conceive of it routinely. We have our physical existence, but selves – or personalities – are not objects in the physical world. Rather, they are part of social reality; constructions we live by. For us, selfhood as lived experience is very real, and the discursive view as it is outlined here might sound like useless philosophical hair-splitting that has no practical value. However, to realize that selves are, after all, constructions we live by enables us, when necessary, to renew ourselves.

Notes

1   Tobias Schneebaum's (1970) ethnography of the Akaramas, a tribe inhabiting the jungles of Peru, reports an extreme case of such a culture. According to Schneebaum, their way of life included no place for the individual. They did everything together, which also meant that if, for instance, someone died or left the tribe, he was not missed or it was hardly noticed.

2   Norbert Elias links this development with more complex interpersonal relationships, with the outcome that an individual's image of others becomes richer in nuances, freer of spontaneous emotions: it is 'psychologized':

> Where the structure of social functions allows the individual greater scope for actions under the influence of momentary impulses than is the case at court, it is neither necessary nor possible to consider very deeply the nature of another person's consciousness and affects, or what hidden motives may underlie his behaviour. If at court calculation meshes with calculation, in simpler societies affect directly engages affect. (1982: 273)

Elias takes it for granted that along with the civilizing process, the personality structure of the individual changes, without noticing the fact that the same process gives birth to the notion of such a structure.

3   We could also put it this way: what did Freud do to the elements of the life-story narrating he heard on his psychiatrist's couch in order to construct his personality theory? By the latter question, I do not mean that we could or should try to reconstruct what Freud actually did; it is rather that as people living in a post-Freudian culture we do this all the time.
    Sigmund Freud is known for his crucial role in shattering the Enlightenment view of the rational self, the individual in control of her- or himself. By introducing the concepts of libido, Id and the unconscious, Freud pointed out that the individual self is not the agent of even his or her own mind. It must, of course, be remembered that the Western view of the self did

not change just because of the genius of Freud. The idea of the possibility that a person is not her or his own master is definitely older than Freud. It is, for instance, reflected in medieval Christian asceticism, which included the idea that certain behaviours, especially pleasures, represent *nature* in the individual, and that is why they have to be overcome, controlled by *reason*. Originally the term *personality* only referred to those who were able to control their urges and impulses (Weber 1971: 118–19); thus implying that the opposite could be true as well. In his uncompleted project Michel Foucault (1980, 1985, 1988) traced the origins of the 'genealogy of the desiring man' (Foucault 1985: 12) to Ancient Greece.

Therefore, what is the significance of Freud? Admittedly, he was just one of the people who formulated the changed and changing conception of the self. Yet the influence of Freud and psychoanalysis probably cannot be overestimated since Freud has provided the Western world with a popular vocabulary with which to talk about the psyche.

4   This interpretation of an individual's action, often named addiction, is real, lived experience for many individuals. By analysing the way this 'Freudian' conception of the self is discursively produced, I do not intend to deny the very real nature of the experience (see Alasuutari 1992a).

7 Identity

Identity has been a highly problematic concept in current social and cultural theory. Recent years have witnessed a 'discursive explosion' around the concept of identity (Hall 1996), and a great many of the discussants and users of the term have been very critical of the old way of defining the concept. Practically all present-day theorists want to reject the Cartesian notion of a central meaner as the basis for an integral, self-sustaining and unified self. Instead, in various ways contemporary theorizing has stressed the contextual and performative nature of self-concepts (e.g., Butler 1990, 1993). Hence, discourse analysis has celebrated the observation that a coherent and integral self or identity is an illusion; the context-bound repertoires that an individual uses are often internally contradictory. Theories of postmodernity have for their part argued that the contradictory or fragmented nature of the self is a historical phenomenon, created by the cultural contradictions of late capitalism. Yet identity continues to interest contemporary theorists and researchers, and that is precisely because it is not seen as an accomplished property but rather as something that is ambiguous, fragile, always in the making, and threatening to split into pieces. Therefore, many authors never give a proper definition of identity, and choose to talk about identification or identity construction rather than identity – in other words, identity as a verb rather than a noun. As Stuart Hall (1996: 2) puts it, the concept of identity is 'operating "under erasure" in the interval between reversal and emergence; an idea which cannot be thought in the old way, but without which certain key questions cannot be thought at all'.

But why is identity a concept that we cannot help using or referring to, even if, or precisely because, it is no more seen as a given property of each individual? Perhaps it is because identity is nowadays seen as an interesting site of (identity) politics, an interface between routines and reflexivity.

For one thing, a coherent identity is a given default assumption in various ways. Despite all the theorizing about fluid, contextual and internally contradictory identities, in everyday life we continue to take the Cartesian unified subject for granted. When we socialize with other people, we start from the default assumption that there is a thread that binds the different acts of a single individual together into a whole, into a consistent person. In fact, this assumption of a 'face' is so strong that we are ingenious in finding consistency, continuity and logic in behaviour that appears totally haphazard at the outset. By doing interpretive face work we support each other's identity. This does not mean that the everyday-life culturally unconscious 'identity frame' expects a totally fixed and frozen identity for each person. On the contrary, the identity frame allows for personal change, growth, development and rethinking one's identity, but at any given time it is routinely assumed that a person has a self or identity, and that his or her acts *reflect* that identity rather than *produce* it as an illusionary notion. Other selves are the other people we know, love, like or dislike, and often we do not give a single thought to their identity. An individual's identity can be experienced as a self-evident fact also in another sense. Identity may refer to a routine, an embodied self-conception due to an individual's identification with a category of people. In that sense an identity may heavily define and determine our action: what we are like; what are our strengths and weaknesses; what we are capable of and what not; and what kind of behaviour is morally or stylistically suitable for us. We may feel very strongly that breaking such self-evident bounds is totally impossible or would at least break us apart and make us into a totally different, unknown person.

On the other hand we also know that even the most strongly felt self-conception, or identification with a social group, can be changed and a new identity can be constructed. For instance, an individual may experience a religious conversion and suddenly become a new kind of person. The rise of political ideologies and movements can be described in a similar vein. A rhetorically skilful and charismatic leader can convince a whole group of people that what he or she suggests is the right way to think and behave, but the political programme in question also *constructs* the group itself, for instance, a nation. In that sense successful ideologies are always identity projects, which provide not only a system of thought but also a whole way of life, complete with a style and taste that a member shares with the others. In a similar way, fans of a band or popular figure, or a purely commercial campaign to sell a product, can develop into such an identity project. That is why religious and political leaders and business people want to make use of identity politics as a form of social engineering. Those who want to make others think or behave in a particular fashion try to consciously and rationally construct attractive identities for people to identify with. Their aim is to produce identities as 'points of temporary attachment to the subject positions which discursive practices construct for us', as Hall (1996: 6) defines the concept.

In recent years there has been extensive cultural research about the ways in which people construct their ambiguous identities out of the materials and discourses available to them. For instance, there has been a lot of research about the identity construction of sexual minorities or people living in multi-ethnic communities. As to the latter, it has been argued that the changing 'ethno-scape' due to globalization has resulted in an increase in 'hybrid' identities (Appadurai 1996).

It can be assumed that identity construction and cultural hybridity attract so much research interest because identities on the whole have become so light, fluid, transient and context-bound. Such postmodernist arguments can be found easily, but the situation is more complex than that. If it were perfectly clear and self-evident that constructing one's identity is just a funny game that we play, there would not be much point in showing how identities are constructed. It is true that sometimes people are quite conscious and even ironic about the way in which they build and express their identity, taste or style, but identity construction would not attract so much interest if it were a totally conscious and rational enterprise. Analyses of identity construction of different groups are interesting when considered against the background that in everyday life we conceive of identities as somehow genuine and natural. Identity construction – for instance becoming a fan of a soap opera, football club or rock star – may be just a part of one's life and people may relate to it in a self-reflective camp spirit, but it would not be something to talk or joke about if even such partial and light identity projects did not also have a serious side. Identity construction is so fascinating because of the magic embedded in such 'deep play'. Although we may be reflexive about it, we are also somehow emotionally attached to the elements of our identity construction – or to the routine, embodied self-conception that it produces as its outcome. That is why identity construction also interests political leaders, decision-makers and social activists; since constructing identities seems to be an effective way to make individuals behave according to a certain code, those who want to influence others need to know how identities are constructed and put to use. In that sense, identity politics can be seen as an important site of social engineering.

The main problem with the concept of identity is that identity and even identity construction are not suitable as analytic concepts. If we want to use identity as a noun, perhaps the best way to define it would be to say that it is the asymptotic outcome of continuous identity construction, but on the other hand, the magic of identity is in the routine lines of thought and action that successful identity projects have instilled in people. Therefore, to get a better grip of the phenomenon we need other analytic concepts that make identity construction conceivable as a process. Four concepts that are used here are: subject position, legitimations, coping strategies, and group consciousness.

Subject Position

Subject position refers simply to the position to which an individual or a whole group of people are placed in their role as holders of that position. In total institutions such as prison or the army, the subject positions of the 'inmates' are also very strict and holistic, so that the positioned subject's activities are very much determined by his or her position. The order of the day is meticulously defined, and the inmates are hardly given any liberties, or free space that they can conquer. Yet even in the case of total institutions, it is not just ironic that we refer to these positions as *subject* positions. It is of course true that people may be subjected to a position by force or threat of violence, so that their possibilities as agents who can act on their given conditions may be very limited or non-existent. However, even in that case they must be called subject positions because the objects of control and supervision are expected to act as human subjects rather than as mechanical objects. If people have to carry out certain tasks, it necessarily entails a measure of autonomy and planning, for instance in regard to the pace, even if the job is done at gunpoint.

Although holistic, strictly defined, full-time subject positions such as that of a prisoner are illustrative as examples, in most cases subject positions are more complexly determined, so that a single individual can possess several subject positions simultaneously. In that sense, subject position is a flexible concept which may refer to the different positions we assume in social life. Different kinds of subject positions may vary in terms of their comprehensiveness, degree of autonomy, duration and uniqueness.

For instance, an occupation can be considered a subject position. In that case the position allows for a fair amount of autonomy, but it often has a long duration for individual subjects who have assumed the position. It is also in many cases a full-time position, at least in regard to its economic consequences: an occupation pretty much determines how much money a person has, and because of that it has all kinds of ramifications for the individual's life.

To take an example, consider peasants in the history of twentieth-century Finland (Alasuutari 1996b: 38–73). The number of small farms, which often provided families with only part of their livelihood, was increased for political purposes, first in the years after Finland's independence in the 1920s and a second time after World War II. In both cases, giving land for farming was a form of social policy that well suited the scarcely populated and not so wealthy country, which had experienced a civil war in 1918. The land given by the state made it possible for hard-working people to make a living, and it prevented massive emigration from the country, whose industry at that time could not provide jobs for the growing population. Furthermore, that policy encouraged people to settle down in the countryside, which in many ways prevented a repeat of the social unrest that the country had experienced in 1918.

To secure and improve the economic conditions of small farming, the government had adopted a policy of protectionist measures: importing agricultural products was allowed only to the extent that it was needed to complement domestic production. The aim was to become self-sufficient. The state also paid farmers who turned marshland or forest into farming land. Later, from the 1950s onwards, when productivity rose rapidly and there was overproduction of butter and eggs for instance, the excess products were exported to the world market. However, since the price level of agricultural products in the protected domestic market was higher than in the world market, the state had to support the exportation by paying the farmers the difference between the agreed-upon domestic price and the world market price. Still later, in an effort to reduce the overproduction of dairy products, peasants were also paid a price for each cow they slaughtered.

We could go on and on discussing the details of Finnish agricultural policy, which changed in 1994 when Finland became part of the European Union. However, the point is that the subject position of peasant must not be seen naïvely as that of a person who lives off the land and whose living conditions are dependent on nature. Instead, it is determined in multiple ways by complex local and global political and economic conditions. They set overall limits and conditions for the peasant's position. Additionally, the social conditions that define a subject position also define the political and economic interests of the people in that position, for instance how different decisions increase or decrease the resources available to them.

Peasant is an example of a subject position that in early twentieth-century Finland hosted a lot of people and is still not that rare. On the other hand, there are subject positions that may be extremely rare or even unique. For instance, there is only one Pope at a time, and the same is true of political leaders, such as prime ministers or presidents of different countries. Yet these positions can be easily defined separate from the person who holds the position at any given time; there are detailed rules that define the rights and obligations of the position-holder. This is not true for what Weber (1978a, 1978b) called charismatic leaders. Likewise, in the case of popular culture stars or self-chosen leaders who have acquired a group of followers, the individual and his or her position as leader cannot be neatly separated. The individual's personal characteristics, such as charisma or personal influence due to respect in wider social circles, may define the features of the position and thus make it unique. On the other hand, it is questionable to talk about a subject position if we only refer to the role a single individual has acquired in a group or society. The idea in talking about subject positions is to pay attention to the way in which an individual member's, even a leader's, place in the social group is defined and determined in complex interaction, which assumes its regular forms in a constellation of a relatively small number of key subject positions. Thus, although the exact position of a charismatic leader may be very much dependent on the individual's personal characteristics, the possibility of any individual rising into such a position is predetermined by certain characteristics of the group in question. For instance, if the leader is chosen because of his or her exceptional qualities, the group in question has to recognize them and for some reason value them highly.

To take a very different example of a subject position, let us consider how different positions are assumed in face-to-face interaction. For instance, Jacoby and Gonzales (1991) show that although the positions of expert and novice have an institutional background and certain consequences, such as different roles in hierarchical organizations, at the micro level the constitution of expert–novice is a much more complicated, shifting, moment-by-moment reconstruction of Self and Other, whether within one speaker's talk or between speakers. By analysing group meetings of a university physics team, Jacoby and Gonzales show that the subject positions[1] of 'expert' and 'novice' can be seen as candidate constitutions of Self and Other, whose ratification or challenging are dependent on at least three interacting dimensions: the individual, the domain (or domains) of knowledge and the recipient. The same individual (for instance the principal investigator or a doctoral candidate) can be constituted as an expert in one knowledge domain but as a novice when traversing to some other knowledge domain. Second, within a single knowledge domain, the same individual can be constituted at one moment as more knowing and at another moment as less knowing. Third, in either of these two situations, the valence of expertise may shift with a change of recipients. At least when dealing with face-to-face interaction in such expert organizations as a research team, any isolation of turns and short sequences to illustrate the status of a particular party as the expert or the novice in a fragment of interaction may be a rather artificial procedure because any next turn can shift the until-then interactionally achieved distribution of expertise. The more knowing subject who can assess others' ideas and suggestions is, in these instances, a shifting context-bound position that is basically independent from historical roles and hierarchical ranking.

The example of the constitution of expertise or novicehood in interaction shows that subject positions are not a fixed place within which an individual is positioned. The same goes for all kinds of momentary positions that participants are temporarily placed in through interaction: for instance, speakers or addressed recipients, questioners or answerers. Yet these roles can rightly be called subject positions comparable to those that are more durable and all-encompassing. For one thing, they are socially or collaboratively constituted: an individual cannot successfully assume a position at will, without a certain kind of consent from other people. People have to have at least tacit knowledge of the existence of the position in question, be it a lecturer, an expert, a leader or whatever. Second, during the time they are held, these different speaker roles set certain limits and conditions on the individual's action. On the one hand, such limits and conditions may constitute the very position in question, so that failing to 'play one's part' also means that the person never held the position in the first place. On the other hand, the limits and conditions imposed on a person placed in a particular position may be realized as expectations for their future action. For instance, a person who is asked a question is expected to give an answer or an explanation for not answering. Failing to do either does not mean that the person is not affected by the positioning; his or her future action is interpreted in terms of a person who was asked a question.

It is of course questionable to use one concept in referring to such a wide variety of phenomena as an occupation, the situation of the inmate in a total institution or a passing speaker role in interaction. However, they all fulfil the same criteria. They are socially defined positions that set certain limits and conditions on individual behaviour. Subject positions must not only be thought of in terms of the limits they impose on individual action; they can as easily be defined in terms of the resources and capacities available to those who hold the position in question. Such resources tied to a position may appear in the form of concrete materials at the individual's disposal, but the bottom line is that a subject position is constituted by a constellation of social relations. The fact that any situation a human being is in can be defined as a subject position at different levels and from different perspectives must not be seen as a problem. Subject positions can be more or less holistic, short-lived or durable, strict or loose, and at any point of time individuals can hold several subject positions that define their situation in various ways.

Justifications and Legitimations

We can analytically think of a subject position irrespective of the way in which it is named and defined by the people involved. By systematically analysing the transcripts of conversations, we can point out the way in which participants co-produce a particular speaker role and how it closes and opens options for the person's next turn of talk. In that sense, a subject position is concrete reality, and it can be studied independently from the participants' ideas about such a position. The same is true of an occupation as a subject position: we can study the statistics to see how the number of agricultural producers has changed or how their average income has developed during past decades.

Yet it is inescapable that names and definitions of subject positions are never wholly unbiased and innocent. Any description of a situation or subject position is also a biased interpretation that systematically forms the object which it appears to describe. Knowingly or unknowingly, the way positions are portrayed and defined in relation to other positions contributes to justifying or problematizing the position in question. For instance, depending on how a group of people, like the unemployed, is defined has an effect on the numbers, which in turn can be used to justify or criticize the existing policy employed toward the subject position in question. Population and labour statistics are an intriguing example of the way in which seemingly objective categorizations are part and parcel of the legitimation of social hierarchies.

Take the income difference between men and women.[2] Throughout the centuries, from William Petty (the founder of political economy and political arithmetic) onwards, statistics have shown that women earn considerably less than men. According to recent international statistics, in the 1990s men's income was bigger than that of women in each country included in the UN statistics (Reskin and Padavic 1994: 109). Statistics from the end of the 1990s in Finland show that the wages of women in full-time employment were 79.5 per cent of men's wages. Thus, statistics prove useful in simply revealing a state of affairs. More elaborate analyses may also be used to test the assumptions that on average men earn more because they have a higher educational level, they are higher in the occupational hierarchy, or they have more demanding jobs. These are all factors that affect differences in individual income and thus partly explain the income difference between men and women, but statistical analysis also shows that even if those factors are controlled so that we compare men and women in similar positions, we find that men tend to earn a little more.

On the other hand, the categories and classifications referred to above are far from objective, neutral or innocent instruments of research that we can use to find out about the state of affairs in the social reality out there. If, for instance, an employer wants to pay a certain employee a higher salary, it cannot be easily done without justifying it somehow. If the person in question does not have more education or training, he or she can be given a promoted job title as a person higher in the hierarchy, but then the tasks he or she performs must be defined as somehow more physically hard, demanding or stress-inducing. When the national statistical bureaux that gather information about working life ask people about their occupation, tasks and position in organizations, the job titles and task descriptions that are used in justifying income differences find their way into the seemingly neutral categories of work statistics. This does not mean that all job titles that include words like chief, principal, executive, head or manager are used only to justify better salaries for some individuals or especially for male employees. In most cases they probably also reflect the social organization of the workplace: individuals in those positions are deemed more skillful, experienced, reliable and trustworthy and are therefore given more power over others and made responsible of certain operations. However, the point is that these categories and titles are only seemingly impartial names for objects in the reality outside discourse. Whether or not an individual's position and salary are generally deemed justified, for the others it is communicated and legitimated by the job title and task description, and therefore titles and descriptions are participants in the contested terrains of discourse within which subject positions are constituted, legitimated or criticized.

Thus the categories and descriptions of subject positions can be approached from the perspective of rhetoric. Rhetorical strategies are used to tacitly strengthen the role these categories and descriptions have in justifying the existing social order. Although talking about strategies implies that it is done consciously, rhetoric is most successful when it goes unnoticed. Therefore, the titles of different positions often make use of 'dormant' metaphors. For instance, in the categorizations of subject positions one often refers to more advantageous positions as higher and to the less advantageous as lower positions. In a similar way, the logical analogue with human body parts is often used: the decision-makers' positions are referred to as heads of the organization (Kinnunen 2001).

But what makes such rhetoric, or the metaphors used in them, go unnoticed? According to Mary Douglas (1986), the stabilizing principle of human institutions is the naturalization of social classifications.

> There needs to be an analogy by which the formal structure of a crucial set of social relations is found in the physical world, or in the supernatural world, or in eternity, anywhere, so long as it is not seen as a social contrived arrangement. When the analogy is applied back and forth from one set of social relations to another and from these back to nature, its recurring formal structure becomes easily recognized and endowed with self-validating truth. (Douglas 1986: 48)

As an example of the naturalization of social relations, Douglas discusses how the sexual division of labour is partly legitimized by an analogy with the complementarity of the right and left hand and the complementarity of gender. According to her, the equation 'female is to male as left is to right' reinforces the social principle with a physical analogy. Douglas also emphasizes that this legitimizing effect only lasts as long as it remains unnoticed. According to her, 'the effort to build strength for fragile social institutions by grounding them in nature is defeated as soon as it is recognized as such. That is why founding analogies have to be hidden and why the hold of the thought style upon the thought world has to be secret' (Douglas 1986: 53).

Naturalization is certainly one of the ways in which the existing situation is tacitly justified. However, naturalization should not be equated with routinization, which we are actually talking about here. The more general idea is the way in which metaphors work (Lakoff and Johnson 1980): an object, like the structure of an organization, is pictured by likening it to something that we are more familiar with. Often, that something used as the source metaphor is derived from the world of concrete physical objects, but that is not necessarily the case. Consider the metaphor 'life is a journey'. Through specific expressions derived from it we can make abstract and difficult situations – like a person 'running out of gas' in his or her career development – easier to understand, but we can hardly say that this is because of natural analogues.

In this kind of legitimation of social hierarchies, natural analogues – or other analogues employed in metaphors used – are often only one part of the rhetorical strategy. The metaphors make the abstract reality of a social organization – that is, regular patterns of interaction and the roles individuals have in them – seem familiar and concrete. The other part is the articulation of a classification of positions – that is, the division into 'higher' and 'lower' ones – with gender. It may be that in some cases articulating male with the right hand and female with the left hand justifies a gendered division of labour by naturalizing it, but it is more common that legitimation is more indirect. Male-dominated positions are easily conceived of as 'higher' and female-dominated as 'lower' in the hierarchy because in prevalent culture people are routinized to conceiving of work roles in terms of a gendered division of labour, not by whether they are legitimated by nature. Routines reproduce themselves in default assumptions, which must be consciously challenged to make a change to people's practices.

In justifying or criticizing the existing order we often make reference to generally approved-of principles or ideologies. For instance, in the example above, the need to justify the fact that certain individuals are paid better than others derives from the implicit principle of equality, or more precisely from the principle 'equal pay for equal work'. Similarly, such commonly respected principles as democracy, justice, free enterprise or freedom of speech are repeatedly implied or openly referred to in the instances where subject positions are justified or called into question.

Racism is a prime example of a situation where it is thought that a deviation from the principle of equality requires legitimation. What we call racism is a legitimation strategy. In other words, behind racism or racist practices there is a society in which equality is a cherished value. In such a situation racist ideology rescues the apparent contradiction by making believe that the principle of equality is not actually violated: the principle of equality cannot or must not be applied to a class of people because they represent a different race. This difference or otherness is then used as the reason for not extending the principle of equality to the others. It may be argued that those excluded do not possess the knowledge or wits required to take part in social life as full citizens. Thus, in Australia, the Aborigines were counted among the fauna of the continent during British rule. Similarly, in many countries suffrage was given first to noble and bourgeois men, next to working-class men and finally to women.

As to titles, they may tacitly contribute to legitimizing subject positions even if there is no reference to an explicit ideology. It is just that in the particular cultural context, certain position descriptions or titles are more valued and respected than others. By framing a subject position within a favourable perspective, they contribute to its legitimation and esteem. The small-farm peasants in Finland again provide an excellent example. As discussed above, small farms were made economically more viable through protectionist measures that prevented imports of agricultural products. Consequently, the price level became higher than in the world market. Moreover, because the state tried to save as much international currency as possible, there was after World War II a scarcity of many products, such as meat, and that scarcity lasted until domestic production gradually rose to meet the demands of consumers. Now, in these conditions the farmers were referred to as producers in contrast to the rest of the population, who were referred to as consumers. Therefore, the small farmers were implicitly – and also explicitly – hailed as hard-working champions who gradually turned more soil into farming land and removed lack and scarcity from the nation.

Such context- and culture-bound descriptions of subject positions may lose their legitimating power along with changing situations, so that justifying strategies are changed. For instance, in the case of the small farmers, when overproduction of agricultural products slowly became a widely known national problem and it then became apparent to the public that agricultural production had to be subsidized by the state, the positive ring of 'the producers' was lost. Farmers became referred to more neutrally as 'agricultural producers', and they – especially small-farm peasants – were now considered as a political problem, a part of the population that needs constant subsidy from the state to survive.

Coping Strategies

In most cases, individuals do not have much choice in assuming the different subject positions in which they are placed, because they are social institutions. In most cases people can have some say as to what they want to do in life, for instance what line of business to work in, but even in these cases the subject positions are there waiting for them, more or less ready-made by the surrounding culture and society. By entering a subject position people cannot much affect the conditions that await them, nor can they willingly undo the public discourses used in describing, justifying, criticizing or reflecting on the position in question.

However, in one way or another people need to make sense of the subject position that they are placed in, especially if the position in question considerably affects their entire existence. A job is a good example of that.

Making sense of one's role and position is not enough; people have to create such an attitude and perspective toward it that they can at least tolerate the given conditions, maybe even find pleasure and enjoyment from them. In this instance we are talking about individual coping strategies in a very broad sense of the word. This entails that people develop an overall view of life within which they can find their role somehow meaningful, can retain their self-respect, and can integrate the subject position into the rest of their life.

Consider the extremely inhuman ways in which people have been treated in concentration camps. In an obvious effort to humiliate people and break their spirit, they have been forced to do something totally meaningless and futile, like digging a hole in the ground endlessly and then filling it. Those who have survived such conditions have developed some kind of coping strategy: they have kept their mind busy with something entirely different, or they have created some specific interest in a job that appeared totally meaningless and monotonous from the outset.

This example shows that when dealing with coping strategies we are not only talking about the human preservation instinct. Even if the tasks individuals are given are not beneficial to them, they may be tolerable if at least someone profits from them. Coping strategies may be built around all kinds of motives, such as resistance of usurpation or refusal to break down under deliberately humiliating oppression, but the common denominator is that coping strategies can only be understood and constructed in a social context. Although coping can be approached from a psychological perspective in the sense that in some details each individual's coping strategy may be unique, the materials of which the strategies are made are socially shared. Constructing one's personal coping strategy is no different from the way in which the position in question is described, justified or criticized in the public discourse. In fact, it is typically constructed out of the materials that the public discourses provide. They may be arranged differently, combined and articulated in unexpected ways, but public discourses are the essential building material. In that sense, an individual's way of creating coping strategies could be likened to the term *bricolage*, which Lévi-Strauss uses when discussing primitive humans' creativity.

Building one's own coping strategy by making use of existing public discourses related to the subject position is not only creative. In one way or another, people simply have to relate their own coping strategy to the existing discourses, because they are the means by which, and frames within which, other people understand the position. It would be quite difficult, if not impossible, for us to create an individual coping strategy that was totally incomprehensible to others. We would have no way of explaining how we related to our position, and in what way it was bearable or even in some ways enjoyable. Besides, a private coping strategy would be lacking because part of the gratification of a working coping strategy is that it can be communicated to others. Individuals whose tasks in the organization seem quite unimportant when seen from the outside may gain pride from their ability to explain their role in such a way that others are seemingly impressed with how important and demanding it is – or alternatively, how easy and leisurely their job is compared to the wages they are paid.

In fact, all the main elements of coping strategies are of social origin, including the need and motive to construct one. For instance, to say that people have to create an attitude to their subject position so that it enables a measure of self-respect already refers to a concept that has a social origin. Furthermore, although an individual may retain self-respect despite others' contempt, respect and contempt are typically justified by ethical principles and socially esteemed characteristics such as industriousness, integrity or compassion.

Thus, in making their individual coping strategies people make use of the discourses within which subject positions are justified or criticized. On the other hand, since coping strategies are communicated to others, it is obvious that they in turn affect public discourses. There is a continuous interplay between individual coping strategies and public discourses. A coping strategy communicated to others often affects public discourses: for instance, it opens another perspective to conceiving a subject position. Changing public discourses may then challenge others to reconsider and rearticulate their own coping strategies in similar, related or oppositional subject positions.

It is also clear that just as public discourses used in legitimating or criticizing a subject position contribute to forming that very position, the same is true of individual coping strategies. The way in which an individual seeks sense and enjoyment in a job affects other occupations such as the supervisor of the employee and the entire organization. A position in a social organization cannot even be thought of without certain in-built expectations about the mentality and attitudes – that is, the typical coping strategies – of the individuals who are put into that position.

Coping strategies adopted by individuals who are assigned or who assume a subject position can be seen from two perspectives. On the one hand they are context-bound, but on the other hand, they depend on the individual who takes on the position in question. That does not mean that each individual has his or her own unique coping strategies, but the strategies an individual adopts in his or her different subject positions affect one another.

By saying that coping strategies are context-bound I emphasize the point made above that to a certain extent a subject position comes with a coping strategy, or with a repertoire of possible strategies. Like actors who have been taught all the major roles in a play, a culture's members who are placed into a position take on the relevant role and play it. Thus, human subjects assume different, even contradictory roles in different contexts and situations. Different subject positions bring out different attitudes and definitions of self because they adapt to the socially constructed rules and discourses that are relevant in that situation. From that perspective it appears that an inner self is merely an illusion; individual behaviour and attitudes expressed can best be explained by the local context of interaction, as is done in discourse analysis and conversation analysis.

However, although individual coping strategies are tightly intertwined with socially and publicly constructed subject positions, a coping strategy is not an entirely collectively determined thing that just comes with the position. For instance, although the materials used in forming a coping strategy are collective property, there are different ways of using them. Different individuals may adopt totally different coping strategies for the same subject position. That may be as a result of different cultural backgrounds and individual preferences, but also because a suitable coping strategy in a subject position is dependent on other spheres of the individual's life, for instance on other subject positions which the individual needs to regularly take into account in the course of his or her everyday life. Even though there is no true inner self, as was assumed in Romanticism, we do make an attempt to seek continuity and coherence in our lives across the varying, sometimes contradictory, positions into which we are placed every day. Although on closer scrutiny we may act in contradictory ways in different situations, according to the common notion subscribed to in all cultures, each person has his or her own identifiable character. In other words, we relate to other people as persons with a history, not as subjects constructed by the situation in question. In some cultures, the history and biography of an individual cannot be separated from his or her family members or from his or her ancestors, but no culture in practice subscribes to the idea that the acts of an individual in one situation do not in any way relate to his or her acts in another situation. Instead, we contribute to constructing, or narrating, continuity and coherence of characters, thus linking and anchoring a body, a physical human being, into patterns of behaviour that we think characterize the person in question, be it oneself or a fellow human being. We share the expectation, in regard both to others and to ourselves, that there needs to be some coherence or integrity in a (moral) person. Therefore, to avoid threatening coherence of the self, we adopt and develop coping strategies that bypass and balance out at least the most striking inconsistencies.

In that sense the gallery of mutually interrelated coping strategies that a person uses gives special flavour to each strategy that he or she uses. On the other hand, such creative moulding of the coping strategies often results in new strategies, which in turn become public property and will be used by others. Thus, the individual and collective aspects of coping strategies are in continuous interplay.

Group Consciousness

Normally, at the macro level of social organization, the subject positions into which people are placed eventually create solidarity and group consciousness. That is especially the case if the position is not particularly enviable: people will realize that by joining their forces they can better defend themselves and perhaps also improve their position. The same is true for those placed high up on the social ladder: to protect their privileges against those who aim to improve their position, they also have it in their interest to unite. In one sense group consciousness can be seen as a coping strategy applied at the collective level.

Social movements are a good example of the way in which political objectives are fought for with the means of collective action. An uprising is the least organized way to stand against oppression, whereas a demonstration shows the potential power of a great number of people in a more symbolic, and in most cases peaceful, way. In a sense, the formation of political parties and voting systems directs the idea of the power of the masses toward a more controlled and bureaucratic direction, but the same basic ideas are also behind labour politics. For instance, workers attempt to fight for better work conditions and wages by forming a labour union, which can make demands as a collective. If the employers are not willing to meet the demands, the union members can go on strike and guard the workplace so that no one is able to do the work. In white-collar occupations, forms of professionalism are a similar attempt to defend and improve the conditions of an occupation. By legal regulations, a profession such as medical doctor is closed off from those who haven't been given a special licence. If the members of the profession have influence in controlling the number of licences granted, they can successfully protect their interests.

The formation of a group that links its members together with ties of solidarity also entails the sharing of common knowledge of the 'tricks of the trade' and of ways to cope with the position. If someone within a trade or occupational position comes up with a good new way of doing the things that need to be done in that position, in most cases others will learn about it. In business, inventions usually give a competitive edge to the one who makes them, and that is why competitors will have to acquire the knowledge needed, for instance by buying, stealing or copying them. In many other positions fellow members of the group are happy to pass on all knowledge that might help others to survive better, but even in business life innovations eventually become shared knowledge; those who cannot keep up with the technical development are forced out of business.

Such shared knowledge is not restricted to technicalities. Coping strategies – that is, ways of finding meaning and enjoyment in a subject position – are also communicated between individuals in similar circumstances. The coping strategy that becomes most popular within the group defines who belongs to it and tells what kind of people they are and how they relate to their lot in life.

Collective action entails much more than just its rationality for human individuals. Even if the formation of social groups may start from individuals realizing that by joining forces they can better defend their interests, it also always entails a complex process within which a whole social structure is transformed and new self-evident notions of categories of people and their characteristics are born. One could even argue that placing people into different subject positions constitutes the whole idea of categories of people and thus produces a social structure. When more than just a single individual is placed in a subject position, it constitutes them as a class of people. Moreover, despite their possible initial differences as individual human beings, placing them under strict rules and conditions as to how to act produces their likeness.

Consider the formation of African-American culture in the United States. When African people were imported to the United States as slaves, they spoke many different languages and had quite different cultural backgrounds. Therefore, they identified themselves as belonging to a tribe such as the Ibo, Yoruba or Fulani. We could of course just as well discuss the social construction of the African tribe system, but let us instead concentrate on the subject position of these people as slaves in the USA. It meant that their own previous categorizations lost meaning because they were placed in a social system in which their legal position was that of a slave. On top of that, they were faced with a system of discourses that was used as a means to justify slavery and social inequality within a culture that also subscribed to the principles of liberty, equality and justice. Therefore, the discourses used served to exempt the slave population from others to whom the noble principles were applied. The discursive system and institutionalized practice of racism referred to them as the 'black' in contrast with the 'white' population (Omi and Winant 1986: 64). The 'colour line', that is, inequality and social segregation based on skin colour, was justified by an ideology that claimed that there were different races among humans, and that the white race was 'by nature' superior to others (Donald and Rattansi 1992; Gilroy 1987). Thus, these discursive and institutional practices constituted 'black' people. Somehow people had to develop coping strategies by which to manage their position, and part of those strategies was to unite as a group and to create some kind of group consciousness despite the fact that from the viewpoint of their previous categorizations they hardly formed a homogeneous community.

The example shows how even a single change in the existing gallery of subject positions triggers complex processes. When a group of people is placed in a position, by doing things together and by organizing joint activities they create shared experiences, concepts and frameworks, and many of these experiences are also emotionally touching. The formation of group consciousness is for the most part a culturally unconscious process, because every human being is at birth already a member of a community. Thus the categories we learn to use and the attitudes instilled in us constitute us as particular human subjects with a plethora of coping strategies.

The building of group consciousness can also be seen as a form of identity politics within which categories of people and bonds of solidarity are constructed and deconstructed. Although the existing subject positions and the corresponding categories of people appear self-evident, we must bear in mind that at any given moment an individual is placed in several subject positions, which are more or less holistic in regard to the constraints they impose on the person. Besides, a subject position can only be separated analytically from the discourses that construct, justify or criticize it. Therefore, it is also always possible to try to propose new *identity projects*. This means that, for instance, a political leader, or a person who aspires to become one, defines a subject position, how people in that position relate to it, and how they as a community form a collective force that fights for a better future for themselves and for the whole world.

When identity projects are perceived this way, they seem to be totally arbitrary constructions, built firmly in the air out of words. However, popular support of such constructions is the true test. For one thing, the target population need to be able to recognize themselves in the description of the subject position. That is an easy task if we are dealing with a narrowly defined position, but on the other hand, forming a successful social group or movement requires that the identity project is potentially appealing to a fairly large proportion of the population. The rhetoric of politicians aspiring to form a new collective force must be very innovative and ingenious because the role of the people in a given subject position must be described in such a way that people feel important.

Conclusion

It is problematic to talk about identity because it easily implies the notion of an integral, self-sustaining and unified subject. It is important to note that we are many: in everyday interaction we take different positions flexibly, and our presentation of self is context-bound. However, it is equally important to acknowledge that in everyday life we are all engaged in mutually supporting each other's personality; we look for continuity and coherence across different situations and encounters in life. This tension between two perspectives on human action is probably the reason why identity construction has attracted so much interest as a concept and phenomenon. The notion of identity is commonly used to refer to the complex way in which human reality works and changes. That is, to talk about identity construction is one way of trying to come to terms with the very gist of human reality. The phenomena that can be described by the concepts of subject position, legitimation, coping strategy and group consciousness form a configuration where a change in any of the elements affects the others, but not in a mechanical way. It is just that these four concepts outline the process wherein mind may turn to matter and matter turn to mind. Subject positions require and produce legitimizing discourses, coping strategies and group consciousness, and any of these elements acts upon the others.

The elements of this Rubik's cube can only be separated from each other analytically. That is, these concepts are not concrete objects out there in reality. Rather, they are concepts created by the analytic discourse that is used to define them. As is commonly emphasized when talking about the starting point of discourse analysis, language not only reflects but also constructs reality. It would, however, be foolish or in any case fruitless to draw the conclusion that since the concepts we use are part of discourses that 'systematically form the objects of which they speak' (Foucault 1972: 49), our concepts are worthless. That would mean that we give up entirely trying to analyse the reality – human or physical – in which we live. We just have to live with the conclusion that our knowledge of reality is conveyed to us through the language system and thus includes a constructive bias.

How can we then come to terms with this bias? In this practical mundane notion of language that we stick to when we use language to make sense of reality, we assume an objective reality in the sense that everything is not some kind of illusion created by the human mind. However, we do not assume that the analytic concepts we use to tackle the world are more or less accurate pictures of objects out there in external reality. Rather, they are products of our practical relation to reality, and work as part of the system insofar as our praxis works. In other words, taken separately, the analytic concepts discussed above could be deemed more or less ingenuous, but what counts is the theoretical model as a whole: it is useful if it accounts for the observations that we can make of reality.

The challenge and rejection of this kind of realist relativism can only stem from a longing for an assumed epistemological Archimedean point. This is the assumption that there is a privileged position from which we can objectively see everything at once the way things really are in the reality out there, without the interference of our own concepts. But there is no such position. Any viewpoint on human reality produces the unseen sector of the cultural unconscious as its own counterpart, as the price we pay to see one aspect of the reality more accurately.

Notes

1 Jacoby and Gonzales do not use this concept.
2 The discussion of this topic is based primarily on Merja Kinnunen's (2001) insightful analysis of the way in which task descriptions and classifications of job titles contribute to legitimating gender inequality in the job market.

8 The Modernization Story as a Reflexive Frame

In a book that claims to give an account of the state of the art of social science by summarizing what we know about human reality, one could easily expect to find a report of what we know about modernization. That is especially because one can justifiably argue that the formation of the social sciences began in the late seventeenth century as a reaction to the great changes that affected European societies from the sixteenth century onward. It can be said that sociology as a discipline was formed as a body of knowledge that analyses modernization: in different ways all the classics of sociology from Marx to Simmel address the question of how to explain the formation of modern society. Similarly, early anthropology centred on the question of cultural evolution, especially how and why primitive societies evolve into contemporary complex society.

Although assumptions about a universal linear development into a single modern model as the endpoint of cultural evolution have been challenged and rejected, the processes of social change and the developments toward contemporary social conditions in world societies have remained a central area of interest in the social sciences. Moreover, because a great deal of research within the social sciences is conducted in so-called 'Western' societies, it is no wonder that the road to modernity and the latest trends in social and cultural development (as seen from the Western perspective) are of particular interest to scholars and the reading public. There is a whole genre of social science literature that is concerned with diagnosis of the time, or *Zeitdiagnose* as the Germans call it, and all kinds of research results are framed within a historical perspective provided by theories of modernization.

However, although the road to modernity is such a central topic in the social sciences, it is only one topic among others. Comparable to other topics that interest human scientists, analysing modernization may give us insights into universal features of human reality but, no matter how widespread the features we associate with modernity may be, the processes of change that we experience today are just particular cases. Even if social scientists were able to reach a consensus between competing theories of modernization, it would not qualify as part of the body of knowledge that we have thus far gathered about the object of the social sciences. Like the natural sciences, that object of the social sciences here called human reality refers to the totality of principles that are assumed to hold not only in particular cases but in any conditions, also in the unforeseeable future.

Contemporary analyses of modern times are, however, interesting as an illustrative example of the role of collective self-reflection in changing or reproducing human reality. Whatever the society or cultural region in question, as natives we are never naïvely ignorant about the features of our society. Rather, within a cultural region there is a repertoire of discourses within which 'insiders' comment on the culture they live in. In that sense, we are reflexive about our own and our fellow citizens' typical habits and thought processes.

Contemporary analyses of modernity are an example of collective self-reflexivity enhanced particularly by social scientists, but we should not overemphasize the role of 'professionals' in this. For instance, among ordinary people in Fiji it is common to hear people complain that 'nowadays too many people drink too much kava, but they never did before' (Tomlinson 2002: 43). This statement, in which native Fijians engage in cultural criticism of their own culture and society, is a prime example of what Greg Urban (2001) calls 'metaculture', culture about culture, as he defines it.

Of particular interest in the Fijian lament over decline and resignation is the fact that such a discourse has existed for a long time. People have made the same complaint about the recent excessive kava drinking for more than a hundred years. From that, one can draw the conclusion that the claimed recent decay of tradition is an erroneous belief. Paradoxically, we could say that the Fijian discourse on cultural decline and resignation is itself a tradition that perpetuates itself in spite of how people's manners and habits actually change from generation to generation.

The same can be said of the whole 'culture of modernity'. Carried on by practically every new generation of social scientists, telling the story of modernization can be seen as a culturally unconscious tradition of repeatedly arguing that everything is right now dramatically changing in a way that may threaten basic human values. New versions of the narrative follow more or less the same story lines, and in that sense the story of modernization can be likened to myth.[1]

The example shows that metacultural reflection and commentary must not be seen as above or separate from everyday life or from the consciousness of common people. It also implies that even though engaging in reflexive discourses about one's own culture and society may appear to be the role of thoughtful and wise persons, reflexivity may serve other functions than the conscious monitoring and adjusting of prevalent routines. It may also contribute to spreading and reproducing prevalent cultural features.

I use the story of modernization in this chapter as an illustrative example of the nature of reflexivity in human reality. Why do social science scholars keep on reproducing the modernization discourse, although its mythical character has been pointed out several times? Related to that, what are its functions for scholars and for society at large? At a more general level, even when devised by social science scholars, if discourses of reflexivity reproduce rather than question routine lines of thought and behaviour, can we justly talk about social sciences? If reflexive discourses on local culture are an inherent part of it, do we have to give up the hope of objectively or rationally researching contemporary society? These are the crucial questions that the story of modernization poses for the social sciences.

In the next section, to show that modernization is an old story I will discuss its history. After that, I will tackle two routine assumptions of modernization, that is, that the sacred and habitual behaviour are disappearing from the world. In the conclusion, I will first address the question why we keep on telling the same story of modernization. Finally, I will return to the bigger question about the functions of the social sciences in society.

The History of the Story of Modernization

Like the topic of excessive kava drinking in Fiji, the history of the idea of modernization clearly shows that it is paradoxically an old tradition. It appeared in its present-day form in the late nineteenth century, but it assumed its main features more than a hundred years earlier. Sidney Pollard's book *The Idea of Progress: History and Society* (1968) gives a good overview of its history.

The origins of the story of modernization can be traced back to eighteenth-century Enlightenment philosophers such as Voltaire, Ferguson and Gibbon. Although these thinkers conceived of themselves as unselfish men fighting for their faith in truth and in humanism, the new view of history which they promoted served an obvious function: they advanced and defended the new economic and social order based on a growing market economy that was developing in the cities. In line with that project, they suggested a new way of conceiving the dynamics of social change. Previous history writing had concentrated on the importance of singular individuals such as kings or popes, which meant that the role of the bourgeoisie in affecting social development as a large group of ordinary merchants was easily overlooked. Therefore it is understandable that the Enlightenment philosophers emphasized the importance of large-scale evolutionary processes on cultural, social and economic levels. They conceived of history in terms of changes in mentality of the general population. To show that the emergent economic and social order was going to be better than previous ones, they introduced a new way of thinking about history in terms of periods. Although the periodizations that the Enlightenment philosophers suggested varied remarkably, they all had the common feature that the present was placed at the dawn of a new, more enlightened era after the 'dark' Middle Ages. It was assumed that there is a universal process in historical development toward increasing rationality. For instance, Condorcet (1743–94) presented a ten-phase periodization model, which can be simplified into four periods with their respective world views. They were: (1) anthropomorphic and theological, (2) metaphysical, (3) mechanistic-materialist and (4) mathematic-scientific.

Although the Enlightenment philosophers' periodizations shared a belief in increasing rationality, not all of them promoted a linear view of progress. For instance, Giambattista Vico (1668–1744) presented a cyclical theory, according to which the history of each nation consists of an alteration of periods of rise and fall. On the other hand Vico's model also includes the seed of a linear model in the sense that according to him the next cycle of development of a nation overcomes the achievements of previous epochs of fruition. It must also be said that although later conceptions of history are clearly linear rather than cyclical, in many cases one can see a cyclical model in the background. The clear linearity of later modernization theories is primarily due to the fact that in them one concentrates on describing the history of Europe from 'the dark Middle Ages' onwards. In doing so, one omits the more 'advanced' Greek and Roman civilizations that preceded it.

One of the main features of the Enlightenment philosophers' narratives of history is their ambivalence about progress. The eighteenth century started with a strong belief in progress, but before the end of the century there appeared doubtful voices. For instance, Montesquieu (1689–1755) was ambivalent in his attitude toward progress. The most pessimistic of the Enlightenment philosophers was Rousseau (1712–78). In many respects he shared the thoughts of his contemporaries but drew the opposite conclusions from them. According to him, the further we advance toward civility, the further away we drift from real happiness. He had a somewhat romantic notion of the happiness and peace of mind of the 'noble savage'. Yet he was not alone in his nostalgic pessimism. For instance, Mably (1709–85) and Morellet (1727–1819) emphasized the dangers and bad consequences of luxury. In 1770 Sebastian Mercier presented a utopia for the year 2440 in which happiness would be achieved by consuming less rather than more. In that sense Rousseau was not an exception.

Classical sociology can be seen as a body of thought that further develops and crystallizes the Enlightenment philosophers' narrative of progress. Unlike their predecessors, classical sociologists at the end of the nineteenth century were not particularly interested in devising periodizations of history. Yet the whole point of the emergence of the new discipline of sociology simultaneously in France and Germany was to address the characteristics of present-day society and expected future social change in light of a reflexive historical consciousness. Classical sociology also carried on the nostalgic ambivalence that characterized the Enlightenment philosophers' narratives of progress. Modern times were simultaneously associated with more civilized habits and certainly more prosperity, but also with a moral decay and individual shallowness. One could even say that one of the prime concerns of sociology has been to ask whether, or on what basis, social integration and solidarity are at all possible in modern times. The nostalgia stems from this: classical sociologists saw that changes are inevitable, but simultaneously they longed for and tried to recapture some of the warmth of the small communities that they associated with the past, or with traditional or primitive society.

The Historicist Method

Although classical sociology and the discipline built on it have a strong self-consciousness as a science that emphasizes that social phenomena are formed historically and change with time, paradoxically the key concepts of traditional and modern that convey a sense of history have little, if anything, to do with real past or present societies. Instead, the formation of the concepts of traditional and modern can be seen as the outcome of a procedure that the classics of sociology used in their research. The periodizations of the Enlightenment philosophers, later further developed and simplified by early sociologists like August Comte and Herbert Spencer, formed the background for classical sociology. For classical sociology, epochs that preceded the present were only interesting as material from which to find contrast in highlighting what were understood as the main characteristics of modernity. Thus, the historical consciousness collapsed into a two-stage dualistic model consisting of 'traditional' and 'modern'. By exaggerating a little the uniformity of classical sociological reasoning, the principles of 'the historicist method' used in laying bare features of present-day social reality can be described as follows.

To get a grasp of the essence of an emergent trend in the present, classical sociologists looked for contrasts in earlier times or in what they thought were less advanced regions or groups of people. Such a contrast was then conceived as a continuum and extrapolated from both ends. The imagined ideal-picture cases at opposite ends of the continuum were then termed 'traditional' and 'modern'.

For instance, in his study *The Division of Labour in Society*, Émile Durkheim (1964) analysed the differences and recent changes in the judicial system and linked them to the extent to which there is an institutionalized division of labour in a society – that is, to what extent people specialize in producing one product or doing one task and engage in exchange economy to get all the products they need. On that basis he constructed two ideal case societies, *primitive* and *modern*.

He associated a low division of labour with a particular form of solidarity, which he called *mechanical solidarity*. According to this, each member of society is expected to behave according to the same normative rules. If that does not happen, the community angered by the breaking of social norms will punish the deviants. The punishment is basically retribution. Durkheim calls a justice system that is based on these principles *repressive*, because the underlying attempt is to prevent individuals from deviating from the uniform ideal of every member of society. According to Durkheim, in such a primitive society, one of the two forms of conscience, the *collective conscience*, prevails over the *individual conscience* and thus determines the prevalent sentiments of the people.

A high division of labour is associated with what Durkheim called *organic solidarity*. According to it, there are different sets of norms applied to different subgroups in society. In this modern type of society, there are an increasing number of laws that define the rules that individuals must obey in their mutual interaction. If such rules are broken, according to the prevalent moral sentiments, the function of the punishment is to re-establish the situation that preceded the crime. Thus, Durkheim calls the judicial system *retributive* justice. In such modern societies, sentiments related to the individual conscience prevail over those related to the collective conscience.

A similar kind of dualism between two ideal types of society, the traditional (or primitive) and the modern, is constructed by all the classical authors of sociology. For instance, Ferdinand Tönnies (1988) constructed a similar dichotomy between two kinds of society, *Gemeinschaft* and *Gesellschaft*. He associated these with two types of motivation or 'will', *Wesenwille*, or 'essential will' and *Kürwille*, or 'arbitrary will'. According to Tönnies, *Gemeinschaft* and *Gesellschaft* are ideal types or *Normalbegriffe*, not empirical categories. They are two forms of social organization that coincide in any society, but he assumed that as modernization progresses, *Gesellschaft*-type social organizations become more and more common.

In theorizing the difference between these two forms of social organization, Tönnies presented a whole list of pairs, in which the idea was that one of the two is closer to *Gemeinschaft* and the other to *Gesellschaft* (see Table 1). It crystallizes very well the 'quasi-historical consciousness' that classical sociology represents: practically every social phenomenon, act or category of people can be approached from the viewpoint of how modern they are. The distinction made between traditional and modern, or later in the 1980s and 1990s between modern and postmodern, is actually a continuum presented in the simplified form of two – and only two – entirely different societies. Although it is clear at the outset that the ideal

TABLE 1.   TÖNNIES' LIST OF RELATIONAL PAIRS THAT EXPRESS
THE GEMEINSCHAFT–GESELLSCHAFT DISTINCTION

Gemeinschaft	Gesellschaft
women	men
countryside	city
city	metropolis
the common people	the educated rulers
the young	adults
folks of the mountains	folks of the plains
provincial towns	the capital city
menial labourers	traders
agricultural labour	industrial labour
the ecclestiastic estate	the secular estate
the landed estates	the capital owning estate

Source: Toennies 1971: 69–72

types of traditional and modern society could never exist as empirical objects, it is still assumed that we are getting closer all the time to the other extreme. Moreover, although it is emphasized that features from both extremes exist in any real society, features associated with the traditional are treated as signs of a gradually vanishing phenomenon.

In addition to Durkheim and Tönnies, there is a whole list of sociologists who have contributed to forming the theory of modernization. For instance, Karl Marx, one of the influential predecessors of classical sociologists, emphasized the importance of the relations of production as the motor of history. For him, the bourgeois era meant an expansion of commoditization. Max Weber was particularly interested in the process of increasing rationality as an outcome of the formation of capitalism. In his early work Georg Simmel approached recent social change from the viewpoint of increasing differentiation, whereas in his later studies he concentrated on analysing the effects of urbanization and capitalist exchange economy on individuals' mentality.

By the 1950s, especially with the influence of Talcott Parsons, the classical sociologists' theorization of Western social change since the Middle Ages had developed into an elaborate modernization theory. By interpreting and further developing the thinking of Durkheim and Weber especially, Parsons conceived of modernization in terms of differentiation. Differentiation for Parsons referred to a process whereby the tasks necessary in a society to guarantee its survival are performed by an increasing number of substructures (or institutions). Rather than overlapping or duplicating their functions, new institutions take over fragments of the activities formerly performed by a single, less differentiated (i.e., specialized) institution. Such a multiplicity of tasks to be performed by an increasingly large number of institutions requires interdependence as well as coordination (Parsons 1964).

Since the 1950s, modernization theory has gradually transformed into a generic quasi-historical perspective practised as part of social theory and cultural critique. This means that every now and then, a new catchy 'ization' term – such as rationalization, individualization or secularization – is introduced to the international social science community. Different kinds of authors, from Alvin Toffler to Jean-François Lyotard, have at regular intervals come up with arguments about the coming of a new age, which is termed for instance 'postindustrial', 'postmodern' or 'global'. In discussing recent social and cultural trends, the participants revisit and recycle the older modernization literature.

The Main Assumptions of the Modernization Discourse

In its various forms, the story of modernization can be seen as a myth that presents us with a story of the origins and development of contemporary culture and society. It is unreal in the sense that it is detached from the concrete history of any particular society, but it has a strong formative function, because it proposes to its readers the self-concept of being 'moderns'. Whether or not actual development in a given moment appears to correspond to the predictions of theories of modernization, the discourses of modernity are a given framework within which we engage in reflexive discussions about the spirit of the times. As said in the previous sections, the myth of modernization promotes a framework in which certain aspects of human reality are seen as receding, or 'traditional', as something that is eventually going to fade away. Correspondingly, the opposite ends of such dimensions of development are presented as emergent, as things that are assumed to become more common.

To sum up what I suggest are the main elements in the myth of modernization, let me quote perhaps the most important early formulation about the experience of modernity. It is Karl Marx's classic text from 1848:

> Constant revolutionising of production, uninterrupted disturbance of all social conditions, everlasting uncertainty and agitation distinguish the bourgeois epoch from all earlier ones. All fixed, fast-frozen relations, with their train of ancient and venerable prejudices and opinions, are swept away, all new-formed ones become antiquated before they can ossify. All that is solid melts into air, all that is holy is profaned, and man is at last compelled to face with sober senses, his real conditions of life, and his relations with his kind. (Marx and Engels 1971: 92)

It has been commonly assumed that Marx and Engels splendidly capture the way people still experience modernity in the lines above. That is why

Marshall Berman named his book about the experience of modernity from the nineteenth century till the 1970s after a citation from that excerpt. According to Berman, to be modern has meant from the nineteenth century onward that one is 'part of a universe in which, as Marx said, "all that is solid melts into air"' (Berman 1982: 15).

However, the modernity discourse includes other, more problematic elements than the stress laid on constant change. In the excerpt above, like the modernization discourse more generally, it is assumed that the transient nature of life in modernity distinguishes it from earlier periods. In other words, it is assumed that all earlier epochs stand in opposition to modernity in the sense that previously – or in 'pre-modern' societies – social change was non-existent or slow. Thus, we have the distinction between traditional and modern society.

The distinction between traditional and modern, often presented as a continuum ranging from old-fashioned or outdated to new and updated, is constructed from two related assumptions. First, it is assumed that the non-existent or slow social change of previous epochs was caused by 'venerable prejudices and opinions' (Marx and Engels 1971: 92) sanctified by religious beliefs. Correspondingly, rapid social change in modernity is possible because 'all that is holy is profaned' (Marx and Engels 1971: 92). Therefore, in the modernity discourse religion and sacred things are also presented as receding phenomena. Second, old and traditional are associated with habitual behaviour, and there is an assumption about increasing rationality and reflexivity.

Let me now discuss these two assumptions by pointing out how they guide the framework within which human reality and human action are perceived.

The Crisis of the Sacred

Social scientists and Western intellectuals have been predicting the disappearance of religion from the modern world for nearly three centuries (Stark 1999: 249), and the term 'secularization' has been used to refer to that prediction from the beginning of the twentieth century onwards (see, e.g., Brown 1912; Geary 1934). From the late 1960s onward secularization was developed into a proper theory and became the 'reigning dogma of the field' (Swatos and Christiano 1999: 210) when several books discussing secularization appeared (Berger 1967; Wallace 1966; Wilson 1966). The concept refers to a diminishing role of the church and the clergy in organizing society whereby other social institutions, especially political and educational institutions, have escaped from religious domination (Stark 1999: 252). Related to that, the secularization theorists assumed that the growing separation of church and state has coincided with a decline in people's religiousness.

When dealing with the subjective side of secularization, theorists often refer to Max Weber, who in his thesis of rationalization as part of modernization also thought that the sacred, or charisma, is disappearing from the world. In Weber's thinking, this trend is related to a change in social organization. According to him, there are three pure types of legitimate domination, or three grounds on which authority may rest: legal, traditional or charismatic. Legal authority rests on a belief in the legality of rules and the right of those elevated to authority to issue commands. Traditional authority rests on an established belief in the sanctity of immemorial traditions and the legitimacy of those exercising authority under them. Charismatic authority rests on devotion to the exceptional sanctity, heroism or exemplary character of an individual person, or on the normative patterns ordained by him or her (Weber 1978a: 215). Since Weber assumed that, along with differentiation, social organization is to a greater degree based on formal rules, as in bureaucracy, it was natural for him to predict that the population's beliefs in the sanctity of traditions or charismatic persons, including gods, would gradually fade away. On the one hand he was concerned about the social consequences, such as weakening ties of solidarity between individuals, but on the other hand he obviously welcomed the triumph of rationality. Thus Raymond Aron, writing at the time when secularization theory was particularly popular, summarizes the Weberian viewpoint this way:

> The world of the primitive contains a distinction between the commonplace and the exceptional, to paraphrase Weber, or between the profane and the sacred, to adopt Durkheimian terminology. If the point of departure for the religious history of humanity is a world peopled with the sacred, the point of arrival in our time is what Weber calls *Entzauberung der Welt*: the disenchantment of the world. The sacred, the exceptional quality which was attached to the things and creatures surrounding us at the dawn of the human adventure, has been banished. The capitalist's world – that is, the world we all live in, Soviets and Westerners alike – is composed of forces or creatures which offer themselves to us to be used, transformed, and consumed, but which no longer carry the charm of charisma. (Aron 1970: 271–2)

At that time, the heyday of modernity, it was particularly tempting to assume that religion was disappearing from the modern world. Americans had just landed on the moon, and it seemed that eventually science and progress would solve all the problems humans might face. In contrast, it seemed that 'traditionalism', patriarchal social order, prejudices and superstition were the most difficult obstacles to progress in the developing countries. As late as the early 1990s Fredric Jameson (1992: 67) wrote that capitalistic modernity had succeeded in killing religion.

Especially against the background of the history of European societies and the Judeo-Christian world it has seemed reasonable to conclude that there is a gradual secularization process going on. In European medieval societies the Roman Catholic church formed an important power centre, and even after the Reformation the European Christian churches took care of many tasks in organizing and controlling people's lives. However, gradually the secular states have taken over, and people's everyday lives have been filled with many other activities than those organized by the church. In addition science first came to challenge and later to beat the church's authority in providing people with a world view. Since it is thought that the very essence of the modern world view is permeated by science, prepared to doubt and question everything that has not been rationally justified and proven, it is easy to assume that there is a crisis of the sacred and that religion is forced into an ever smaller corner of people's minds.

From the late 1970s onwards, however, secularization theory has been increasingly criticized. Behind the researchers' increasing willingness to reconsider their views was, for instance, the rise of socially radical movements that instead of Marxism and communism swore in the name of Islam. In 1979, fanatical Muslims overthrew the Shah of Iran, whose government was believed to symbolize modernization. The simultaneous rise of Christian fundamentalism, for instance Creationism, which opposes Darwinism, also cast a shadow on the secularization thesis. Furthermore, the collapse of the Soviet Union showed that several decades of institutionalized atheism had not been able to remove religion from the Eastern bloc. Instead, by 1990 church attendance had already recovered to levels comparable to Western Europe, and forms of religiousness still continue to rise (Stark 1999: 266).

A systematic analysis of the modernization theory has shown its weaknesses, and leading researchers, including one of the theory's most influential proponents, Peter Berger, have changed their minds and come to the conclusion that it was mistaken. As Berger puts it:

> The world today, with some exceptions attended to below, is as furiously religious as it ever was, and in some places more so than ever. This means that a whole body of literature written by historians and social scientists over the course of the 1950s and '60s, loosely labeled as 'secularization theory', was essentially mistaken. In my early work I contributed to this literature and was in good company so doing – most sociologists of religion had similar views. There were good reasons for holding these views at the time, and some of these writings still stand up. But the core premise does not. (Berger 1997: 3)

Practically all elements of the secularization thesis have proven to be mistaken, or else empirical evidence does not support them. For instance, the assumption that religiousness has declined from earlier days is mere nostalgia. Most prominent historians now agree that there never was an 'Age of Faith' (Stark 1999: 255). As to more recent research on people's religiousness, the existing data do not show any dramatic changes. For instance, the annual reports of US citizens' religiousness can be characterized by stability. Basic religious beliefs, and even religious practice, differ relatively little from the levels recorded since the beginning of polling in 1935 (Hadden 1987: 600). The same can be said about religion in Europe: there has been no long-term decline in religious participation, and a considerable part of the population say that they believe in God (Stark 1999).

Although empirical evidence does not give support to the secularization theory, the idea that the sacred is a receding feature still seems to lurk behind different variants of the story of modernization. In them, the new rise of religion and belief in sacred principles is associated with 'anti-modern' extremism in one form or another. Although the writers may stress that religion is not dying out, the argument is made in the spirit of cultural pessimism. The new rise of religion is presented as a backward phenomenon, as proof that modernity or part of the modern world is drifting further away from its unfulfilled promises. For instance, in some of the globalization discussion (religious) fundamentalism has been placed at the opposite pole to modernization. For Barber (1995), one of the adherents of this theory, the polarization is between Jihad and McWorld, between religious fundamentalism and global consumer capitalism. For Huntington (1996), the polarization is between civilizations, especially between the West and an emergent Islamic–Confucian axis. Finally, for Giddens fundamentalism opposes modernity and in that sense does not belong to it. According to him, fundamentalism means an 'assertion of formulaic truth', which can be seen as a reaction to the difficulties of living in a world of radical doubt (Giddens 1994: 100).

Like all myths, the assumption of the crisis of the sacred in the modern world effectively organizes our experience by making us pay attention to certain phenomena from a particular perspective, and by making us overlook some other features or viewpoints. For instance, in discussing the future of the sacred we tend to concentrate on groups or movements that are referred to as religions or religious sects in public discussion. Much of the discussion deals with the state of established religions: for instance, how their position has changed, how the membership has developed or how active the members are. This tendency to concentrate on established religions overlooks a much broader definition of religion proposed by Émile Durkheim (1965). According to him, what is shared by all world religions, even the small primitive ones that have not established a church as a worldly power centre, is the distinction made between sacred and profane. In other words, certain things are given a special, honoured place in people's life. In this sense it is hard to think of a society where everything has lost the members' respect. Although we may be well aware that there are principles – such as freedom, equality or 'Western values' more generally – that most people honour, they are seldom taken into account when discussing the disappearance of the sacred.

In a similar way, the modernization myth makes us sensitive to a trend of individualization that seems to support the secularization assumption. Thus, concomitant with modernization, it appears that society splits into innumerable sects or segments that do not share the same values. One could even go so far as to argue that in fully modern society, each person has his or her own individual set of values. Therefore, if anything is left of the sacred, it appears that everyone has his or her own gods and churches. In this line of thought we overlook the fact that instead of pulverizing societies into ever smaller communities, economic and technological development has instead created larger areas than previously that share the same dominant language and political agenda. From the medieval era onwards, geographically large areas have turned into political units within which the population is subjected to the same administration, justice system and education; an effective means of communication, such as newspapers and the electronic media, has formed citizens into 'imagined communities' (Anderson 1991). The enlargement of 'nations' in this sense can also be seen in the fact that the number of languages spoken in the world has decreased during recent centuries, and the pace of extinction of world languages is predicted to increase.[2] As for the population, these nation states are not just cold administrative units. Most citizens develop a feeling of patriotism toward them, partly because the states design and organize public and private rituals to foster the sacred unity of the nation.

Increasing Reflexivity

In addition to suggesting that the sacred is a receding phenomenon in modern societies, the modernization story promotes the assumption that, because of a trend toward rationalization, people are becoming more and more reflexive about everything they do, and therefore habitual behaviour is fading away. This assumption of increasing reflexivity is typically related to rapid social change, which was already the case with Marx's famous argument, according to which, in the bourgeois epoch, constant revolutionizing and disturbance of social conditions create everlasting uncertainty and agitation, so that people's attitudes and opinions 'become antiquated before they can ossify'.

In the modernization myth, habitual behaviour is presented as a receding feature via two different routes, but often these paths cross and form an unclear pattern. This can be seen in Max Weber's (1978a) famous treatment of different types of action.

To demarcate the newly established discipline of sociology, Weber makes a distinction between meaningful action and 'merely reactive behaviour to which no subjective [or social] meaning is attached' (Weber 1978a: 25). Weber seems to think that such unconscious habitual behaviour lies totally beyond the scope of sociology, which is social action. It is as far away as possible from instrumentally rational action, which according to him gains more ground with the development of capitalism. Therefore, Weber implies that habitual behaviour is a receding phenomenon.

There is also another reason why Weber thought that habitual behaviour was becoming obsolete as a result of modernization. According to him, habits represent tradition in people's behaviour. That assumption is evident in the name: Weber talks about traditional action as one type of social action. It is of course traditional in the sense that habits do not appear all of a sudden. However, when talking about traditional action Weber also thought that habits exist because they are legitimated by a tradition. In other words, people follow certain behavioural patterns because they honour a tradition. In this latter sense traditional action comes close to another action type that Weber distinguished, value-rational action.

These two ways to conceive of habitual behaviour are mixed with each other, which further strengthens the conclusion that habitual behaviour is a thing of the past. Weber argues:

> Strictly traditional behaviour, like the reactive type of imitation discussed above, lies very close to the borderline of what can be justifiably called meaningfully oriented action, and indeed often on the other side. For it is often a matter of almost automatic reaction to habitual stimuli which guide behaviour in a course which has been repeatedly followed. The great bulk of all everyday action to which people have become habitually accustomed approaches this type. Hence, its place in a systematic classification is not merely that of a limiting case because, as will be shown later, attachment to habitual forms can be upheld with varying degrees of self-consciousness and in a variety of senses. In this case the type may shade over into value rationality. (Weber 1978a: 25)

By grading habits as low or traditional in his conceptual system, Weber is by no means alone among the classical sociologists. As Erkki Kilpinen (2000: 13–39) points out, it is characteristic of the whole classical tradition of sociology to make a distinction between (rational and conscious) action and (mere mechanical) behaviour, and the reason seems to be the same as with Weber: habitual action is associated with traditional or pre-modern society. For instance, when discussing Durkheim's treatment of the concept of habit, Jeffrey Alexander (1982: 108) says that the notion of habit implies mechanical adaptation, and holds the same view throughout his four-volume treatise on classical sociology. The same tendency to favour intentional 'action' over and above 'mere behaviour' persists in present-day social theory.

The persistent tendency in social theory to treat habits as a receding or less valued feature of social reality is a logical conclusion of the myth of modernization, which celebrates creativity and progress. In doing that, it guides our vision of routines in several ways. It makes us pay attention to habitual behaviour as something that hinders or slows down social change or development, and it hides the part routines play in learning and acquiring new skills. It also implies that self-conscious and rational action excludes habits, thus forming a one-sided view of human action.

Conclusion

At the beginning of this chapter I argued that theories of modernization must be considered as variants of a myth rather than as scientific theories of social change. The social history of the idea of modernization discussed here gives support to that argument. Instead of being a logical conclusion from theory building, theories of modernization are a direct successor of the Enlightenment idea of progress, which served to promote the future that the Enlightenment philosophers thought was best for society. The philosophers acted more like ministers of a civil religion of progress than as scientists. The same appears to be the case with contemporary modernization theorists, although in both cases the individuals themselves do not seem to notice that aspect of their activity.

I have shown that the narrative of modernization guides us quite poorly in understanding contemporary societies. The two main assumptions entangled in the narrative, that is, that sacred and habitual behaviour are disappearing from the world, cannot be properly defended on empirical grounds. This also supports the inference that the modernization discourse functions in other ways than its apparent ability to provide people with a historical perspective to their everyday life.

Therefore, I think it is relevant to ask: why is it that social and cultural theory carries on the tradition of the modernization discourse? What are its functions for scholars and for society at large?

Let me start with a prosaic and somewhat cynical explanation. One reason for the appearance of ever-new theories about a recent historical turn resides in the social science publishing market. Universal theory sells well. As book market customers we easily discard monographs analysing developments in a particular region, and instead choose to buy a book that promises to explain recent developments across the globe. Therefore, at any time a sizeable portion of social science publications discuss a new trend and concept, such as postmodernity, globalization or reflexive modernization.

Another reason for the success of such concepts is their usefulness in justifying or criticizing political decisions. As I pointed out in discussing the history of the idea of modernization, the eighteenth-century Enlightenment philosophers promoted the future development they hoped for by framing the past in such a way that it supported their vision and presented it as an unavoidable outcome. The same is still true of the political uses of this genre of social science literature. If and when globalization is conceived of as an irreversible, law-like global process, national decisions can be justified by arguing that there are no alternatives to adjusting to global market demands. Alternatively, a national or international duty to defend precious things (such as 'national cultural heritage') against the evils of globalization can justify many kinds of political demands.

One important precondition for the endless modernization discussion is that when discussing recent events and the 'spirit of the time' in the public sphere or even among social scientists, we do not seem to notice its repetitive character. The role of the ever-renewed story of modernization as a creation myth of the culture of modernity seems to go unnoticed. There are probably several reasons for this.

To start with, we could assume that there is a social-psychological explanation for it. Although we have good historical records and excellent histories about past decades, individual memory and experience of previous times dates back only a few decades. From the perspective of each new generation, older generations are stuck with hopelessly outdated habits, manners and styles, which they seem to defend in the name of tradition and the good old times, when things were still simple and in their right place. For the older generations, their manners and habits may sound rational and modern, even radical during the time they acquired them. Thus recurring arguments about recent modernization can go largely unnoticed because of humans' short memory, and the persistent modernity discourse serves as a framework within which the 'spirit of the times', social change and the older and younger generations are assessed.

More generally, it is apparent that both the success of ever-new modernization theories and our tendency not to notice how they largely recycle old themes is because the idea of modernization strikes a chord in the culture of modernity. For instance, we are used to the experience that science and technology develop all the time; technical problems are solved and the standard of living gets higher. That is why the culture of modernity esteems all that is new, which is easily assumed better than old objects or ideas. As Greg Urban (2001) puts it, the 'metaculture of newness' has a dominant position in Western societies. As to changes in society, the discourse of modernity is often ambiguous or worried about new developments, but such concerns also appear to be guided by our experience of constant technological development. The assumptions that traditional habits and religion are disappearing, and that the warmth and solidarity of small communities will be replaced by impersonal city life, all seem to assume that people will resemble the mechanical world of machines and computers. The threat of losing the main features of human reality feels so real that, despite all recycling, the narrative of modernization does not lose its captivation.

To turn to the broader question about the function of reflexivity in human reality, what are the implications for the case of the modernization discourse? If we can generalize from that case, it would seem that discourses of reflexivity reproduce rather than question routine lines of thought and behaviour. On that basis, is there any real potential in social sciences? If reflexive discourses about local culture are an inherent part of it, is there any way we can rationally research human reality and the very conditions we live in?

To acknowledge that the modernization discourse does not get very far from the local cultural unconscious does not necessarily mean that we have to deem it worthless. On the contrary, to be useful at all, all knowledge about human reality has to address questions that are pertinent, or at least understandable, to the members of the society in question.

It can be argued that the case of modernization discourse represents one of the two forms in which the social sciences can make themselves relevant in society. As a form of *Zeitdiagnose*, the modernization discourse addresses its consumers by raising concerns about unwanted development or by building up positive expectations about a better future. In other words, it assumes a form of moral assessment. For instance, within the modernity discourse social changes are measured from the viewpoint of humaneness: whether people under changing conditions are still able to preserve authenticity, integrity, solidarity and compassion toward others. The answers to these burning questions may be presented in a shocking fashion, for instance by arguing that at that very moment structural changes in society are leading to a general corrosion of character, but that may be only to increase the dramatic effect of the writing. Whether the interpretations of the current situation or predictions about the future are deemed justified or not, these studies nevertheless approach the contemporary condition from viewpoints that members deem morally relevant. Thus *Zeitdiagnose* makes people reflect on the current state of affairs in terms of their central values.

The tradition of empirical social research represents the other form in which social science makes itself useful for society. Within this tradition, one normally puts emphasis on the reliability of the observations and measurements and avoids highly speculative interpretations. Empirical social research is useful because it provides facts that serve to monitor and control social development.

In actual practice, social science scholarship can be seen as a continuum from pure *Zeitdiagnose* to pure empirical social research, and at the *Zeitdiagnose* end it competes for popularity with art and religion. In some ways modernization stories can be likened to sermons, which also warn about morally questionable features of our time and about dangers that individuals should avoid. In this sense social science is a form of religion, and the modernization discourse represents a secular treatment of the dominant religious values. The relationship of social science to forms of art, especially literature, is also blurred.[3] On the other hand positivist social research, which assumes natural science as the model for a scientific study of society, is hardly more successful in distancing itself from culturally given frameworks. Although the observations of social facts may be conducted in a precise manner, the classifications that construct the facts and the measurements by which they are examined are largely taken for granted. Even if they are reflected on, they cannot really be questioned because it is precisely their moral or administrative relevance that makes the whole research useful.

It seems, therefore, that as a form of reflexivity social research is destined to stay within the confines of culture. But although there is no total escape from our limitations as humans, deliberate ethnocentrism is hardly the conclusion we must draw. The more we know about past and present social and cultural systems around the globe, the better we are able to understand human reality. The case of the modernity discourse reminds us that meta-culture is part of culture, and the promotion of reflexive frames about the current condition always has potential political uses and consequences.

Notes

1   To say that the modernity discourse is not a truly scientific theory is not a totally new argument. For instance, Jeffrey Alexander (1994: 170) makes the same point when discussing post-war modernization theory in the United States. According to him, it was a symbolic system that functioned not only to explain the world in a rational way but also to interpret the world in a manner that provided meaning and motivation. Alexander also refers to Pocock (1987), who has emphasized that 'modernity' must be understood as the consciousness rather than the condition of being modern.

2   Of the 6,000 languages currently spoken in the world, half are thought to be in danger or dying out. Some experts go as far as to predict that more than 90 per cent of all the world's languages will die out in the next century (Geary 1997; Waas 2001).

3 For an empirical study of the relationship between literature and sociology, see Wolf Lepenies' study *Between Literature and Science: The Rise of Sociology* (1988). Lepenies shows how in the early nineteenth century literature and sociology competed for recognition as the chief analysts of the new industrial society in which they lived. Sociology was conceived as the third major discipline, a hybrid of the scientific and literary traditions.

9 The Enigma of Human Reality

I have tried to describe the state of the art of social science by telling what we know about human reality. To sum up, the main features of this fascinating object of research are as follows.

First of all, human reality consists of routines, that is, every kind of taken-for-granted, and in that sense culturally unconscious, aspect of human activity. Routines not only comprise automated, conditioned activities like chopping wood or washing dishes, there are routine aspects in all realms of human reality. To take a prime example, our ability to use language is based on the fact that we routinely understand the meaning of most of the words used and can thus concentrate on following the substantive points made in the course of communication. The same is true of all higher mental activities, like solving mathematical problems. In fact, one could argue that the more complex the task, the more it entails internalized routines.

Routines are the explanation why humans have been so successful as a species. Through the routines that we are taught, once painstakingly made inventions are passed on from previous generations and from our contemporaries to us, and we do not even need to understand why an invention works. Routines are a form of institutionalized intelligence, which frees us from needing to rebuild everything from scratch. They enable us to concentrate each time on what is at stake at that particular moment, which means that we do not have to be like walking supercomputers, and yet, or precisely because of that, we can solve urgent problems.

As default assumptions about how other members of society will act and what different options of action in a given situation mean, routines also coordinate social interaction and make it more predictable. This does not mean that the set of routines that members are socialized into in a given society determine or guide the coordination of individual acts, it is only that the contradictions, disputes and negotiations between actors stay within limits, which depend on the cultural proximity of the interacting people. The closer people are, for instance linguistically, the less there is a need to build from scratch the activity in which the parties are engaged.

Thus routines increase predictability in human reality and are therefore the mainstay of social order. This does not mean that harsher or more visible ways of maintaining order, such as coercion, use or threat of violence, normative social control or references to social norms, are insignificant, but after turbulent times, when the existing order is challenged, the status quo is rapidly channelled into routine lines of thought and behaviour, and even in times of crisis and radical change a total break with pre-existing routines is not possible. In clever, insignificant ways, routines are at the background of even the most radical phenomena.

Routines cannot be entirely challenged because most of them are not of our own making. Every individual member is born into a society that follows certain routines at different levels of social life. We do not know why we follow the routines in our practices because we learned most of them through practice, without anyone explicitly putting into words how things are done and why. Thus there is no point zero at which members consciously agree on certain procedures. Instead, human reality entails a constant two-directional process in which old routines are challenged and new ones are formed.

The constant interplay between routines and reflexivity that character-izes human reality is always mediated through the body and bodily expe-riences. Our practical mastery of any routine is stored in our body, not just as information in the brain but as if written in the flesh, conditioned in our reflex-like behavioural and emotional reactions. When we learn or unlearn these bodily aspects of routines, this may take place entirely with-out conscious deliberation; the physical facets of social practices speak directly to our bodies. As was discussed in Chapter 5, rituals and ritual-like activities are particularly important from this viewpoint. Of course, everyday social life always entails that we are placed in different positions and behave in certain ways, but certain occasions are stronger as bodily experiences and thus leave a deeper memory trace on our bodies. One way of making an event memorable is through strictly defining and styl-izing the movements of the participants. When not just the mind but the whole body is involved in such events, they speak directly to our body and make us routinely behave in a particular way. Because the mainte-nance of power relations by voluntary means is crucial to the smooth functioning of a society, it is no wonder that institutional interaction takes on such ritual-like features.

Related to routines, language has a central role to play in human real-ity. It is not that language or discourse simply forms the counterpart to the cultural unconscious as the realm in which humans engage in reflecting on their routines. Language itself depends on routine mastery of a vocab-ulary that makes reflexivity possible. Nevertheless, language is the best tool people can use to distance themselves from what they do and reflect on, or play with, other possible options.

But language is more than just a tool of reflection. It also constructs human reality in various ways. First, language is a further developed extension or aspect of human interaction, in which each act changes or affects the previous state of affairs. This is the case in any conversation, in which each turn of talk drives the coordination of the participants' acts forward, but the same is true of what could be called institutional interaction in the large sense of the term. That is, often utterances have an ability to change the state of affairs because the participants are in institutionally defined positions and because the interaction itself is part-and-parcel of the institutions. After all, institutions, or social structures, are nothing but patterned forms of interaction, in which talk and texts have central roles.

On the other hand, language cannot be reduced to a plain expression or function of institutional interaction. It has an active, creative role in constructing and modifying social institutions. It is not possible for an individual speaker to make any kind of description of a situation acceptable, because other participants judge the relevance of each reference to it against their own observations and understanding, but a convincing new framing of the state of affairs may radically change existing practices and thus the reality in question. In conjunction with social practices, language thus has the intriguing double role that on the one hand one can make descriptions of reality with it, but on the other hand it forms reality. When practices are perceived from the viewpoint of signification they can be called discourses, which do not morely consist of groups of signs but, as Foucault, (1972: 49) puts it, are 'practices that systematically form the objects of which they speak'.

From this viewpoint, whether or not a description accurately corresponds to its object, that is, whether it is truthful, is one type of discourse that we may resort to in human reality. In order for a description to be granted the unchallenged status of truth, the community in question needs to routinely agree that it matches its experience of the object in question. This of course means that the description works in practice, for instance that new practices or applications built on the premises of the prevalent truth function as they should. If they don't, the existing truths are easily challenged, or the community finds another way to account for the discrepancies.

As a practice, the discourse of truth is seldom reflected on. Even when conflicting descriptions are assessed and tested, such practices are routinely seen as ways to compare descriptions with reality itself. That is because within the mundane notion of language, discussed in Chapter 3, we treat language as a realm that is seen as being apart from and placed against reality. It is conceived as a transparent lens which itself does not interfere with its role as an instrument that provides us with a view of reality. Of course, when we take into account that with the help of language humans are able to coordinate their interaction and pass on knowledge about their environment, such a notion of language is not unsubstantiated – it is only that it has its limits when it comes to other aspects of human reality.

When compared with the natural sciences, social sciences have quite a different function in society. While the natural and technical sciences discover natural laws and thus enable new inventions, the social sciences provide us with reconstructions of our tacit practices which, if they are deemed accurate, 'ring a bell' among those whom the interpretation in question concerns. It is as if the people whose routines are explained recollect from memory the bigger picture that makes the details of the practice understandable. Yet this does not necessarily mean that the participants in the routine under scrutiny have consciously known – and later forgotten – the explanation given, because it may have never been put into words before. Routines are learned in practice, and many of them are passed on from a previous generation of 'practitioners'. Their meaning is typically so self-evident that putting it into words does not occur to the members.

Routines are self-evident also in the sense that they constitute human agents; as was discussed especially in Chapter 8, people are what they are through adopting certain culture- and context-specific practices. However, to appreciate an explanation of the details of a routine or a set of routines, one does not need to be a member of the same culture. Even if a practice is not only unintelligible but unethical from the viewpoint of an outsider, a social science explanation may be deemed sensible if it is able to account for the observations made about the phenomenon and if the inner logic reconstructed in the explanation matches people's experience about the ways in which humans may behave.

There are, however, also other conditions that determine whether an interpretation is deemed valid. A social science explanation may not necessarily be deemed reasonable, truthful or accurate simply because it is able to give an account of the facts concerned. For instance, if an explanation strikingly goes against the ideals and moral principles of the people concerned, or if it does not match a strongly prejudiced conception of the group, it may be denied and replaced by an interpretation that is more in concert with people's conscious values and preconceptions.

Thus there is always a politics of truth involved in accounting for phenomena that prompt our attention and require an interpretation. This does not, however, simply mean that such politics sometimes prevent us from hearing or accepting the truth. Although in many instances the ability of language to represent reality works well, especially when dealing with human activities and with characteristics attributed to actor roles and persons, the situation is more complex. Giving an explanation to a routine does not only mean that we become reflexively conscious of something that we mastered in practice and never bothered to think about. As was discussed especially in Chapter 3, it must be emphasized that the act of putting a routine into words, of bringing it to discourse, is also a move in discursive practice, an act in its own right. For one thing, prompting a routine and reflecting on the rationale behind it must have a reason; it typically shows that, in one way or another, the self-evidence of the routine is questioned. And even if questioning the sense or meaning of something that thus far has gone unnoticed comes unexpectedly, for instance because the community in question comes in close contact with a foreigner or another culture, questioning an old habit makes people relate differently to it and thus change its meaning or add a new element to it. Also, if a routine is given an interpretation that is commonly accepted, it affects and guides its future occurrences. When this bringing to discourse happens, it does not much matter whether the interpretation given to a routine really is a recollection or whether it re-collects existing materials and thus gives it a brand new meaning.

The Inherent Tensions in Human Reality

When we consider the overall picture of the human condition, we can see that human reality is indeed a tricky object. For instance, if we take seriously what was said about the constructive character of language, it follows that in human reality, descriptions and their objects cannot be neatly kept apart from each other. The concepts and tropes we use to describe reality are unavoidably derived from the same source, and it could be argued that therefore we are basically unable to distance ourselves much from the intersubjective world that has constituted us as human agents. Additionally, each description of reality must be considered as an act upon it – a move that, at least in principle, makes a difference to it.

Because descriptions of human reality are an inseparable part of it, we lack a privileged position from which to give a coherent, contradiction-free description of it. Nor do we have a logical language that could be used to give that account. Instead, key elements of human reality such as language can be approached from different angles in such a way that the theories work in practice, but there does not seem to be any means to form a single grand theory within which these building blocks can be fitted together in a consistent manner.

Does this mean that we should give up on even trying to describe human reality? Within the social sciences, there are a plethora of opposing positions that represent such surrender in the face of difficulties. On one hand, different forms of positivism or scientific realism reject the constructive aspects of language and demand a social science that studies social reality as if it were second nature. On the other hand, an extreme post-modernist attitude stems from the reasoning that since there is no way of giving an objective account of social reality, a human scientist may as well be open about his or her standpoint – that reflexivity and sincere reporting are the last solid ground (Salzman 2002). According to this line of reasoning, which can be dated back to Nietzsche's perspectivism, no one else but people who are in a particular position can understand their reality and experience (Gilmour 1990; Hales and Welshon 2000; Nietzsche 1968; Reginster 2000; Salzman 2002).

Thus, according to these extreme standpoints we have two options. We can restrict ourselves to treating human reality as if it were part of nature and thus save science at the expense of losing any grasp of human reality. The other option is that we wholeheartedly embrace constructionism and relativism and end up unable to make any difference between art and science, or between research-based and other arguments made about the reality we encounter as humans.

I suggest that the dead end we easily face when trying to take human reality seriously is due to a taken-for-granted model for a satisfactory account of it. Admittedly, there are a plethora of 'root metaphors' employed in approaching human societies, or aspects of social reality, from different angles. For instance, among these are game, play and network (Brown 1989). However, when we assess the quality of different theories, the metaphors we use as resources in trying to make a complex reality understandable are a much smaller group. When it turns out that different elements of human reality cannot be fitted into a coherent whole, we are not satisfied. That is because we automatically conceive of a proper theory of human reality as if such a theory were a map or a picture of another physical object. Thus, the metaphors we try to use are taken from the material world of concrete objects. Yet, as has been pointed out in this book, human reality is quite different. Physical reality – or rather as it is conceived in knowledge about it – cannot serve as the model by which to make sense of it.

To avoid this blind alley, we have to reconsider the criteria of scientific knowledge about human reality. The social sciences cannot ignore the physical world as a condition for, and in various ways constitutive of, all human practices. However, to understand human reality in its entirety we have to go beyond physics, indeed into the meta-physics of human life and experience. In this sphere, we have to accept that our partial regimes of knowledge about human reality do not always add up. There remain unsolvable tensions and contradictions between alternative ways of analysing the human condition. For instance, accounts can be assessed from the viewpoint of their truthfulness, on their ability to reflect reality. Yet the same accounts can be analysed from the perspective of rhetoric or semiotics. Furthermore, they can be seen as speech acts, as moves in end-lessly unfolding interactions that systematically form the objects of which the subjects speak, including the subjects themselves. There is no way that the results of these different analytic enterprises could be merged into a coherent total view of the object in question. However, different view-points cannot be treated as wholly independent regimes of truth. The results of one analytical perspective cannot be treated as a yardstick in assessing the truthfulness of another one. The quality of any type of analysis can only be assessed by using its own particular criteria, although one general criterion is shared throughout the natural and social sciences: one has to make rational conclusions based on the observations that the angle of vision enables one to make.[1]

Human reality thus consists of parallel regimes of knowledge that form a kaleidoscopic whole. Based on the perspective one takes, things look a bit different. Each perspective has its core area where it is particularly relevant, and the further away one goes from it, the more relevant it becomes to complement or replace the perspective with other angles and means of producing observations. For instance, the descriptive function of language works well when dealing with the physical world and with largely shared 'basic facts' of social reality, but the more one is dealing with descriptions and prescriptions of social action and human subjects, the more useful it becomes to take into account the constructive and argumentative aspects of language. Yet there are no clear lines that delineate the area of validity of one perspective from another one.

As has been emphasized in this book, it is precisely this multifaceted character of human reality that makes it such a rich resource for the human collective intelligence. Whatever the facts or whatever the situation, through language that stores the experience of previous generations, we always have at our disposal different ways of questioning and reflecting on what appears to be taken for granted. Internal tensions and contradictions of human reality are the source of our creativity.

The Sociology and Ethics of Scientific Knowledge

I have more or less equated the accumulated knowledge of human reality with that reality itself, but of course we have to bear in mind that what was said about the use of language as action also concerns statements about human reality. If we take seriously the point that language not only describes human reality but also forms it, we have to accept that the same goes for this treatment and for all the social sciences. What kind of role do our meta-cultural discourses about societies and cultures and their present conditions have in maintaining and transforming society? What implications should human scientists draw from the fact that we are necessarily partisans, whether we like it or not?

It is indeed reasonable to extend the idea that statements have a formative role to scientific discourse also. Doing so gives science and scientists a healthy reminder that the knowledge we produce is not entirely different from other forms of knowing. What goes as science is a knowledge production institution that has become increasingly powerful, partly because the commonly taken-for-granted assumption that knowledge comprises descriptions of external reality hides the role of science as a creator of society. We must also bear in mind that, whether they are considered scientifically valid or erroneous, when assumptions about reality are deemed real they become real in their consequences. Since from the practical viewpoint scientific knowledge consists of statements about reality validated by a relatively small, often highly esteemed scientific community, nothing would be more dangerous than to blindly believe in science as the received truth and thus let a small elite form society in the image of scientific truth.

On the other hand, when I say that statements about reality must be considered as moves that affect the existing situation, I have already reoccupied the same position that I tried to abandon, and made another argument about reality. The impossibility of giving up on what was termed the mundane notion of language nicely illustrates the kaleidoscopic character of human reality: there are several valid regimes of knowledge that are in contradiction with each other. In other words, we have to take the formative function of human scientific knowledge seriously but knowledge cannot be reduced to it; it not only constructs but it also describes reality. The conclusions to be drawn from this are as follows.

Social science must be related to other forms of meta-cultural commentary about present conditions, which have always had a role in human societies. Like other sciences, the particular strength of the social sciences, as compared with other forms of reflexivity, is its aim to be rational and systematic: when analysing the object of research to consistently follow the set of rules that a particular method honours. That way, the analysis may produce a picture of the object that cannot be seen with the naked eye.

Scientific research does not reveal to us the truth and nothing but the truth, but it is the best known practice with which to pursue systematic analysis of the conditions in which people live. It is pointless to chew over the true nature of human reality because, as Marx (1969) puts it in his *Theses on Feuerbach*, the question of whether objective truth can be attributed to human thinking is a *practical* question, but precisely because of it, arguments about social reality can be weighed against practice. That is, they can be evaluated by testing how consistent they are with the observations used as evidence: how reliable or indisputable the observations are; whether there are several independent observations that support the case; and if it is possible to come up with another interpretation about the same facts. Most importantly, and what makes truth a practical matter, rulings about truthfulness are made by a community, by the people whom the interpretation concerns. This also means that no matter how solid the arguments that a scholar makes, they can only be considered as suggestions to the academic community.

Even if one thinks that with the help of scientific research it is possible to gradually form an objective picture of social reality, human scientists also need to consider their reports from a formative viewpoint. The results of a study can be used as evidence and justification for measures that change social conditions. The concepts and classifications introduced can be put into practice, so they become real in their consequences. This brings us to the problem that human scientists also need to assess their research from an ethical viewpoint. In writing and publishing a report we need to think of our audience and other potential audiences: what could be the political implications drawn from our research, and how can we make sure we can live with them?

There is no simple answer to this problem. Although authors can take it as their duty to put their words in such a way that unwanted political implications of their work are avoided, there is no way scientists can prevent misuse of the knowledge they produce. It is of course possible to abstain from posing and answering questions that might lead into politically incorrect implications. However, such a policy would jeopardize the main principle of science – that is, to systematically follow the rules of one's analysis, regardless of where they lead. If the self-defined rules of research are not observed, there is nothing that differentiates such practice from other forms of reflexivity and social commentary.

Toward More Reflexive Human Science

To cherish the particularity of social science among other forms of reflexivity and meta-cultural commentary, we should be critical toward the kind of social science literature that is called *Zeitdiagnose*. The modernization story constantly recycled in that genre of social science has a function as a form of preaching. For instance, it may call for the values of humaneness by warning that people are getting increasingly individualistic, egoistic and reflexive about everything. It is understandable that social scientists employing the modernization story take part in public discussion about the spirit of the times; it is one of the reasons why the social sciences exist as a social institution. However, the premises of the modernization story do not withstand critical inspection. For instance, increasing reflexivity is a practical impossibility: becoming reflexive about something necessarily means that we take some other things for granted.

Instead of engaging in the modernization discourse, I suggest that we pursue a more reflexive social science in another sense. When studying social phenomena, in addition to being reflexive about the theories and methods we use, we should also be reflexive about the role in which the research places the researcher within the institution being studied and within society at large. Do researchers, for instance, smuggle their own prejudices and cultural constraints into the research design, into the methods used, and into the way results are presented, so that unknowingly or against their best intentions they contribute to particular developments? The antidote against this is not that individual researchers try to be honest and sincere or that they openly disclose their own standpoint. Like other people, researchers have their different political opinions and conceptions about how things should be. Some may think it is their duty as researchers to advance their goals with their research, while others may want to distance themselves from their role as citizens. The only antidote against social science blindly promoting political goals is that the scientific community and the general public are constantly reflexive about social science literature. That way we can best contribute to the critical function of social science in social life: reflexive monitoring of our routines of thought and behaviour.

Notes

1   This conclusion about a fundamental aspect of human reality resembles the postmodernist argument, according to which all ideas must be understood as originating from specific perspectives and thus the claims to unsituated knowledge are suspect because they deny that most fundamental characteristic of knowledge (Riley 2002: 243). This viewpoint owes to, and is influenced by, Friedrich Nietzsche's perspectivism. As Nietzsche (1968, 481) puts it: 'Against positivism, which halts at phenomena – "There are only facts" – I would say: No, facts is precisely what there is not, only interpretations. We cannot establish any fact "in itself": perhaps it is folly to want to do such a thing.' In postmodernist writings, perspectivism is often seen as an outcome of the recent move toward the postmodern age (see, e.g., Lyotard 1984). When this view of reality and science is taken to its extreme, it follows that no justifiable claims about reality can be made; a particular viewpoint is as good as any because they all represent different forms of situated knowledge.

   The point made here about the kaleidoscopic nature of human reality represents a weaker version of perspectivism. It only argues that forms of knowledge about human reality can be validated within the practical framework in which they are used, and in that sense the facts constructed are hard within their area of qualification. However, although it seems that different frameworks overlap, the maps of corresponding aspects of human reality cannot be neatly fitted together to form a total picture.

References

Abrahamsson, Ulla (1988) *Publikens television* [The Public's Television]. Stockholm: Sveriges Radio, publik- och programforskning.

Adorno, Theodor and Max Horkheimer (1979) *Dialectic of Enlightenment*. London: Verso.

Alasuutari, Päivi (1992) Ehkäisyn kiellon synty ja umpikuja vanhoillislestadiolaisessa herätysliikkeessä [The Birth and Impasse of the Ban on Birth Control in the Old Laestadian Revivalist Movement]. *Sosiologia* 29 (2), 106–15.

Alasuutari, Pertti (1986) Alcoholism in Its Cultural Context: The Case of Blue-Collar Men. *Contemporary Drug Problems* 13, 641–86.

Alasuutari, Pertti (1992a) *Desire and Craving: A Cultural Theory of Alcoholism*. New York: State University of New York Press.

Alasuutari, Pertti (1992b) 'I'm Ashamed to Admit it but I Have Watched *Dallas'*; The Moral Hierarchy of TV Programmes. *Media, Culture & Society* 14 (4), 561–82.

Alasuutari, Pertti (1993) *Radio suomalaisten arkielämässä* [Radio in the Everyday Life of the Finns, includes English summary]. Helsinki: Yle, Research & Development, reports 3/1993.

Alasuutari, Pertti (1995) *Researching Culture: Qualitative Method and Cultural Studies*. London: Sage.

Alasuutari, Pertti (1996a) Television as a Moral Issue. In Ian Crawford and Sigurjon Baldur Hafsteinsson (eds), *The Construction of the Viewer: Media Ethnography and the Anthropology of Audiences*. Höjberg, Denmark: Intervention Press, 101–17.

Alasuutari, Pertti (1996b) *Toinen tasavalta: Suomi 1946–1994* [The Second Republic: Finland 1946–1994]. Tampere: Vastapaino.

Alasuutari, Pertti (1997) Why Does the Radio Go Unnoticed? *The Nordicom Review of Nordic Research on Media and Communication, a Special issue on Radio Research in Denmark, Finland, Norway and Sweden*. No. 1/1997, 161–72.

Alasuutari, Pertti (ed.) (1999) *Rethinking the Media Audience*. London: Sage.

Alexander, Jeffrey (1982) *Positivism Presuppositions and Current Controversies: Theoretical Logic in Sociology*, Vol. 1. Berkeley: University of California Press.

Alexander, Jeffrey (1994) Modern, Anti, Post, and Neo: How Social Theories Have Tried to Understand the 'New World' of 'Our Time'. *Zeitschrift fur Soziologie* 23 (3), 165–97.

Anderson, Benedict (1991) *Imagined Communities: Reflections on the Origin and Spread of Nationalism*. London: Verso.

Ang, Ien (1985) *Watching Dallas: Soap Opera and the Melodramatic Imagination*. London: Methuen.

Ang, Ien (1991) *Desperately Seeking the Audience*. London: Routledge.

Appadurai, Arjun (1996) *Modernity at Large: Cultural Dimensions of Globalization*. Minneapolis: University of Minnesota Press.

Aron, Raymond (1970) *Main Currents in Sociological Thought: Durkheim, Pareto, Weber*. Harmondsworth: Penguin.

Atkinson, J. Maxwell and Paul Drew (1979) *Order in Court. The Organization of Verbal Interaction in Judicial Settings*. London: Macmillan.

Atkinson, Paul (1985) Talk and Identity: Some Convergences in Micro-Sociology. In H.J. Halle and S.N. Eisenstadt (eds), *Micro-Sociological Theory: Perspectives on Sociological Theory*, Vol. 2. London, Sage, 117–32.

Atkinson, Paul and Amanda Coffey (2002) Revisiting the Relationship Between Participant Observation and Interviewing. In Jaber F. Gubrium and James A. Holstein (eds), *Handbook of Interview Research: Context & Method*. London: Sage, 801–14.

Austin, John L. (1962) *How to do Things with Words*. London: Oxford University Press.

Baacke, Dieter, Uwe Sander and Ralf Vollbrecht (1990) Medienwelten Jugendlicher: Ergebnisse einer sozialökologischen Forschungsprojekts. *Media Perspektiven*, 5, 323–36.

Barthes, Roland (1969) *Elements of Semiology*. London: Cape.

Barber, Benjamin R. (1995) *Jihad vs. McWorld: How Globalism and Tribalism are Re-shaping the World*. New York: Random House.

Beck, Ulrich (1994) The Reinvention of Politics: Towards a Theory of Reflexive Modernization. In Ulrich Beck, Anthony Giddens and Scott Lash, *Reflexive Modernization: Politics, Tradition and Aesthetics in the Modern Social Order*. Stanford: Stanford University Press, 1–55.

Beck, Ulrich, Anthony Giddens and Scott Lash (1994): *Reflexive Modernization: Politics, Tradition and Aesthetics in the Modern Social Order*. Stanford: Stanford University Press.

Bell, Catherine (1997) *Ritual: Perspectives and Dimensions*. New York: Oxford University Press.

Benjamin, Walter (1989) The Task of the Translator. In Andrew Chesterman (ed.), *Readings in translation theory*. Helsinki: Oy Finn Lectura Ab.

Berger, Peter (1967) *The Sacred Canopy: Elements of a Sociological Theory of Religion*. New York: Anchor Books.

Berger, Peter (1997) Secularism in Retreat. *National Interest* 46, 3–12.

Berger, Peter and Thomas Luckmann (1966) *The Social Construction of Reality: A Treatise in the Sociology of Knowledge*. New York: Anchor Books.

Berlin, Brent (1970) A Universalist-Evolutionary Approach in Ethnographic Semantics. In Ann Fischer (ed.), *Current Directions in Anthropology*. Washington, DC: American Anthropological Association, 3–18.

Berlin, Brent and Paul Kay (1969) *Basic Color Terms: Their Universality and Evolution*. Berkeley: University of California Press.

Berman, Marshall (1982) *All That Is Solid Melts Into Air: The Experience of Modernity*. New York: Simon & Schuster.

Bloch, Maurice (1989) *Ritual, History and Power: Selected Papers in Anthropology* (London School of Economics Monographs on Social Anthropology, No. 58). London: Athlone Press.

Blumer, Herbert (1986) *Symbolic Interactionism: Perspective and Method*. Berkeley, California: University of California Press.

Boden, Deirdre (1994) *The Business of Talk: Organizations in Action*. Cambridge: Polity.

Boden, Deirdre and Don H. Zimmerman (eds) (1991) *Talk and Social Structure: Studies in Ethnomethodology and Conversation Analysis*. Cambridge: Polity Press.

Bourdieu, Pierre (1977) *Outline of a Theory of Practice*. Cambridge: Cambridge University Press.

Bourdieu, Pierre (1990a) *The Logic of Practice*. Palo Alto, CA: Stanford University Press.

Bourdieu, Pierre (1990b) *In Other Words: Essays Towards a Reflexive Sociology*. Palo Alto, CA: Stanford University Press.

Brown, Penelope and Charles C. Levinson (1987) *Politeness: Some Universals in Language Usage*. Cambridge: Cambridge University Press.

Brown, Richard Harvey (1989) *Poetic for Sociology: Toward a Logic of Discovery for the Human Sciences*. Cambridge: Cambridge University Press.

Brown, Samuel (1912) *The Secularization of American Education as Shown by State Legislation, State Constitutional Provisions, and State Supreme Court Decisions*. New York: Russell & Russell.

Bryce, Jennifer and Hope J. Leichter (1983) The Family and Television: Forms of Mediation. *Journal of Family Issues* 2, 309–28.

Burgos, Martine (1988) Life Stories, Narrativity, and the Search for the Self. *University of Jyväskylä: Publications of the Research Unit for Contemporary Culture* 9.

Butler, Judith (1990) *Gender Trouble: Feminism and the Subversion of Identity*. New York: Routledge.

Butler, Judith (1993) *Bodies that Matter: On the Discursive Limits of 'Sex'*. New York: Routledge.

Carolan, Mary (2002) Reflexivity: A Personal Journey during Data Collection. *Nurse Researcher* 10 (3), 7–14.

Clifford, James and George E. Marcus (1986) *Writing Culture: The Poetics and Politics of Ethnography*. Berkeley: University of California Press.

Coffey, Amanda (1999) *The Ethnographic Self: Fieldwork and the Representation of Identity*. London: Sage.

Delany, Paul (1969) *British Autobiography in the Seventeenth Century*. London: Routledge & Kegan Paul.

Donald, James and Ali Rattansi (1992) *'Race', Culture, and Difference*. London: Sage.

Douglas, Mary (1986) *How Institutions Think*. New York: Syracuse University Press.

Douglas, Mary (1991) The Idea of a Home: A Kind of Space. *Social Research*, 59 (1), 287–307.

Drew, Paul and John Heritage (eds) (1992) *Talk at Work: Interaction in Institutional Settings*. Cambridge: Cambridge University Press.

Durkheim, Émile (1964) *The Division of Labor in Society*. New York: Free Press of Glencoe.

Durkheim, Émile (1965) *The Elementary Forms of the Religious Life*. London: Allen & Unwin.

Durkheim, Émile (1982) *The Rules of the Sociological Method*. New York: Free Press.

Eco, Umberto (1971) *Den frånvarande strukturen* [The Absent Structure]. Staffanstorp: Bo Cavefors.

Eco, Umberto (1979) *Theory of Semiotics*. Bloomington: Indiana University Press.

Elias, Norbert (1978) *The History of Manners: The Civilizing Process,* Vol. I. New York:

Elias, Norbert (1982) *Power and Civility: The Civilizing Process*, Vol. II. New York: Pantheon Books.

Etzioni, Amitai (2000) Toward a Theory of Public Ritual. *Sociological Theory* 18 (1), 44–59.

Foucault, Michel (1972) *The Archeology of Knowledge*. New York: Pantheon Books.

Foucault, Michel (1973a) *Madness and Civilization: A History of Insanity in the Age of Reason*. New York: Vintage Books.

Foucault, Michel (1973b) *The Order of Things: An Archeology of the Human Sciences*. New York: Vintage Books.

Foucault, Michel (1975) *The Birth of the Clinic: An Archeology of Medical Perception*. New York: Vintage Books.

Foucault, Michel (1979) *Discipline and Punish: The Birth of the Prison*. New York: Vintage Books.

Foucault, Michel (1980) *The History of Sexuality*, Vol. I: *An Introduction*. New York: Vintage Books.

Foucault, Michel (1985) *The Use of Pleasure:* Vol. 2 *of The History of Sexuality*. New York: Viking.

Foucault, Michel (1988) *The Care of the Self: The History of Sexuality,* Vol. 3. New York: Vintage Books.

Freud, Sigmund (1978) Civilization and Its Discontents. *The Standard Edition of the Complete Psychological Works of Sigmund Freud*, Vol. 21. London: The Hogarth Press, 57–146.

Garfinkel, Harold (1967) *Studies in Ethnomethodology*. Cambridge, UK: Polity Press.

Geary, Gerald Joseph (1934) *The Secularization of the California Missions*. Washington, DC: The Catholic University of America.

Geary, James (1997) Speaking. *Time Magazine*, 7 July.

Geertz, Clifford (1973) *The Interpretation of Cultures*. New York: Basic Books.

Geertz, Clifford (1983) *Local Knowledge: Further Essays in Interpretive Anthropology*. New York: Basic Books.

Geis, Michael L. (1982) *The Language of Television Advertising*. New York: Academic Press.

Gergen, Mary and Kenneth J. Gergen (1984) The Social Construction of Narrative Accounts. In Kenneth J. Gergen and Mary M. Gergen (eds). *Historical Social Psychology*. Hillsdale, NJ: Lawrence Erlbaum Associates, 173–89.

Giddens, Anthony (1984) *The Constitution of Society: Outline of the Theory of Structuration*. Cambridge, UK: Polity Press.

Giddens, Anthony (1990) *The Consequences of Modernity*. Stanford: Stanford University Press.

Giddens, Anthony (1992) *The Transformation of Intimacy: Sexuality, Love and Eroticism in Modern Societies*. Stanford: Stanford University Press.

Giddens, Anthony (1994) Living in a Post-Traditional Society. In Ulrich Beck, Anthony Giddens and Scott Lash, *Reflexive Modernization: Politics, Tradition and Aesthetics in the Modern Social Order.* Stanford: Stanford University Press, 56–109.

Gilmour, John C. (1990) Perspectivism and Postmodern Criticism. *Monist* 73 (2), 233–47.

Gilroy, Paul (1987) *There ain't no Black in the Union Jack: The Cultural Politics of Race and Nation.* London: Hutchinson.

Goffman, Erving (1967) *Interaction Ritual: Essays on Face-to-Face Behavior.* New York: Pantheon Books.

Goffman, Erving (1971) *Relations in Public: Microstudies of the Public Order.* New York: Basic Books.

Greimas, Algirdas Julien (1987) *On Meaning: Selected Writings in Semiotic Theory.* Minneapolis: University of Minnesota Press.

Grice, Herbert Paul (1975) Logic and Conversation. In Peter Cole and J.L. Morgan (eds), *Syntax and Semantics,* Vol. 3: *Speech Acts.* New York: Academic Press, 41–58.

Grice, Herbert Paul (1978) Further Notes on Logic and Conversation. In Peter Cole (ed.), *Syntax and Semantics,* Vol. 9: *Pragmatics.* New York: Academic Press, 113–28.

Gubrium, Jaber F. (1992) *Out of Control: Family Therapy and Domestic Disorder.* Newbury Park, CA: Sage.

Gubrium, Jaber F. and James A. Holstein (1995a) Biographical Work and New Ethnography. In Ruthellen Josselson and Amia Lieblich (eds), *Interpreting Experience: The Narrative Study of Lives.* Thousand Oaks, CA: Sage, 45–58.

Gubrium, Jaber F. and James A. Holstein (1995b) Life Course Malleability: Biographical Work and Deprivatization. *Sociological Inquiry* 65, 207–23.

Gubrium, Jaber F. and James A. Holstein (1997) *The New Language of Qualitative Method.* Oxford: Oxford University Press.

Gubrium, Jaber F., James A. Holstein and David R. Buckholdt (1994) *Constructing the Life Course.* New York: General Hall.

Gusfield, Joseph R. (1981) *The Culture of Public Problems: Drinking-Driving and the Symbolic Order.* Chicago: University of Chicago Press.

Hadden, Jeffrey K. (1987) Toward Desacralizing Secularization Theory. *Social Forces* 65 (3), 587–611.

Hagen, Ingunn (1994) The Ambivalences of TV News Viewing: Between Ideals and Everyday Practices. *European Journal of Communication* 9, 193–220.

Hales, Steven D. and Rex Welshon (2000) *Nietzsche's Perspectivism.* Urbana. University of Illinois Press.

Haley, Jay (1985) *Problem-Solving Therapy.* New York: Harper Torchbooks.

Hall, Stuart (1996) Introduction: Who Needs Identity? In: Stuart Hall and Paul du Gay: *Questions of Cultural Identity.* London: Sage, 1–17.

Harré, Rom and Grant Gillett (1994) *The Discursive Mind.* Thousand Oaks, CA: Sage.

Hawking, Stephen W. (1988) *A Brief History of Time: From the Big Bang to Black Holes.* Toronto: Bantam Books.

Heath, Christian and Hubert Knoblauch (2000) Technology and Social Interaction: The Emergence of 'Workplace Studies'. *British Journal of Sociology* 51 (2), 299–320.

Heritage, John (1984) *Garfinkel and Ethnomethodology*. Cambridge: Polity Press.

Holland, Dorothy and Naomi Quinn (eds) (1987) *Cultural Models in Language and Thought*. Cambridge: Cambridge University Press.

Holzkamp, Klaus (1976) *Sinnliche Erkenntnis: Historischer Ursprung und gesellschaftliche Funktion der Wahrnehmung*. Kronberg: Athenäum Verlag.

Huntington, Samuel P. (1996) *The Clash of Civilizations and the Remaking of World Order*. New York: Simon & Schuster.

Jacoby, Sally and Patrick Gonzales (1991) The Constitution of Expert-Novice in Scientific Discourse. *Issues in Applied Linguistics* 2: 149–82.

James, William (1983) *The Principles of Psychology*, Vol. I. New York: Dover.

Jameson, Fredric (1992) *Postmodernism, or the Cultural Logic of Late Capitalism*. London and New York: Verso.

Jefferson, Gail (1984) On the Organization of Laughter in Talk about Troubles. In Max Atkinson and John Heritage (eds), *Structures of Social Action*. Cambridge: Cambridge University Press, 269–346.

Jefferson, Gail and Jim Schenkein (1978) Some Sequential Negotiations in Conversation: Unexpanded and Expanded Versions of Projected Action Sequences. In J. Schenkein (ed.), *Studies in the Organization of Conversational Interaction*. New York: Academic Press, 155–72.

Kay, Paul and Chad K. McDaniel (1978) The Linguistic Significance of Meanings of Basic Color Terms. *Language* 54, 610–46.

Kay, Paul, Brent Berlin and William Merrifield (1991) Biocultural Implications of Systems of Color Naming. *Journal of Linguistic Anthropology* 1, 12–25.

Keskinen, Raimo (1989) Fyysikon Aika [Physical Scientist's Time]. In Pirkko Heiskanen (ed.), *Aika ja sen ankaruus* [Time and Its Mercilessness]. Helsinki: Gaudeamus, 172–79.

Kilpinen, Erkki (2000) *The Enormous Fly-Wheel of Society: Pragmatism's Habitual Conception of Action and Social Theory*. Department of Sociology, University of Helsinki: Research Reports No. 235.

Kinnunen, Merja (2001) *Luokiteltu sukupuoli* [Classified Gender]. Tampere: Vastapaino.

Kraybill, Donald B. (1994) The Amish Encounter with Modernity. In Donald B. Kraybill and Marc A. Olshan (eds), *The Amish Struggle with Modernity*. Hanover: University Press of New England, 21–34.

Kraybill, Donald B. and Marc A. Olshan (eds) (1994) *The Amish Struggle with Modernity*. Hanover, USA: University Press of New England.

Kuhn, Thomas S. (1970) *The Structure of Scientific Revolutions (2nd, enlarged edn)*. Chicago: University of Chicago Press.

Kytömäki, Juha (1991) Täytyy kattoo, jos saa kattoo: Sosiaalipsykologisia näkökulmia varhaisnuorten televisiokokemuksiin [I Must Watch It If I'm Allowed to Watch It: Socio-psychological Perspectives on the Television Experiences of Subteens]. Helsinki: Helsingin yliopiston sosiaalipsykologian laitos, Sosiaalipsykologisia tutkimuksia 1.

Kytömäki, Juha (1998) Parental Control and Regulation of Schoolchildren's Television Viewing. *Nordicom Review* 2, 49–61.

Laclau, Ernesto and Chantal Mouffe (1985) *Hegemony and Socialist Strategy: Towards a Radical Democratic Politics*. London: Verso

Lakoff, George and Mark Johnson (1980) *Metaphors We Live By*. Chicago: University of Chicago Press.

Lane, Christel (1981) *The Rites of Rules: Ritual in Industrial Society – the Soviet case*. Cambridge: Cambridge University Press.

Langacker, Ronald W. (1990) *Concept, Image, and Symbol: The Cognitive Basis of Grammar* (Cognitive Linguistics Research, No. 1 Part 2). Berlin: Walter de Gruyter.

Le Roy Ladurie, Emmanuel (1978) *Montaillou: Cathars and Catholics in a French village, 1294–324*. London: Scolar.

Lejeune, Philippe (1989) *On Autobiography*. Minneapolis: University of Minnesota Press.

Lepenies, Wolf (1988) *Between Literature and Science: The Rise of Sociology*. Cambridge: Cambridge University Press.

Lévi-Strauss, Claude (1963) *Totemism*. Boston: Beacon Press.

Lévi-Strauss, Claude (1966) *The Savage Mind*. London: Weidenfeld & Nicolson.

Linde, Charlotte (1987) Explanatory Systems in Oral Life Stories. In Dorothy Holland and Naomi Quinn (eds), *Cultural Models in Language and Thought*. Cambridge: Cambridge University Press, 343–66.

Lynch, Michael and David Bogen (1994) Harvey Sacks' Primitive Natural Science. *Theory, Culture & Society* 11, 65–104.

Lyotard, Jean-François (1984) *The Postmodern Condition: A Report on Knowledge*. Minneapolis: University of Minnesota Press.

Malinowski, Bronislaw (1948) *Magic, Science and Religion and other Essays*. Boston: Beacon Press.

Marcus, George E. and Michael M.J. Fischer (1986) *Anthropology as Cultural Critique: An Experimental Moment in the Human Sciences*. Chicago: The University of Chicago Press.

Marcuse, Herbert (1968) *One-Dimensional Man*. London: Routledge & Kegan Paul.

Marx, Karl (1969) Theses on Feuerbach. *Marx/Engels Selected Works*, Vol. 1. Moscow: Progress Publishers.

Marx, Karl (1970) *A Contribution to the Critique of Political Economy*. Moscow: Progress Publishers.

Marx, Karl and Friedrich Engels (1971) *Communist Manifesto*. New York: International Publishers.

Maslow, Abraham H. (1987) *Motivation and Personality*. New York: Harper and Row.

Mauss, Marcel (1979) A Category of the Human Mind: The Notion of Person, the Notion of 'Self'. In *Sociology and Psychology: Essays*. London: Routledge & Kegan Paul, 57–94.

Maynard, Douglas W. (1989) On the Ethnography and the Analysis of Talk in Institutional Settings. In James Holstein and Gale Miller (eds), *New Perspectives on Social Problems*. Greenwich, CT: JAI Press, 127–64.

MacIntyre, Alasdair (1981) *After Virtue: A Study in Moral Theory*. Chicago: University of Notre Dame Press.

Mead, George Herbert (1934) *Mind, Self & Society from the Standpoint of a Social Behaviourist*. Chicago: The University of Chicago Press.

Melkas, Jussi (1985) Lestadiolainen televisioideologia elämismaailman puolustuksena [The Laestadian TV Ideology as a Defence of Life-World]. *Sosiologia* 22 (4), 261–72.

Misch, Georg (1969) *Geschichte der Autobiografie, I–IV*. Frankfurt am Main: Verlag G. Schulte-Bulmke.

Moerman, Michael (1974) Accomplishing Ethnicity. In Roy Turner (ed.), *Ethnomethodology: Selected Readings*. Harmondsworth: Viking Press.

Moerman, Michael (1988) *Talking Culture: Ethnography and Conversation Analysis*. University of Penn. Press.

Moerman, Michael (1992) Life After CA: An Ethnographer's Autobiography. In Graham Watson and R.M. Seiler (eds), *Text in Context: Contributions to Ethnomethodology*. London: Sage, 30–4.

Mouzelis, Nicos (1991) *Back to Sociological Theory: The Construction of Social Orders*. Basingstoke: Macmillan.

Nelson, Christian Kjaer (1994) Ethnomethodological Positions on the Use of Ethnographic Data in Conversation Analytic Research. *Journal of Contemporary Ethnography* 23 (3), 307–29.

Nietzsche, Friedrich (1968) *The Will to Power*. New York: Random House.

Nofsinger, Robert E. (1991) *Everyday Conversation*. Newbury Park, CA: Sage.

Nonaka, Ikujiro (1994) A Dynamic Theory of Organizational Knowledge Creation. *Organization Science* 5 (1), 14–37.

Omi, Michael (1986) *Racial Formation in the United States: From the 1960s to the 1980s*. New York: Routledge & Kegan Paul.

Palmer, Gary B. (1999) *Toward a Theory of Cultural Linguistics*. Austin: University of Texas Press.

Parsons, Talcott (1964) *The Social System*. Glencoe, IL: Free Press.

Parsons, Talcott (1967) *The Structure of Social Action: A Study in Social Theory with Special Reference to a Group of Recent European Writers*. Glencoe, IL: Free Press.

Peirce, C.S. (1901) MS 692, 1901 [MS refers to the manuscripts of Charles S. Peirce kept in the Houghton Library, Harvard University].

Peräkylä, Anssi (1995) *AIDS Counselling: Institutional Interaction and Clinical Practice*. Cambridge: Cambridge University Press.

Peräkylä, Anssi and David Silverman (1991) Owning Experience: Describing the Experience of Other Persons. *Text* 11, 441–80.

Perelman, Chaim (1982) *The Realm of Rhetoric*. Notre Dame: The University of Notre Dame Press.

Perelman, Chaim and Olbrechts-Tyteca, Lucie (1971) *The New Rhetoric: A Treatise on Argumentation*. Notre Dame: The University of Notre Dame Press.

Pocock, J.G.A. (1987) Modernity and Anti-Modernity in the Anglophone Political Traditions. In S.N. Eisenstadt (ed.), *Patterns of Modernity*, Vol. I: *The West*. London: Frances Pinter, 44–59.

Pollard, Sidney (1968) *The Idea of Progress: History and Society*. New York: Basic Books.

Pollner, Melvin (1987) *Mundane Reason: Reality in Everyday and Sociological Discourse*. Cambridge: Cambridge University Press.

Pomerantz, Anita (1984) Agreeing and Disagreeing with Assessments: Some Features of Preferred/Dispreferred Turn Shapes. In J. Maxwell Atkinson and John Heritage (eds), *Structures of Social Action: Studies in Conversation Analysis*. Cambridge: Cambridge University Press, 57–101.

Potter, Jonathan and Margaret Wetherell (1987) *Discourse and Social Psychology: Beyond Attitudes and Behaviour*. London: Sage.

Propp, Vladimir (1975) *Morphology of the Folktale*. Austin and London: University of Texas Press.

Rabinow Paul (1977) *Reflections on Fieldwork in Morocco*. Berkeley: University of California Press.

Reginster, Bernard (2000) Perspectivism, Criticism and Freedom of Spirit. *European Journal of Philosophy* 8 (1), 40–62.

Reiss, David (1981) *The Family's Construction of Reality*. Cambridge, MA: Harvard University Press.

Reskin, Barbara and Irene Padavic (1994) *Women and Men at Work*. Thousand Oaks, CA: Pine Forge Press.

Riley, Alexander Tristan (2002) Durkheim contra Bergson? The Hidden Roots of Postmodern Theory and the Postmodern 'Return' of the Sacred. *Sociological Perspectives* 45 (3), 243–65.

Sacks, Harvey (1992) *Lectures on Conversation* (2 vols). Oxford: Blackwell.

Salzman, Philip Carl (2002) On Reflexivity. *American Anthropologist* 104 (3), 805–13.

Sapir, Edward (1958) *Culture, Language and Personality*. Berkeley, CA: University of California Press.

Saussure, Ferdinand de (1966) *Course in General Linguistics*. New York: McGraw Hill.

Schaefer Henry 'Fritz' (1996) *Stephen Hawking, The Big Bang, and God*. Real Issue. location: www.iclnet.org/clm/real/ri9404/bigbang.html

Schatzki, Theodore R., Karin Knorr Cetina and Eike Von Savigny (eds) (2001) *The Practice Turn in Contemporary Theory*. London and New York: Routledge.

Schegloff, Emanuel A. (1992a) Introduction. In Harvey Sacks, *Lectures on Conversation*, Vol. I. Oxford: Blackwell, ix–lxii.

Schegloff, Emanuel A. (1992b) Repair after Next Turn: The Last Structurally Provided Defence of Intersubjectivity in Conversation. *American Journal of Sociology* 97 (5), 1295–345.

Seidman, Steven (1998) Are We All in the Closet? Notes Towards a Sociological and Cultural Turn in Queer Theory. *European Journal of Cultural Studies* 1 (2), 177–92.

Shore, Bradd (1996) *Culture in Mind: Cognition, Culture, and the Problem of Meaning*. Oxford: Oxford University Press.

Schneebaum, Tobias (1970) *Keep the River on Your Right*. New York: Grove.

Silverman, David and Jaber F. Gubrium (1994) Competing Strategies for Analyzing the Contexts of Social Interaction. *Sociological Inquiry* 64 (2), 179–98.

Silverman, David and Anssi Peräkylä (1990) AIDS Counselling: The Interactional Organisation of Talk about 'Delicate' Issues. *Sociology of Health & Illness* 12, 293–318.

Sokal, Alan (1996a) A Physicist Experiments with Cultural Studies. *Lingua Franca* May/June 1996, 62–4.

Sokal, Alan (1996b) Transgressing the Boundaries: Toward a Transformative Hermeneutics of Quantum Gravity. *Social Text* 14, 217– 52.

Stark, Rodney (1999) Secularization, R.I.P. *Sociology of Religion* 60 (3), 249–73.

Svenning, Marianne (1988) *Barn, massmedia och samhälle* [children, Mass Media and Society]. Lund: Studentlitteratur.

Swatos, William H. and Kevin J. Christiano (1999) Secularization Theory: The Course of a Concept. *Sociology of Religion* 60 (3), 209–28.

Tomlinson, Matt (2002) Religious Discourse as Metaculture. *European Journal of Cultural Studies* 5 (1), 25–47.

Toennies, Ferdinand (1971) *On Sociology: Pure, Applied, and Empirical. Selected Writings*. Chicago: University of Chicago Press.

Tönnies, Ferdinand (1988) *Community and Society*. New Brunswick, NJ: Transaction Books.

Torfing, Jacob (1999) *New Theories of Discourse: Laclau, Mouffe, and Zizek*. Oxford, UK: Blackwell Publishers.

Turner, Stephen (1994) *The Social Theory of Practices: Tradition, Tacit Knowledge, and Presuppositions*. Chicago: University of Chicago Press.

Urban, Greg (2001) *Metaculture: How Culture Moves Through the World*. Minneapolis: University of Minnesota Press.

Valtaoja, Esko (2001) *Kotona maailmankaikkeudessa* [At Home in the Universe]. Helsinki: Ursa.

van Dijk, Teun A. (1980) *Macrostructures: An Interdisciplinary Study of Global Discourse, Interaction, and Cognition*. Hillsdale: Lawrence Erlbaum Associates.

Waas, Margit (2001) Taking Note of Language Extinction. Location: http://www.colorado.edu/iec/alis/articles/langext.htm. Originally published in *Applied Linguistics Forum* 18 (2), 1, 4 and 5.

Wallace, Anthony F.C. (1966) *Religion: An Anthropological View*. New York: Random House.

Watzlawick, Paul, John H. Weakland and Richard Fish (1974) *Change: Principles of Problem Formation and Problem Resolution*. New York: Norton.

Weber, Max (1969) *Basic Concepts in Sociology*. Westport, CT: Greenwood Publishing Group.

Weber, Max (1971) *The Protestant Ethic and the Spirit of Capitalism*. London: Unwin University Books.

Weber, Max (1978a) *Economy and Society*, Vol. I. Berkeley: University of California Press.

Weber, Max (1978b) *Economy and Society*, Vol. II. Berkeley: University of California Press.

Weintraub, Karl Joachim (1975) Autobiography and Historical Consciousness. *Critical Inquiry*, 1 (4), 821–48.

Weintraub, Karl Joachim (1978) *The Value of the Individual: Self and Circumstance in Autobiography*. Chicago: University of Chicago Press.

Williams, Gareth (1984) The Genesis of Chronic Illness: Narrative Reconstruction. *Sociology of Health and Illness* 6 (2), 175–200.

Whorf, Benjamin Lee (1956) *Language, Thought and Reality*. Cambridge, MA: MIT Press.

Wilson, Bryan (1966) *Religion in Secular Society*. London: C.A. Watts.

Wilson, James Q. (1993) *The Moral Sense*. Glencoe, IL: Free Press.

Winch, Peter (1971) *The Idea of a Social Science and its Relation to Philosophy*. London: Routledge & Kegan Paul.

Wittgenstein, Ludwig (1999) *Philosophical Investigations* (3rd edn). Englewood Cliffs, NJ: Prentice Hall.

Yates, Frances (1969) Bacon and the Menace of English Lit. *New York Review of Books*, 27 March, 37.

Index